An Interpersonal Approach to Child and Adolescent Psychotherapy

An Interpersonal Approach to Child and Adolescent Psychotherapy

Stanley Spiegel, Ph.D.

JASON ARONSON INC.
Northvale, New Jersey
London

First softcover edition 1996

Copyright © 1996 by Jason Aronson Inc.
Copyright © 1989 by Columbia University Press

The hardcover edition was titled *An Interpersonal Approach to Child Therapy:
The Treatment of Children and Adolescents from an Interpersonal Point of View.*

Library of Congress Cataloging-in-Publication Data

Spiegel, Stanley.
    [Interpersonal approach to child therapy]
    An interpersonal approach to child and adolescent psychotherapy /
Stanley Spiegel.
       p.   cm. — (Personality, psychopathology, and psychotherapy)
    Originally published under the title: An interpersonal approach to child therapy.
    Includes bibliographical references and index.
    ISBN 1-56821-838-9 (sc : alk. paper)
    1. Child psychotherapy. 2. Adolescent psychotherapy.
3. Interpersonal relations. I. Title. II. Series: Personality, psychopathology, and psychotherapy (New York, N.Y.)
RJ504.S59   1996
618.92'8914 — dc20
                                                 96-6159

Manufactured in the United States of America. Jason Aronson Inc. offers books and cassettes. For information and catalog write to Jason Aronson Inc., 230 Livingston Street, Northvale, New Jersey 07647.

For Julia, Joseph, and Laura

TO THE READER

Throughout the book I use "he" rather than "he or she" or "s/he" (except in self-explanatory cases). This is merely a way of making the book easier to read and I don't intend to offend anyone.

Contents

Foreword

One of the most difficult things to do in the field of psychotherapy is to represent accurately how and what one does in the therapeutic sessions. There are obvious obstacles. There is the translation of an oral communication to a written one. The multiple impressions (aural, visual) which the therapist has of the person in front of him have to be communicated to an unknown audience. We take these fleeting impressions and translate them into an observation. The observation is presumably value-free, nonintrusive, and calculated to help increase awareness of what is going on inside and outside the person designated as patient. The therapist also has to be able to distinguish between what he is seeing and what he has learned from experience in both theory and practice. He has to note and comment on the uniquely individual detail of the patient's experience.

Surely anyone who undertakes the double task of spelling out the principles of his approach and then illustrating their usefulness in treatment with individual patients is assuming almost an impossible task. How well does Stanley Spiegel do?

His writing is lucid. There can be no mistaking what he means. He starts without using arcane language or terms difficult to comprehend. The assumptions behind his language are clear. He wants therapy to help the child to be what he would have been if such and such had not happened to him in an interpersonal field with significant others. He discusses the differences between treatment of children and of adults—he emphasizes the use of metaphor. He details the importance of being alert to nuances from the first phone call to the final. He tells us how he would set up a play room. He gives us the details of specific treatments from the inception to the termination.

How well does he succeed? I would say admirably. While adhering to the principles he enunciates so well, he is no idealogue. He expertly tailors the treatment to the needs of the child, he is alert to the details of the family experience, he meets the child at his own level and thereby facilitates the growth process.

Dr. Spiegel fulfills the role of the scholar ideally. He stands on the shoulders of his predecessors and sees more than they could see. He then takes his vision and crafts an approach to child therapy which owes some to his predecessors but is his unique creation. This book will prove invaluable both to tyros and old hands.

Earl G. Witenberg, M.D.

Preface to the Softcover Edition

Since this book was first published in 1989, there have been a number of changes in mental health approaches that have strongly affected the field. The two most significant influences have been managed care and increased emphasis on medication as the treatment of choice. Certain cultural factors also coalesce with the effects of managed care and a biological orientation and encourage a symptom-oriented approach to therapy that I find antithetical to effective treatment.

Managed care, largely for economic reasons, operates best with clear-cut diagnosis and prescribed treatment. Diagnosis is based on apparent symptoms. It is assumed that if a disorder is labeled accurately, then the treatment required can be fairly standardized. As a result the length of treatment is highly predictable and managed care can control cost by allowing a prescribed number of sessions for each disorder. This point of view is in concordance with a biological approach to treatment, for if one knows what medication will work and how long it will take, it is assumed then that emotional disorders can be effectively treated.

Patients do not read the *DSM-IV* before they develop symptoms, and a need for precise diagnosis is not in concordance with the dynamic structure of personalities. Symptoms that may be prominent at one time may readily disappear and other symptoms become substitutions with the same underlying dynamic disorder. Varying symptoms may exist concurrently and the diagnostician may be forced into a somewhat arbitrary choice to select the most prominent symptom. The DSM system itself, in an attempt to accommodate for this, has become somewhat cumbersome by utilizing varying levels of description. The movement is toward more finely tuned definitions, and as a result these must have many qualifiers, whereby the system becomes unwieldy.

Medical research has moved in the direction of finding neurological correlates to behavioral manifestations and biological effects of varying medication. Consequently there is a refinement of medication that can target specific moods and provide such benefits as reducing anxiety, depression, and aggression with minimal side effects. While this may have the advantage of making one more accessible to psychotherapy and in that way be beneficial, I believe it does not attack the underlying causes of these symptoms, and without other changes in lifestyle I do not believe it can provide lasting results. Medication may be quite effective as an ancillary form of treatment, but it is my feeling that emotional disorders are a result of problems of living and biological imbalances may well be a result rather than a cause. Good treatment needs to deal with the methods people have developed or are developing in the way they manage their lives and their interpersonal relationships.

Unfortunately, there are other factors that are increasingly contributing to a symptom-oriented approach to treatment and away from dynamic-oriented psychotherapy. An additional input in the direction of medication and symptom orientation is the movement society has made toward encouraging people to be spectators rather than participants in their life endeavors and recreational activities. Children seldom make up their own games that require the imagination to construct their own play objects, and there is little encouragement toward constructive fantasy. This is particularly unfortunate because an ability for good constructive fantasy helps one to absorb the shocks of everyday living and protects one from serious adverse reactions. The Zeitgeist is away from interpersonal skills and toward television, spectator sports, and computer games, albeit some of these may be interactive (but only with machines). Transportation is quick, communication instant, and there is little time to think through problems and consider solutions. Part of the result of this is a population that expects a "quick fix." People take aspirin for headaches, mood elevators for depression, depressants to reduce anxiety, and use the correct toothpaste or deodorant to solve their interpersonal problems. This attitude is well suited to a predilection for medication that one hopes will provide relief and solve the problems of daily living.

All of these influences as well as others not described here work together so that the orientation toward a biological approach and an attempt to merely provide symptom relief in emotional disorders have become more intense.

Many studies of the effect of medication and psychotherapy on emotional disorders clearly indicate that psychotherapy is an effective form of treatment and strongly suggest that in the long run it is more effective than drug treatment. The effect of psychotherapy alone does not differ in efficacy from medication and psychotherapy.[1] Treatment by medication alone may appear to be worthwhile, but it is not my orientation nor the approach presented in this book. Symptoms are a result of many influences, not the least of which are personality factors, and to make people merely symptom free without attacking the underlying etiologic factors is an unrealistic goal for people with problems in living. If symptoms are attacked directly and removed by medication or other pragmatic approaches, the effect is likely to be short lived, and the symptoms are likely to reappear or patients will probably develop new symptoms, some of which may be less effective for adaptation to their life situation.

This book is written with minimum emphasis on diagnostic categories and terminology. It is written about people, not systems and disorders. People are shown here to be complex dynamic entities. They seek treatment for themselves or their children because they have

---

1. For a recent full discussion of the effectiveness of psychotherapy see Seligman, M.E.P. 1995. "The Effectiveness of Psychotherapy: The *Consumer Reports* Study." *American Psychologist,* Journal of The American Psychological Association, December, 50(12):965–974.

problems in living and while medication may change their mood, no matter what the biological factors, it is the problems in living that must be solved. Interpersonal Psychotherapy is oriented toward dealing with these problems. People do not live alone and it is primarily the interpersonal factors that make for personality structure and determine methods of relating to other people. That is what Interpersonal Psychotherapy and this book are all about.

A dynamic interpersonal approach realistically must deal with knotty problems including speculation about etiology of disorders, which often includes blame and recrimination. One must look to the nature of interpersonal influences and the structure of parents as well as children, in order to understand the total nature of personality disorders.

There are many influences on the personality of children other than directly interpersonal ones. Interpersonal Theory includes such components as economics, physical appearance, religion, color, race, language, temperament, intellect, television, and other societal influences.

While Interpersonal Psychotherapy requires a considerable amount of skill and competence, it is not completely antagonistic to managed care in that it is oriented toward efficiency. Good treatment should be provided in an efficacious manner. I do not believe in extending treatment to result in some kind of "normality" and I do not wish to confuse pathology with unique character structures. I do want to encourage, not discourage or interfere with, creativeness and the variety of effective ways of adapting to life. And centrally I do not believe it is possible, nor is it the job of the good child therapist, to attempt to make a complete, efficient, happy adult of any child. It is the job of the good therapist to assist the child in a natural developmental, maturational process. Good therapy gives the child the necessary equipment, tools, attitudes, and character structure to enable him to competently face life problems in a healthy, constructive manner. In effect, therapy seeks to help him become the best person he can be.

Child psychotherapy need not be a long-term process. Children are far more plastic and malleable than adults. To help therapists treat children efficiently and effectively with minimal "tampering" and in short order is a major purpose of this book. If there are restraints of managed care, the nature of Interpersonal Psychotherapy lends itself to a kind of flexibility so that the treatment, even if curtailed by time restraints, can still be quite effective.

In this book emphasis is often placed on the importance of self esteem, indicating ways in which this can be created and enhanced. While much naturally developed behavior is directed toward protecting self esteem, it is often not in the most constructive manner and may include the denigration of other people. Self esteem is not something that can be purchased in a supermarket. Good treatment must seek out the basis of one's assessment of oneself and contribute to a view that is in keeping with reality and is not hurtful to the self or others. This is no easy task, but competent treatment will make a substantial move toward that goal. I believe this book will provide the child therapist with a theoretical framework as well as a practical approach to therapy, free of contradictions and pat solutions.

As a final note to further illustrate the orientation of this book, here is an analogy. In Japanese carpentry there is a very complex joint that is extremely strong and efficient. It is primarily an internal structure and not visible from the outside. But it does its job even though only the carpenter may know it is there. I believe that this is the function of good psychotherapy, to build an internal structure of security, self esteem, and adaptive mechanisms that enables the individual to deal with problems of life as they arise in an effective, enriching manner.

Preface

For several years I have been teaching courses in child therapy and have always had difficulty in compiling a comprehensive bibliography for an interpersonal approach to child therapy. There were many references from varying theoretical orientations that I have been able to provide to students that have been helpful regarding aspects of the problems, theory, and practice of child therapy. However, I have never felt they came sufficiently close to a generally accepted interpersonal viewpoint, nor did they satisfactorily integrate theory with practice. It is for this reason that I have decided to write this book.

Since interpersonal therapy has its roots in the thinking and writing of many theoreticians, the explication and documentation of its principles is subject to many variations. Nevertheless, it has always seemed to me that there are consistent and reliable underlying principles and while not all are directly attributable to specific theoreticians, such principles are still congenial with interpersonal theory. In this book I have spelled them out. In themselves the principles may appear axiomatic and thus be considered simplistic, but in the context of this volume I believe I have effectively demonstrated their real value when applied to the treatment of children.

It is difficult to trace the source of my own thinking. I am aware that in my earlier days as a psychologist my approach was somewhat eclectic, and as a result I was troubled by the contradictions of my work. With the influence of my teachers I gradually honed and refined my methods. Among the many who challenged my methods and caused me to be curious and self critical were Doctors Erich Fromm, Geneva Goodrich, Earl Witenberg, Ernest Schachtel, and Rollo May. In addition to having allied themselves with the William Alanson White Institute, all had in common their general avoidance of technical terms and their attempt to convey clearly and simply the basis of their beliefs. It is in this tradition that I have written this book. Technical terms can be useful as shortcut methods of relating complex ideas, but they tend to convey different things to different people. In order to preserve the uniqueness of people it is necessary to avoid diagnostic labels; people do not read the *DSM III* or Freud or Sullivan before they develop an emotional disorder. It is for these reasons that theoretical beliefs and methods are spelled out in descriptive dynamic, rather than diagnostic, terms.

My principles and practices have evolved as a result of not only the teaching of those scholars whom I have just named, but also the reading I have done over the years. I have accepted some ideas, rejected others, and refined my own views. Most of all, however, it has been in the very practice of working with children that I have been able to observe and improve my methods and beliefs. Fortunately for parents and clinicians alike, children are remarkably resilient and forgiving of our mistakes.

I have tried to write this book as clearly and simply as I could, but I think its simplicity is deceptive. It is not a cookbook designed to provide a recipe for the treatment of specific disorders and problems of living, but rather, through case material it is intended to provide principles and a point of view to guide one in a methodology of treatment that adapts to the individual needs of the child patient and his own special problems. From these principles, technical moves might be deduced. It is my hope that this book will help the therapist to understand the meaning of the child's words and behavior and the meaning of the therapist's own actions with the child so that the methodology and actual procedures utilized will be based on sound, consistent principles and will provide the most effective treatment. The reader will find it most useful to read the book in its entirety, not in parts.

Conceiving of a book is only the first part of completing one. Getting ideas into printed words is the major task. In this process, including the reading and rereading of my manuscript, I give special thanks to Doctors Eric Singer and Jay Greenberg for their care in reviewing the work and making many helpful suggestions. I also wish to acknowledge with gratitude Elinore Kobrin's editorial assistance.

Finally, I am most grateful to my remarkably patient and insightful wife, Julia Hunkins, for the many days and hours she spent in reviewing and editing the manuscript and for her most useful suggestions that enabled me best to convey my ideas and beliefs.

Introduction

Those who practice child therapy or psychoanalysis with children show rather remarkable diversity in what they do. Approaches often are pragmatic; they do not always adhere to major theoretical positions. A looseness in the application of psychoanalytic theory is a necessary consequence of the attempt to adapt to the therapy of children theoretical positions that were devised to describe therapy with adults or from the application of theories of dynamics and development rather than of treatment. In addition, the practice of child therapy was devised primarily from experience and the passing on of varying methods and techniques more or less empirically. If one is to avoid attempting to integrate ideas and theories that are essentially mutually exclusive, there is a need for a treatment approach that is fully compatible with theories of development.

Few established training programs are expressly designed for the teaching of child therapy, although the move toward establishing such programs has been intensified over recent years. Because there is such diversity in approach, training programs tend to be all-encompassing, embodying the broad spectrum of points of view. While such a "cafeteria curriculum" has the advantage of allowing the student to select from different viewpoints, it and the empirically oriented methodology that is often taught may lead to some confusion because some students may cross theoretical lines indiscriminately. Hence, the combining of methods and ideas that are contradictory may be self defeating. It is therefore important that in teaching alternative views of child therapy similarities and differences be carefully delineated.

Examining methods of child therapy is a complex venture. Most theories of development emphasize the lacunae or distortions (in Sullivan's words, warps) in development that lead to pathology, but these same theories do not adequately show ways to correct the gaps. Furthermore the varying theories of treatment or "cure" that are postulated in the literature are complicated and often in dispute. At the least, it is hoped that therapists might be able to maintain consistency in approach so that what they do in child therapy has a reasonable basis in a theory of therapy as well as in a theory of development. If therapists fail to do this, the course of the therapy is handicapped, for techniques that seem efficacious may actually interfere with each other. Providing theoretical principles in concordance with sound therapeutic practices in the treatment of children is, of course, no simple task. As Chrzanowski said, "Theory and therapy strike me as an odd couple who despite good intentions, are more harmful than helpful to each other" (1986a:446). And in Witenberg's view; "We all make a living by being with patients, yet we do not have a theory from which we can deduce actual technical moves with a patient" (1987:189).

A sustained but somewhat loosely organized view of psychological development, pathology, and treatment is subsumed under the heading the *interpersonal approach*. The emphasis, as the phrase implies, is on the relationships between people as the source of both emotional health and pathology. More specifically, the concern is with the anxiety or security provided by the interpersonal relationship and the consequent good or poor integration of the self. If this then is the source of pathology, one must infer that psychological change is brought about through the relationships of people. The interpersonal approach is represented by the thoughts and ideas of theoreticians and clinicians who, because of their disparate views, tend to be thought of independently, but because of their emphasis on the influences of social and interpersonal forces, a "school" is thus comprised. Certainly among the founders of this group are Fromm, Sullivan, Arieti, Thompson, Searles, and May. At least partly because of its emphasis on respect for the human condition, interpersonalism is a combination of considerable diversity of views. Nevertheless, there is, I believe, an underlying unity to it that can be extracted by examining its precepts. Moreover, I believe that out of interpersonalism emerges a theory of child treatment that is compatible with a theory of development and that provides an outline of the most effective ways to treat pathology in children.

This approach to a dynamic understanding of psychological development and behavior shows sound and sustained internal consistency, overall comprehensiveness, and widely agreed on views. Of course, I do not believe that I have found final answers, but in this book I strive for consistency and efficacy in my approach. I attempt to show that what one does in treatment with children should and can follow a developmental format as well as a theory of therapy in full concordance and compatibility with that format. Such an approach to treatment is ultimately most effective in bringing about desired therapeutic change.

At the book's outset I have set down what I believe to be central underlying principles that govern an interpersonal approach. To arrive at these precepts, and in the light of many years of treating children, I examined the interpersonal approach from the views of a number of leading theoreticians of the interpersonal school. The core writings I selected are those of Harry Stack Sullivan, and these provide the essential guide for abstracting principles. In these principles, which I believe govern the work of interpersonal practitioners, there is an implicit underlying theory of development as well as an underlying theory of treatment and "cure." Although these principles are not always specifically noted throughout the book, they are the underpinnings of all treatment of children outlined in this volume.

Following the exposition of the principles, special emphasis is

placed on the use of metaphor, a concept consistent with an interpersonal approach. Metaphor—that is, indirect but symbolic communication—accomplishes an interpersonal transaction, frequently
avoiding the miscommunications that are often the result of literal
use of language. I believe that the use of metaphor is the most
effective way of bringing about improvement in children with few-
est risks. Because I so strongly believe metaphor is the basis of
good treatment of children, this concept is explored in detail: what
is meant by metaphor and how it can be applied. The central focus
of the chapter on metaphor is the delineation of the extreme care
necessary for verbal interpretation and transactions with children.

Next, therapeutic issues are presented in a way that generally
conforms to the procedure for treating children. Since all aspects
of theory and treatment must be considered at all phases of treatment and since central problems and issues of individual children
are reflected in all aspects of child therapy, there is a necessary
overlap in some chapters. Even in the interest of consistency, a
therapist cannot apply formula methods that ignore individual problems and individual differences in children. For optimal understanding of my approach, it is therefore important that the reader
consider the book in its entirety.

The treatment aspect of the book contains descriptions of practical problems involved in actual interaction with the child patient
and discussion of approaches and solutions to these problems that
follow the principles outlined, with emphasis on metaphor. The
reader is taken through the initial stages of contact with parents
and children—through discussions of such issues as who is to be
seen first, parents or children, and when and where. Although in
some ways these concerns may seem simplistic, the manner in which
they are resolved is not arbitrary and is vital to good treatment.
Much like the conducting of experiments, if the initial arrangement
and controls are carefully designed, fewer allowances need be made
for extraneous or deleterious variables that could have been avoided.

The playroom, which is the essential workroom of the child therapist, must be equipped with extreme care. The use and misuse of
toys, games, and other equipment are examined in detail. I recognize that optimal conditions are not always available—that is, few
playrooms can be equipped with a sandbox—but it is not only the

inclusion of certain materials that is important; it is also the exclusion of some items that requires attention. Items that should or should not be in the playroom are examined in detail, showing the pros and cons of each. Of further significance in this regard, certain items ought to be available for some children and not for others. Because it is important that play objects be used most efficaciously, recommendations are made for their optimal use.

In chapter 4, "The Playroom," as throughout the book, there is an examination, with clinical details, of alternative methods of providing child therapy. Through a critical exploration of what I feel are the flaws of many other approaches, I demonstrate what I believe to be the more appropriate methods of child treatment. It is not my intent to be unduly harsh in my criticism—one can hardly overstate the contribution of traditional psychoanalytic theory—but it appears to me that there are so many basic errors built into the application of traditional psychoanalytic, psychoanalytically oriented, and other methods of child treatment that I would be remiss not to discuss them.

The initial contact with the child is of vital therapeutic as well as diagnostic importance. How the therapist conducts the initial contact depends on many factors, including the age of the child, the nature of the child's problems, the aims of the treatment, the setting of the therapy, and the characteristics and predilections of the therapist. Since the interpersonal developmental schema to which I subscribe holds that development can be uneven in many aspects and areas of life, a description of a child of six will not always conform to an ideal about 6-year-olds. To say that a child is mature or immature is insufficient. Rather, areas of maturity or immaturity need to be described and understood, with subsequent treatment designed to dovetail with the particular needs and levels of functioning of the individual child. Because diagnosis must lend itself to therapeutic application, exploration of the history as well as a complete description of the present personality are required. It is vitally important to diagnose the problem thoroughly in order to provide treatment.

When a therapist attempts more precision in diagnosis, there is often a tendency to lean heavily on diagnostic labels. Good diagnosis, however, consists not of appropriate diagnostic labels, which take on a kind of autonomy, but rather of competent dynamic descriptions. Satisfaction with a diagnostic label leads to a false sense of security. It is as if the security achieved by knowing the name "Rumpelstiltskin" in the fairy tale is valid. The process of treatment itself requires continuous inquiry to obtain more information and effectively arrive at a more precise diagnosis in terms of understanding present and underlying dynamics. Good treatment requires that the therapist remain constantly curious. There is always more to learn. The therapist must be able to be comfortable without knowing everything but always seeking to know more. That is why the principles presented are principles, not formulas.

The problems of limit setting appear to be of such magnitude that they are given a special chapter. Problems of limits are encountered in all phases of child treatment, including the relationships with parents and others as well as in the individual activities and interaction with the child in treatment. In chapter 6 I present and examine a detailed interaction with a child from the point of view of limits; the same session might well have been examined in terms of other underlying dynamics or in use of play equipment. The flow of issues among chapters is not to be avoided: its very presence emphasizes the need for a consistent attitude and a view of treatment and techniques that follow basic principles.

Similarly, the problems of treating adolescents require special attention. Because the transition between child and adult is not consistent among different children and because many children can be adolescent or adult in some aspects of their lives and childlike or even infantile in other ways regardless of chronological age, the problems of adolescence show considerable variability. In addition, the treatment of adults is based on a model different from that of the treatment of children, and the treatment of people somewhere between these stages requires unique consideration and techniques. Depending on the personality configuration and dynamics of the particular adolescent, a therapist may in some cases use methods more suitable to young children, and in others the therapy may be essentially the same as it might be with an adult.

Following the principles outlined, with emphasis on the use of metaphor with young children, ways in which these principles can be applied to advantage with adolescents are described. Chapter 7, on adolescence, includes a detailed discussion of the treatment of an adolescent based on a traditional Freudian model along with an explication of why this appears to be an ineffective treatment and in fact may be a form of iatrogenic therapy. Such other issues as engaging adolescents in treatment and the special questions related to the specific manner of working with adolescents are discussed in some detail. It is important that in work with adolescents the clinician recognize that failures are sometimes pandemic and that with some adolescents a direct therapeutic approach is not always the most successful one.

In chapter 8, "Ongoing Treatment and Special Issues," I consider such matters as ethical issues, especially as they pertain to adolescents. These issues are not confined to matters of confidentiality or the use of drugs, which are discussed at some length, but also include the therapist's relationship to school personnel, to pediatricians, and to family members. Many therapists have their offices in some way connected with their homes, and factors involving the home and members of the therapist's family must be considered in child treatment. Taking the child outside of the playroom for therapy raises certain ethical and essentially therapeutic questions that are worthy of special consideration. During the course of treatment many factors that affect treatment change: financial, geographic, transportational, and unpredictable fluctuations in the family structure. These variations must be managed in a manner that follows sound principles for effective treatment.

Alternative forms of child treatment, such as family therapy, behavior modification, and a detailed method of working with children in groups are discussed in chapter 9. While these methods are not the focus of this book, they are frequently considered as appropriate alternatives or as adjuncts to individual treatment and thus are certainly worthy of careful consideration.

In the final chapter, treatment termination with children and adolescents is examined. Here again I emphasize the difference between child and adult therapy and the need for many special considerations that must be made for children. Separation as a major underlying dynamic is especially considered. Changes in frequency of sessions should be placed in the context of the problem that brought the child to therapy as well as his or her history and underlying dynamics, so that the decision to separate is a result of a comprehensive understanding of the child. Because therapy with children is not confined to contacts with the child, in the matter of termination one must also consider relationships and factors that involve parents and other family members.

The course of treatment with children, frequently even more than with adults, is remarkably unpredictable. Specific issues and consistent methods that follow the given principles appear through this book. The examples provided cannot cover all events that might occur in the course of child therapy. Certain behavior in children might not be evidence of pathology at all; the child therapist must be able to differentiate pathology from uniqueness in accord with a principle of compassion and respect that recognizes individual differences in personality and style without labeling it as disorder. In this book it is proposed that the therapist's orientation be toward nurturance, gentleness, and a respect for potential disruptions to the child's privacy and self-esteem.

It is my intention to provide guidelines and principles based on the application of interpersonal theory in specific situations in the hope of giving the reader a conceptual framework that will enable her or him to use imagination and ingenuity in performing the task of an effective child therapist.

An
Interpersonal
Approach
to Child and
Adolescent
Psychotherapy

1

Interpersonal Principles

A brief review of the history of what is generally known as the interpersonal school will reveal some of the roots of the approach and the principles that guide it. These principles reflect the development of interpersonal theory.

At least in theory the particular method of psychotherapy one selects is largely dependent on one's concept of psychopathology. For instance, if a particular therapist's concept of psychopathology is derived from some form of learning theory, then the applied approach to treatment will be behavior modification, with its emphasis on modifying behavior through conditioning or desensitization. On the other hand, if one leans heavily on drive theory as an explanation for personality organization and development, then the general approach will be classical psychoanalysis. Even then, however, the approach is not clearcut. The body of knowledge that defines classical psychoanalysis has become muddied by considerable revision over the years. When, at the turn of the century, Freud first conceived of it, psychoanalysis was quite different from what it is today. Over the last few years, with the influence of attachment theory and the object relations approach, psychoanalysis has moved in the direction of becoming an interpersonal theory.

As various analysts broke with Freud to develop their own theories, a variety of psychoanalytic schools of thought developed. A full, clear, but somewhat dated discussion is found in Munroe (1955). As each offshoot of Freudian psychoanalysis emerged and therapists adopted one or another orientation—Jungian, Reichian, or Adlerian—for example, there was even further differentiation and development. While psychoanalysts attempted to adhere to sound and scholarly principles, a multiplicity of factors, not the least of which was the politics of psychoanalysis, exerted their influence to push or pull for whichever theory came into vogue, and an effort to include cultural and interpersonal influences on the development of personality became sufficiently significant to account for some major changes in both the political and the theoretical structure of psychoanalysis. The evolution of the field was additionally complicated by the question of "lay" analysis. There was splintering: some of the movements survived, and others retained only a few adherents over the years.

Disagreement arose among some psychoanalysts who were oriented toward cultural influences on psychological development, and after a major schism with the followers of Karen Horney—Harry Stack Sullivan, Frieda Fromm-Reichman, Clara Thompson, Erich Fromm, and others founded the William Alanson White Institute in New York in 1947. Largely because of the influence of Sullivan, the White Institute, along with the Washington School, became known as those institutions representing the interpersonal approach. Since its founding, the White Institute's leading members have reflected and developed ideas, attitudes, and directions about theory and developmental constructs; within the school there is disagreement and controversy but certainly sufficient unity of thought and approach to warrant calling it a school of thought. The institute's interpersonal approach may perhaps be defined more by what it is not than by what it is: while some of its advocates do use aspects of other approaches, the White Institute's is essentially non-

Freudian, nonbehavioral, non-Adlerian, non-Reichian, non-Jungian. It is, above all, interpersonal in that most adhere to the "schema devised by Sullivan . . . a relational model which attempts to bridge biological, sociocultural, physiochemical, and psychological dimensions of human existence" (Anchin and Kiesler 1982:26).

Some contemporary thinking that is considered to be interpersonal has in fact been revealed to vary considerably from beliefs of the founders of the White and Washington Institutes. For example, the recent *Handbook of Interpersonal Psychotherapy* (Anchin and Kiesler 1982) has seventeen chapters by twenty-four different authors, only one of whom is associated with the William Alanson White Institute, and none is known to have been connected with the Washington School. Moreover, there is in the book only a single mention each of Clara Thompson and Erich Fromm, and none of Frieda Fromm-Reichman or Rollo May. This lack of historical grounding may not mean less of an interpersonal approach, but it does indicate the broad range of modalities that go by the name "interpersonal" as well as the degree to which they have become disconnected from their origin. We at the White Institute have no proprietary rights to the interpersonal approach. For a long time we were considered to have taken a radical approach to psychoanalysis, although we are now often thought of as the more conservative end of interpersonal theory. Nevertheless, the William Alanson White Institute is generally considered to be the leading proponent of Sullivanian theory and the interpersonal approach. There is considerable diversity of perspectives among the different members of the White Institute, but there are essential principles to which most of us affiliated with the institute generally adhere.

Principles of Work With Children

Few basic assumptions can be made about psychotherapy that are acceptable to all therapists. But it is reasonable to say that most psychotherapy with adults is, or should be, an alliance in which two people join in examining the psychic life of one of them in an attempt to help that person through verbal rather than biological, chemical, or physical means. Although the treatment of children is also based on an alliance of two people, child patients obviously do not have as their aim the examination of their psychic lives, nor should they conceive of therapy in this light. Therefore, the initial conception of an interpersonal interactional model, one in which the aim is a mutually accepted, essentially verbal search for the basis and modification of the pathology—the adult model—must be modified.

Toward that end, I have derived the following principles that were developed and distilled from the application of the interpersonal approach to my therapeutic work with children. These principles are neither definitive nor uncontroversial. Some of them have their origin specifically in writings of interpersonalists; some have been derived from other models; and others reflect my own views. All, however, are congenial to an interpersonal approach, or at the least they do not contradict interpersonal views. These principles are essentially of equal importance and to me represent the core of an interpersonal view. While they may seem to be deceptively simple or even axiomatic, their proper application requires considerable skill, and, if carefully taken into account in the process of treatment, their full importance for their therapeutic efficacy will be appreciated.

PRINCIPLE 1. The Essence of Psychopathology is Problems of Living.

In an extensive study sponsored by the National Institute of Mental Health at three research sites, a comparison using an identical research protocol was made of two forms of brief psychotherapy (cognitive behavior therapy and interpersonal psychotherapy) with the use of medication in the treatment of depression in a group of 239 outpatients (Elkin et al. 1985). In this instance interpersonal psychotherapy was defined as being "based on the premise that depression occurs in an interpersonal context. The techniques are intended to help patients achieve a better understanding of their interpersonal problems and to improve their social functioning. The rationale is that if improvement in interpersonal relations can be effected, improvement in other areas will follow" (p. 311). The study concluded that psychotherapy was clearly as effective as drugs in bringing about cure.

This study is one of many that could be cited. Obviously, there are scores of studies that either support or deny biological as well as psychological factors in the etiology of pathology as well as those that point out the importance of both (Bergin and Strupp 1972; Weil-Malherbe and Szara 1971; Arieti 1974; Will 1967; Normand and Bluestone 1986; Cohen 1980). Methods of measuring the effectiveness of treatment, selection of patient populations, and other factors that are difficult to control always enter into such studies. The study is mentioned here only to emphasize the complexity of the problem and the variations in experimental findings.

Although there may be biological components of disorders of adjustment, it is one's relationship to one's world and to other people that is of central importance to the practice of psychotherapy. The explication of this principle is appropriately restrictive in neither seeking out nor concentrating on the biological or genetic factors that may influence the development of the disorder. Biological factors are, of course, significant insofar as they affect the manner in which the individual operates in relation to his world. A critical aspect of these factors from the interpersonal view is how the child understands these factors and integrates or fails to integrate them into his personality configuration. If antipsychotic drugs, mood elevators, antidepressants, and tranquilizers are included in the treatment of the child or adult, they must be considered as simply affecting his mood or reducing his confusion, not solving his problems of living. Specifically regarding depression, Arieti, for example, states, "I have never seen a patient about whom I could say his depression was unrelated to prior anguish, or about whom I could say that his depression came from nowhere and its origin had to be sought exclusively in a metabolic disorder" (1978:5).

Sullivan articulated the relationship between life experience and mental illness when he said:

But I should say that the genetic influences that are strongly conditional of a subsequent psychosis cannot go further than limit the possibility of psychosis, just as they limit the possibility of developments in other directions. There is no shadow of doubt in my mind that mental illnesses arise out of life experience. . . . In fact, we can cure patients only because there is nothing fixed and immutably ordained. (1956:359)

Psychotherapy cannot cure a deformed spine or repair a damaged brain or correct biological deafness, but addressed to problems of living, it can help people to adjust to these disorders so that their limitations do not keep them from developing satisfying and secure interpersonal relationships.

PRINCIPLE 2. Personality Structure and Dynamics are Essentially a Result of Interpersonal Relationships.

When emphasis on inherited and other biological factors as components in personality disorders is increased, the interpersonal factors tend to be understated. It is true, of course, that some people have more energy than others because of differing biological factors: temperament may be inherited. These factors may affect the intensity of certain feelings, but they do not determine how these feelings are expressed nor the characterological structure of the individual. From birth to death one is constantly learning ways of relating to other people [as a result of prior interactions with other people]. This learning occurs at an accelerated rate in infancy and becomes a more studied, cautious progression in later years (Stern 1985). Some patterns become more fixed than others and are harder to modify, but their formation is a result of interpersonal interaction and, just as in any "cure" through psychotherapy, is modified primarily through interpersonal interaction. Learning ways of behaving may be considered in terms of positive or negative reinforcement, but the significant issue is the nature of the reinforcement. The learning is a result of a complex phenomenon involving verbal and nonverbal communication and interaction with the specific biological and emotional needs of the growing human being. Because of the nature of language development and the use of metaphor as the primary mode of communication with children, development of a child is still very much the result of interpersonal relationships, the emphasis in understanding their development as well as their treatment is on nonverbal communication. The use of language complicates the process, particularly because of the unique coding and signal systems that evolve in different families.

PRINCIPLE 3. *Everyone is Much More Simply Human than Otherwise.*

This concept simply stated here as principle 3 was a central view of Sullivan (1953b:32) and is often referred to as the "one-genus postulate." In his assertion of this postulate Sullivan indicated that it is possible for us to understand the nature of the dynamic operations in people in whatever form these operations appear: their extreme forms in pathological manifestations have much in common with simple forms that are present in all of us where there are no pathological manifestations. Sullivan stresses the commonality among people. He focuses on our ability to understand each other's personalities because we are more like each other than we are different. Zaphiropoulos wrote that the one-genus postulate is "definitely intended to note that, no matter what the difference in endowment, environment, or achievement and whatever the degree or manifestations of mental health or psychopathology in a given person, that person is more likely to show behavior pertinent to the human race than to anything outside of it" (1985:427). R. Spiegel translates the one-genus postulate to "But for the grace of God, there go I" (1980).

According to Sullivan, most aberrations in behavior—what he would call security operations guarding against anxiety—can be viewed on a continuum. Speaking of them as parataxic processes to minimize anxiety, Sullivan said:

I believe that there are no peculiarities shown by the morbid; there are only differences in degree—that is, in intensity and timing—of that which is shown by everyone. Thus whenever I speak of dynamisms I am discussing universal human equipment, sometimes represented almost entirely in dreadful distortions of living, but still universal. And the distortions arise from misfortunes in development, restrictions in opportunity, and the like. (1953b:305)

For example, even if one is neat and orderly and prefers everything that way, one may not merit the label of compulsive, but simply orderly. If the orderliness, however, takes on an aspect of psychological pain or of discomfort in the presence of disorder, the label "compulsive" might be well deserved. Or, to take another example, one may occasionally count fence posts as one goes by them or avoid cracks in the sidewalk. But invariably counting fence posts or avoiding cracks may be considered a serious symptom in an adult.

Similarly and even more seriously, if one must go back and recount fence posts if one has lost track or return to step over a crack one had previously stepped on, the behavior takes on more pathological proportions. As the behavior approaches ritual—lining up loose change in order of size or value before retiring or checking each door and window four times before leaving the house—the symptom can be considered to be even more pathological and its effect more deleterious to the quality of life.

As part of the routine at a quality hospital for the emotionally disturbed, all patients, regardless of the degree of their pathology, were required to walk well-worn paths on the hospital grounds on a daily basis. One seriously disturbed schizophrenic, who had been walking paths for some ten years, had established a ritual in his daily walk. It was a complicated system that apparently had a private meaning requiring a specific number of steps forward before a certain number could be taken backwards. The ritual included such procedures as stopping to touch a leaf or kiss the ground or mumble some "magic" words. Surely this was serious pathology hardly in the same class as keeping a neat notebook and far more serious than simple obsessiveness or compulsiveness—it was clearly psychotic. However, if one follows the logic of the continuum outlined here, then this behavior can be seen as an extreme form of the progression from neatness and orderliness to obsessional and finally ritualistic behavior. Thus, the carefully observing clinician is able to some degree to understand empathically the terror of the anxiety and the uncanny emotions to which he too is susceptible, but to a lesser degree, and thus understand the ritualistic behavior of the schizophrenic on his daily walks.

Other classes of human experience can be traced on a continuum. For example, there is the progression from irritation to anger to rage. Or there are vague feelings of uneasiness at one end of a spectrum and intense anxiety at the other. All human experience has much in common, and an awareness of this shared experience makes it possible to be empathic, to understand how others think and feel.

In keeping with the one-genus postulate, there is always the potential for empathy and understanding. Men can never know from personal experience what it is like to be pregnant or to give birth, but all of us have experienced events that have altered our body images and all of us have suffered some physical pain.

Empathic understanding is crucial to working with children. Adults do not face the same problems that confront children, but we can empathize with them because of the isomorphic representation and transformations of experiences we have had that have a similar structure. As adults, we are not likely to have to obey or defy an unreasonable parent, nor are our toys stolen from us by older siblings. Some children may react to such situations by withdrawal, others with temper tantrums. Adults are not likely to have temper tantrums. If something is stolen from us or if we have a disagreeable supervisor who gives unreasonable orders, it is assumed that we have more mature ways of reacting. But all of us have had enough experience with the feelings engendered by such circumstances to enable us to understand, at least on an unconscious level, the feeling beneath the action or response of the child.

PRINCIPLE 4. Common Symptomatology Does not Assume Common Etiology.

It is easy to make assumptions about the origin of behavior on the basis of standard theoretical beliefs. In the days when dementia praecox first became known as schizophrenia and then was subtyped into simple, catatonic, paranoid, and heberophrenic, it was necessary only to ascertain which of the types the patient fell into. To account for exceptional behavior, however, new terms were coined—"borderline schizophrenia," "schizoaffective," "incipient schizophrenia," and "true paranoia." While diagnostic labels are useful ways of describing people, they carry with them certain assumptions about the origin of the pathology that may be far too rigid to afford an accurate description of the individual being examined.

As Erwin Singer said:

What strikes me as more important than the question of the correctness of the shortcomings of a particular theoretical position is the dangerous possibility that he who is the originator or the vociferous proponent of a given approach becomes the captive of his own creation and is in danger of subsequently not fully hearing his patient, for he may become wittingly or unwittingly more interested in proving himself right and in proving the value of his creation than in genuinely listening and hearing the other person. (1970:389)

In general, proponents of the interpersonal approach are more likely to describe people in terms of dynamic formulations than to use "shortcut" labeling, which does not do justice to the richness of the material and often precludes careful inquiry into the history of the specific disorder encountered.

It is easy to say that all alcoholics had passive fathers and aggressive mothers, but careful examination of individual dynamics indicates that this often is not so. Even when it is so, the terms are not sufficiently specific and reflect very different kinds of interpersonal integrations among parents and children. People who use alcohol may become addicted for varying reasons: some to feel more alive, some to feel more relaxed or less alive, some to feel more convivial with others, and some to feel more comfortable when alone. How can one make an assumption about the origin of such behavior when its function is so varied? For a fuller exploration, see Levenson (1983). The interpersonal approach is a pragmatic one that requires careful and complete inquiry.

As principle 3 suggests, there is a wide range to all human behavior including compulsive behavior. But, assuming compulsiveness as a separate entity, the strict Freudian explanation is that the problem has its origin in the "anal" phase and has much to do with toilet training. Indeed, toilet training is frequently a time for the transmission of anxiety (Sullivan 1953b:143–145). Not all compulsive people, however, had problems during toilet training. Some *may* have had, for a parent's trying to convey a need for extreme tidiness may have given rise to anxiety in the child, and compulsiveness might then have become a method of trying to avoid the anxiety. Toilet training is certainly an area of development where compulsivity can have its origin. Of course, it is also possible that as a result of interactions having to do with defecation some children may be so inclined to oppose their parents that they intentionally become quite disorganized rather than becoming excessively orderly. It is the nature of the interaction that determines the specific developmental inclination around significant areas of upbringing. As for compulsivity, there are many possible origins for this characteristic style of behavior. For example, a child might develop an extreme sense of order to protect himself against a household of turmoil or disorder. Or if a parent constantly gives unclear or mixed messages, the child's manner of dealing with confusion may be constantly to seek precision or clarification, to know "where he stands," and his character structure may then incline toward compulsivity.

To illustrate further the complex origin of symptoms, there is the label "hystrionic," which is given to people who seem to exaggerate the importance of the issues they confront in life. They believe their feelings to be more intense than anyone else's. Their physical disorders frequently terrify them, for they most often see any disorder as evidence of severe physical pathology. They may shout and scream because they come from families where members were not heard unless they called attention to themselves and the person who shouted the loudest won the argument. Often, people who still merit the label "hysteric" by virtue of their exaggeration of issues or who technically and more accurately might be called "hystrionic" may come from families where the preferred way of calling attention to oneself was by giving people the "silent treatment." That is, their way of handling anger was to stop talking with the party assumed to be the offender.

While hysterical behavior frequently serves as a way of calling attention to oneself, it can also be used to distract people from more significant issues. By showing exaggerated behavior, the hysteric can avoid revealing feelings of uncertainty or hide information whose disclosure might have deleterious consequences (or so he or she parataxically believes).

The principle that common symptomotology does not assume common etiology as it more specifically applies to children may be illustrated by the fact that some children bring toys with them to the playroom. They may do so to comfort themselves because these are their own toys; they may be showing you that they own toys; they may be avoiding playing with certain objects that are in the playroom; they may wish to show you their ability to master those toys; they may be using their toys as ways to discourage a therapist whom they find too intrusive with language; or they may bring toys for some other reason that needs to be discovered. Only inquiry, both verbal and nonverbal, will disclose the basis for this behavior. Bringing a toy from home is not necessarily an indicator of pathology, but its meaning must be understood by the therapist, and no ready generalization can explain its significance without risk of missing the real meaning of the behavior.

Good interpersonal psychotherapy must include a careful and detailed study of the individual's total development so that all symptoms can be understood in terms of their specific origins. The essential process of treatment is effectively continuous and thorough inquiry.

PRINCIPAL 5. Cultural Factors have a Vital Influence on Personality Development.

In addition to one's parents and other significant figures, there are many influences on a child's life; all must be understood if individual behavior is to be comprehended. As Fromm put it, "The most beautiful as well as the most ugly inclinations of man are not part of a fixed and biologically given human nature but result from the social process which creates man" (1941:12).

A child brought up in ghetto conditions may show behavior that could be considered to be paranoid or at least indicate that the child is highly suspicious and protective of his possessions. In psychotherapy learning about trust would be different for this child than it would be for a child who came to a similar attitude by virtue of having a greedy sibling or an intrusive parent.

The following illustrations, presented as evidence more of culturally idiosyncratic influence than of a total cultural value or standard, exemplify the specificity of effect and the crucial need for complete understanding of the etiology of an attitude.

An analyst treating an immigrant from a traditional Japanese background notes that his patient consistently understates his abilities; in speaking Japanese, English, and even in his ability as a professional photographer. The analyst notes that the patient speaks English quite well, assumes he can speak Japanese well because of the patient's ability to deal with people who speak only Japanese, and has learned that the patient's work as a professional photographer has met with consistent approval and admiration. The natural inclination of the analyst not cognizant of the traditional Japanese cultural emphasis on modesty and self-deprecation would be to assume that the patient has a very poor self-image. However, an understanding of the patient's background would preclude the making of such an assumption on the basis of this evidence.

A recently emigrated Nigerian teenager once described his family to me. He made frequent reference to different male members as being very strong or powerful. The language was somewhat misleading, and I began to wonder why there was so much emphasis on physical prowess. Careful inquiry disclosed that his use of the words strong and powerful had nothing to do with physical ability but rather referred to the degree of influence or importance in this extended family. In the same way, when asked to tell me about his family, he said that he had twelve mothers, since bigamy was culturally and legally accepted. However, through careful inquiry and attention to individual dynamics, I was able to parcel out the influence of specific significant figures. Such cultural influences were noted by Fromm-Reichman, who said:

In evaluating the contents of patients' communications, the psychiatrist must consider with equal care the colloquialisms and slang expressions, the use of which may frequently be conditioned by differences in patients' cultural and social backgrounds.

In the case of a foreigner it may happen that he uses the wrong words because of a lack of command of the language, which, if used by an American-born patient, might permit psychological conclusions regarding his state of mind. In the instance of a foreigner who uses the word "homely" when meaning to express appreciation for a "homelike" environment, this slip may be attributed to his unfamiliarity with the language. If an American-born person makes such an error, it may be assumed that it is due to a hostile impulse. (1950:51)

To further illustrate the various possibilities in the origin of behavior, one might note that a child who gives excessive attention to a flowering plant in the therapist's playroom may be indicating nurturing qualities, identifying with the plant, or giving it excessive value because there are few if any flowering plants in the ghetto neighborhood from which he comes—or any combination of the above.

Principle 5 thus emphasizes that a variety of factors—geography, neighborhood, school, race, sex, religion, teachers, playmates, mores, intrafamily structure—influence the formation of particular character and dynamics.

PRINCIPLE 6. Normal Development Requires the Maintenance and Enhancement of Self-Esteem.

This principle is not merely an elaborate way of saying that we all like to hear nice things about ourselves. The principle should be considered as a basic and intense underlying force in operation in all people. Self-worth is a primary goal of much of our behavior, albeit the method of achieving this may show considerable variation and may even include behavior that is considered illegal, immoral, or sadistic. The search for self-worth may, for example, involve stealing or inflicting pain on others; stealing might be a way of enhancing such esteem by indicating that one has more or better things than others, and inflicting pain may be a way of enhancing self esteem by showing superior strength. I do not mean that in the search for self-esteem one ignores all moral or ethical values but rather that one attempts to feel good about oneself in order to maintain satisfying relations with other people and to deal with the normal problems of living while feeling comfortable about oneself. On the other hand, if one cannot permit bad thoughts about oneself because they would lower self-esteem, one may go to great lengths to prevent these thoughts, to the point of dissociating many events and experiences in life.

If we think pejoratively about patients in their interactions with the therapist, it is difficult to assist them in maintaining self-esteem. Some therapists assume a kind of paranoid orientation in their approach to patients. They think in terms of what the patient is trying to do to them. They may be correct in their analysis, but the emphasis is not the most useful to the patient. It is much more helpful for the therapist to think in terms of what the patient is trying to do for himself. If, in this process of doing something for himself, the patient psychologically injures the therapist, the therapist should call attention to the hurtfulness of the behavior but should not assume that the primary motivation of the patient was to hurt the therapist, get even, or otherwise injure the therapist's feelings. If we assume that one's self-image is essentially the result of the reflected appraisal of others, then, although the patient may behave badly, we must be careful in how we react and describe the patient's action to him. It is all too easy to criticize patients if we think of their actions as having malevolent intent, and expressing such criticism in the interest of confrontation "for the patient's own good" easily becomes the avenue of approach. But we do not help them by making pejorative statements about their personalities.

Pejorative statements are especially hurtful to children, who do not have the verbal or physical ability to protect themselves in order to maintain their self-esteem. They are trusting and forgiving and tend to assume the best motivation about adults. Thus, they may assume that an adult's hurtful verbal or physical behavior directed against them is valid and justified and the injury to their self-esteem can be quite profound even when the adult was speaking in jest. It is for this reason that adult criticism should be clearly directed toward *behavior,* not toward personality.

A simple example of the importance of careful use of language by the therapist is illustrated in an incident in which an adolescent reported to me dishonest acts he performed as part of his school behavior. These included lies about his homework, cheating on examinations, and stealing pencils from the teacher's desk. To deal with this directly and at the same time to make it palatable, I said, "How did such a nice guy like you come to take up stealing?" Not only was this not injurious to self-esteem but by saying "such a nice guy like you," I was enhancing self-esteem.

PRINCIPAL 7. People Are Not Free to Change Until They Are Free to Be What They Are.

At first reading, this may appear to be double talk. It is my impression, however, that we have many kinds of mechanisms to maintain and enhance our self-esteem and that direct attacks on people—on what they are or think they are—result in defensiveness and thus obstruct change. In fact, if the attacks are so severe that normal modes of protecting oneself, such as denial or simply discounting the attacks or the attackers, are insufficient to maintain a sense of self, then more extreme forms of defense are utilized and psychotic behavior may be a result. An extreme example of this is that of a psychotic child who on admission to a hospital attacked and fought with the attendant, tearing his shirt, because she believed the attendant to be the devil. She experienced being admitted to the hospital as so humiliating that, to justify her own behavior, she had to hallucinate. The following day the girl apologized to the attendant, saying that she was sorry she had torn his shirt but that she had thought he was the devil. This is a rather complex piece of behavior involving a child who was unable to deal with stresses with more acceptable and less distorted means. Her whole internal world was badly fragmented; her behavior represented an intricate distorted self-system manifested in psychotic behavior. This aspect of her behavior illustrates the function of psychotic behavior in the maintenance of self-esteem.

Less extreme protective behavior is seen when a therapist says something to a patient that evokes tears. If the patient needs to maintain an image of not being hurt or upset, of never crying or showing sadness, the patient may claim to be wiping her eyes because something blew into them—to save face. It becomes important that such patients accept their vulnerability so that they can build adequate and appropriate defenses and then be able to admit their hurts and cry openly.

Often, psychotherapy is oriented toward confrontations of the worst kind, confrontations that give therapists an opportunity to express their own unresolved hostilities. I have seldom seen such confrontations result in psychotherapeutic improvement. While the old expression "no gain without pain" is often applied to psychotherapy or psychoanalysis, I strongly disagree with this contention. There certainly will be painful moments in the therapeutic treatment process, but these should not be intentional. It is unfortunate that such moments occur, but it is not always essential that they do. I suspect that "no gain without pain" has its roots in a quasi-superstitious concept that if we suffer we will then be rewarded, or if we have something fortuitous happen to us, we are likely to suffer because of it afterwards. There are many people who still retain the notion that an antiseptic must be painful in order to kill bacteria; they prefer iodine to mercurochrome because iodine hurts and therefore must be more effective. Good treatment can be an enriching, enlivening, and even joyful experience; hurt or pain is not an essential ingredient. Those painful times that do occur should emanate from the patient's own discoveries, not because of hurtful, harshly presented confrontations initiated by the therapist.

If adult patients can see how they came to be the way they are, through insight they can demystify their own behavior and understand its use and justification. They can discover how, for example, at one time in their lives lying may have been necessary but is now inappropriately and needlessly used, resulting in few people trusting them. Information about themselves can become palatable, and the patients are then freer to change their behavior and eliminate this manner of operating. I do not deny the value of selective confrontation with adults, but in view of the importance of maintaining self esteem, it must be done without humiliation.

With children, avoiding injury to self esteem is even more critical. One must be particularly cautious in correcting their errors to be sure to attend to the errors and not the character of the child. If children are called clumsy, stupid, or ugly, they tend to take it literally as descriptive of their whole personality. Take, for instance, a 10-year-old running up the stairs to the playroom with his shoe laces dangling. The therapist observing this is genuinely concerned that the child could trip and be injured. It would be foolish to ask, "Why don't you tie your shoelace?"—although that is perhaps better than saying, "Tie your shoe lace," which would be perceived as an order or a demand. Children are frequently admonished by parents, who say, for example, "Tie your shoelace. You always leave them untied," and the parents may then go on to thoroughly discuss the child's character and failings. A more appropriate response from a thoughtful therapist might be: "Isn't it amazing that you are able to run up the stairs without tripping on your dangling shoelace?" It would certainly be a way of calling the child's attention to the untied shoe, which he may not be aware of and which might be a result of carelessness, without *requiring* him to change, so that if he wishes to leave his shoelaces untied, he is free to do so.

PRINCIPLE 8. Treatment Requires Movement in the Direction of an Undistorted View of Oneself and the World.

In Sullivan's words, "No one has grave difficulties in living if he has a very good grasp of what is happening to him" (1970:22). A major goal of psychotherapy is to enable the individual to make judgments based on real evidence so that unreasonable expectations do not interfere with personal relationships. Evidence of faulty expectations may be found in distortions and/or selective inattention.

The term "parataxic distortion," as used by Sullivan (1956), is different than the Freudian term "transference," and refers to a private mode of experience though over the years they have come to be used somewhat interchangeably and inexactly. Distortions of identity, however, take place not only in the analytic situation but throughout life's experiences. One way of viewing the matter is to use learning theory as a model and assume that because of varying and sometimes quite traumatic factors, people make faulty generalizations. For a simple example, a man who was severely bitten or mauled by a dog may thereafter be fearful of all dogs, no matter how gentle they are. A woman who was deserted by her father and whose later contrary experience has not been sufficient to overcome an expectation of being abandoned may extend that expectation to all men later in life. Fear of desertion on the part of a woman who would like to be married may be extended, and she may assume that the tendency to discard women is a characteristic of all men— an assumption that may cause considerable difficulty throughout the woman's life.

Another form of distortion is selective inattention, which is a method of avoiding anxiety or denying information that might contradict one's strongly held beliefs by failing to include or take note of experiences that could change one's beliefs or distortions. Selective inattention is a remarkable phenomenon that underlines the hazy distinction between conscious and unconscious and allows for varying levels of awareness. In order for people not to hear or see something that may give rise to anxiety, they must in fact hear it or see it or else they would not be able to select the information to be screened out.

In the context of the dissociated systems Sullivan explains:

Whenever dissociated systems of motives are involved, we find a relative suspension of awareness as to any effects that these motives have. That suspension of awareness may be as minor as the relatively trifling and almost ubiquitous disturbance of awareness to which I give the term *selective inattention,* in which one simply doesn't happen to notice almost an infinite series of more-or-less meaningful details of one's living. But even selective inattention is very impressive when one observes that it could not possibly act so suavely, and so eternally at the right times, unless there was continuous vigilance lest one notice what for some obscure reasons one is not going to notice. (1953b:319)

Psychotherapy should heighten patients' awareness of and place in proper perspective all experiences in which they participate. Broadening the scope of inquiry is a major function of psychoanalysis (Wolstein 1988).

The issue of distortion is crucial with children. While it is important that they learn to make distinctions among people that are based on reality rather than some kind of projected or misidentified image, they are still developing and involved in a complex learning experience. Depriving them of their distortions too quickly leaves them with no concept of other people that has any reliability or constancy. A child who refers to the therapist by his teacher's name first needs to be assured that in some ways the therapist *is* like a teacher. It is only later that the child should be gradually assisted to see what the differences are.

PRINCIPLE 9. Anxiety Is a Noxious State That People Seek to Avoid.

Levenson (1983) suggests that Sullivan sees avoidance of anxiety as the underlying force for all behavior or as the essential drive behind all activity. Sullivan did emphasize the commonality of the human need to guard against the potential for anxiety. While I believe this is indeed important, I do not believe it is sufficient to explain the motivation of all behavior. In fact, I believe Sullivan assumed additional motivation when he stated, "I have come to feel sure that we may depend on everyone's drive toward more adequate and improved ways of living; in a word, toward improved mental health" (1953b:373). For Singer (1970), who sees the avoidance of anxiety as the motivator for Sullivan, the drive is toward interpersonal relatedness. However one chooses to conceive of the

matter, it is clear that anxiety plays an important part in psychody-
namics and is a very unpleasant feeling that people will go to great
lengths to avoid, frequently not too successfully. In treatment some
therapists as well as patients will avoid talking about some subjects
as a way of staving off anxiety. I believe that on the contrary, talking
about something reduces anxiety; it does not increase it. What's
more, not talking about it is collusive and suggests that the problem
is so disturbing or shameful that even the therapist does not wish
to discuss it. Unfortunately, many therapists see this as a directive
to encourage confrontation, which may have elements of accusation
and hurtfulness and, if not handled in a most skillful manner, may,
as noted earlier, result in feelings of humiliation or at best in defensiveness. Instead of avoiding discussion of anxiety, therapists should
offer opportunities and encouragement for patients to reveal and
discuss their feelings of anxiety and the things that make them
anxious.

Most people have experienced a feeling that is commonly referred to as free-floating anxiety, in which the anxiety does not seem
to be attached to any particular cause. Most likely, if its underlying
connection were understood, the anxiety would be injurious to self-
esteem. Understanding the underlying cause in its proper perspective and dealing with it in a direct but supportive manner usually
results in a more satisfying internal state.

With children the differentiation of feelings is an important developmental task that can be greatly assisted in therapy. Locating
fears and separating them from feelings of anxiety, guilt, dread, and
remorse is not easily accomplished. Because of the strong but con-
flictual desire children have to be "grown-up," admitting fears may
seem to them to be a way of acknowledging that they are still babies. Conveying the acceptance and understanding that certain events
make people anxious can be most helpful to children in therapy.

PRINCIPLE 10. The Therapist Is a Participant Observer in the Treatment Process.

Most therapists of all schools accept the fact that they are a part
of the therapeutic process, and today there is little reference to the
therapist as a "blank screen." However, within broad parameters

there is considerable variation. There are those who wish to remain essentially anonymous to their patients and, particularly unfortunately, discount completely any influence they may have on the therapeutic process (Greenberg 1986a, 1986b). And there are those who become so thoroughly intertwined in the lives of their patients that they lose their objectivity. The natural involvement that the therapist has with the child patient is usually far more extensive than with adults by virtue of the therapist's having to deal with many significant others in the child's life. This arrangement can too readily lead to an attitude of control on the part of the therapist and a diminishing of respect for the child's autonomy in the growth process.

The concept of participant observer contains not merely the influence of the therapist on the behavior of the patient or of the patient on the behavior of the therapist (Epstein and Feiner 1979) but also the field that is a result of the interplay between patient and therapist. I do not believe in "wild analysis," where anything goes and where therapists are all too revealing of their personal lives. However, children, like adults, may inquire about the private life of the therapist. Such issues as whether or not the therapist is married or has children may be of vital importance to the patient, particularly a child. Of course, the central issue is what the information means to the patient, adult or child, and this needs to be explored. Underlying factors that may partly determine how the therapist deals with these issues may have to do with his own attitudes about his life and about issues of confidentiality and secrecy. However, withholding information that is not highly personal would at best be rude and is in itself likely to resonate with issues of secretiveness and withholding that might well be part of the family experience of the patient. The fundamental meaning of personal questions is likely to be somewhat different for adults than it is for children. For the adult patient a question about the therapist's age or marital status might have implications for some remote fantasy about his eligibility as a potential mate, whereas for the child who is particularly cautious it may be a way of asking if the therapist has children of his own. What the child may have in mind is the consideration of the possibility that he or she could come and live with the therapist. With some children who may feel that the therapist is able to love only one child (for reasons that will be described later) the presence of the therapist's own children precludes the possibility that he can love the patient. With a child it is important to recognize that withholding information in response to direct questions can be particularly deleterious, for it is unlikely that the child can accurately conceive of the classically defined role of "therapist" as some kind of catalyst.

The concept of participant observer is more complex in relation to children than it is with adults particularly as it applies to the therapeutic sessions. As a participant observer the therapist must be fully aware of his own feelings and with adults be fully able to share them. It is in the process of unraveling issues of transference and countertransference that the reactions of the therapist and the role he fills by virtue of his action in the therapeutic encounter becomes most useful. With children, if the therapy is play therapy, then the issue of participating in the play must be considered. There are some therapists (Ginott 1961b) who do not participate in any play with the children. Others become fully involved, but their roles may become so diluted that they function as playmates rather than as therapists. (For a more lengthy discussion of this issue see chapter 6, "Limit Setting.") If the therapist participates in play with a child, which I generally recommend and will discuss in later chapters, then there is a opportunity for him to play varying roles, as a police officer, parent, child, sibling, or teacher. In this way the transference is specifically directed and dealt with but not generally interpreted as transference.

PRINCIPLE 11. Stages of Development are Continuous Throughout Life.

The idea of discrete stages of development that require mastery before the next stage can be encountered is neither accurate nor useful in the conception of psychodynamic formulations that lead to effective psychotherapy. To some degree Sullivan anticipated the findings of Stern (1985) in suggesting overlapping of stages of development. As Zaphiropoulos, describing the interpersonal school, noted:

Sullivan outlined sequential modes of experiencing—sequentialness that is likely, although uncertain, with possible overlapping—pertaining to the maturational unfolding of the organism's endowment. Arrest or persistence in those modes that seem chronologically inappropriate may account for certain peculiarities of personality or for specific forms of pathology. (1985:428)

Stern's research (1985) has clearly established this notion of sequence regarding infancy. To the extent that people must learn to crawl before they can walk or that they must be able to understand arithmetic before they can understand algebra, the concept of completion of stages is useful. However, if one considers such sequential issues in regard to sexual development, such as adhering to a concept of an Oedipal stage when development is supposed to be complete, one precludes the possibility of change in later life. Problems having to do with sexuality, for example, may not appear until preteen years, during teen years, or sometimes not until adult years. The circumstances that contribute to such development must be carefully considered rather than assumed to be a result of problems that occurred during the so called pre-Oedipal or Oedipal years. Some men who experience impotence for the first time in later life never had such difficulties in their youth. One cannot literally return to childhood years to undo or redo critical periods, but the treatment process is a kind of reconstruction. If the sequence of developmental tasks had been completed, psychotherapy could not be effective in bringing about changes in orientation, attitudes, and beliefs.

Development is so uneven that adherence to stage-specific concepts of the origin of pathology tends to blur variability in personality. For example, a child could be remarkably mature in his table manners or his intellectual development and most immature in his attention to cleanliness or appearance. Certain tasks are usually completed during different periods of life, but for some people the tasks are accomplished sooner or later than expected, or are only partially completed. To extend the findings and implications of Stern's work (1985), one may be fairly specific about the point of origin for a particular developmental aspect of the character structure to appear, but the completion of development and modifications may well continue throughout life. Even when people have shown a certain "maturity" in one or another aspect of personality, under some trying circumstances these people may regress and display atypical immaturity. Rigid, stage-related conceptualizations deprive us of fluidity and deny an appreciation of the full richness and complexity of personality. The function of therapy with children is not to make them into mature adults in any sense, but rather to bring them to a level of maturity that is relatively appropriate for their age.

PRINCIPLE 12. Communication in Therapy is Largely a Semiotic Process.

While the use of the term "semiotic" as it applies to therapy might best be attributed to Levenson (1972), its meaning is close to attunement as described by Stern (1985) in relation to the mother-infant relationship. Effectively, the term refers to communications between people that is not dependent on literal use of language and can include intonation and volume as well as nonverbal cues. Obviously communication by other than verbal means is of vital importance in all therapy. The actual or authentic message is the significant ingredient in communication within or outside of psychotherapy. The "right" words with the wrong inflection, facial expression, or tone of voice may take on a completely different meaning than the words would otherwise seem to convey. Nonverbal communication is more primitive and in many ways much more reliable than verbal communication.

The therapist who gives verbal permission to be messy with finger paints and then spends time guarding his or her clothes or office against the ravages of such play is, at best, giving a very mixed message. This principle, that communication is largely a semiotic process, is an important aspect of my discussion of interpretation and communication through metaphor.

PRINCIPLE 13. The Preferred Method of Interpretation with Children is Through Metaphor.

This point is not a direct extraction of an interpersonal principle. It is deduced as one congenial with such principles, and it deserves considerable emphasis. The total function of insight must be examined in the light of enhancing natural development. Providing information that bypasses normal growth process (Spiegel 1973) can have serious deleterious effects on later adjustment. This point is so important that the next chapter is devoted to it, and throughout the book the methods of utilizing metaphor are frequently illustrated and explained. The goal of good therapy with children is to change internal conceptualizations, not to provide cognitive understanding of unique dynamics.

2

Metaphor

Almost all symptoms of pathology can be considered as functions of regressed or arrested development. At one or another time during growth the symptoms were appropriate methods of coping. While this is evident with adults, it is especially apparent in working with children, where the goal of treatment is to bring the child only to a level of psychological development commensurate with his age. It is of primary importance not to try to make an adult of the child.

While I do not believe that Anna Freud always honored this position, she did propose that one *need* not take a child further than the position in which all children are at that developmental stage (1946). I would alter this to say that one *should* not take a child further. It is important for the child to be aware of and connected with his feelings; but to provide the child with information about the origin and etiology of his disorder—in effect for him to analyze the transference in his behavior—would bypass a natural maturational process by depriving him of the development of normal defenses and would likely lead to serious problems in later development. It appears to me that this is a basic error of much analytic and therapeutic work that is done with children—a point that cannot be overemphasized.

Psychoanalytic Origins of Play Therapy

With the exception of the rather remarkable analysis of Little Hans, which Sigmund Freud (1909) performed as a kind of family treatment through the child's father, the major avenue by which psychoanalysis of children developed was by the utilization of the same method as in the individual treatment of adults, even to the point of having the child free associate on the couch. The limitations of a child's vocabulary became an obstacle, so that play readily became the vehicle by which the analysis could take place. Nevertheless, the underlying assumption was that the child was to learn the basis of his behavior in terms of transferential distortions.

Preserving Healthy Development Through Play

While the use of play as the vehicle for therapy with children was recommended primarily because the child is not sufficiently able to use language, its value goes far beyond that. If the goal of treatment with the child is to bring that child to the level of development commensurate with and appropriate to his age, then the means of accomplishing this should also be age appropriate. Infants do not begin development with a spoken language; full mastery is not attained until relatively late in childhood. Treatment with children (as with adults) should be in the lexicon of the patient. The patient should not be forced to use the lexicon of the therapist.

The natural form of communication for a child is play, just as the natural form of locomotion for a child is running. The therapist who uses play objects to convey messages to the child is communicating directly. As Ekstein stated, "the royal road to the unconsciousness of the child is his play" (1983:169). When a therapeutic message is conveyed through play and the interpretation is inaccurate, premature, or otherwise inappropriate, the child can readily reject it

without having to confront the therapist and risk rejection or dis-
approval. Of course, the child's preference might not be the sole
criterion for choosing play or verbal therapy as the method of treatment. Some children who genuinely prefer to talk may be too intellectualized for their age and should be encouraged to play more
than talk. This would be especially true if the verbalizations tend
to be dissociated from feelings. A major problem often encountered
in metropolitan and presumably sophisticated parts of the country
or with sophisticated families is that children (and adults) obses-
sively talk too much about their feelings to the point where many
of them cannot adequately differentiate between real feelings and
those about which they believe they are talking.

I am always willing to discuss directly with children some of their
concerns and fears if they so choose and when they indicate that
they are fully aware of the problems and wish to talk about them,
but I never force the issue. Of course, one never knows: an elementary school teacher reported that a 6-year-old child who came
from a troubled family had recently entered psychotherapy. The
teacher was quite pleased and told this to the child. The child responded by saying she liked it fine, but that she thought she was
going to see someone whom she could talk with "and all he wants
to do is play." This child is an exception and more likely to be
seen in a metropolitan area, but a request such as this should certainly not be ignored. Depending on the issues involved—for example if the child has been pressured into being too adult for her
age—it might still be appropriate to discourage language and continue to encourage play.

Unlike many child therapists, I do not see the aim of good therapy with children as getting them to talk about their concerns and
problems in a straightforward manner. That could be part of the
process, but the purpose of the treatment is to enhance their self-
esteem, to affect their concept of themselves and others so that
their view is realistic, to be aware of what their feelings are, and
to assist in the cure of specific neurotic or psychotic processes. All
of this need not be accompanied by insight about origin and dynamics of their disorder, and for the most part I hope that it is
not.

The Nondirective Approach Placed in Context

An essentially nonpsychoanalytic approach to the treatment of children came about through the work of nondirectivists: Rogers (1951), Allen (1942), Axline (1947), and others. Their underlying assumption was that, given the proper nurturing and accepting environment, the child would grow in the appropriate direction. This point of view is also reflected in the work of Sullivan (1956). There was recognition that feelings need to be experienced and recognized by the child and that the job of the therapist was frequently to reflect verbally the feelings displayed.

An example of this is taken from Axline:

(*Jack filled his mouth with water. He leaned over and spat it on the floor.*)

JACK: Look I spit on my home.

THERAPIST: You spit on your home.

(*Jack jerked off the nipple and filled his mouth again and once more spat on the floor.*)

J: I spit on my brother. I spit on my father. I spit in their very faces. They wouldn't give me the toys. He broke my gun. I'll show them. I'll spit on them. (*Again and again he filled his mouth with water and spat on the floor.*)

T: You are very angry with your brother and your father. You would like to spit right in their faces because of the way they have treated you.

J: They broke my gun. (*He went over to the drinking fountain and filled the nursing bottle again and continued to spit on his father and brother. They had a new rug back home.*) Look . . . I'll spit on the rug. I'll get it all wet. I'll ruin it. And my brother's new suit! I'll spit on his new suit and I'll ruin that.

T: You'll ruin the new rug and the new suit. You'll get even with your father and brother.

J: (*violently*): I hate my father! I hate my brother!

T: You hate your father. You hate your brother.

(*Jack sat down across from the therapist, suddenly very calm. He lowered his voice. He put the nipple back on the bottle and began to suck on it again.*)

J: I didn't know how long I was going to stay when I went home.

I didn't take enough clothes with me. I stayed longer than I had planned. I never know. They never tell me. [I assume that the child is in some kind of institution or else he lives with his mother and makes periodic visits to his father.]

T: You never know what to expect. You can't make plans for your visits unless they tell you how long you can stay. You didn't have enough clothes with you because they didn't tell you. 103–4)

Many children would find this kind of treatment annoying. Early in my training merely verbalizing and reflecting feeling was considered an acceptable and even preferred approach, but I first began to question the utility of this method when a child said to me, "How come you say everything I say?"

What Axline accomplished in this session is difficult to determine. She did elicit a very direct expression of the child's anger. From her theoretical standpoint, by acknowledging and repeating the child's words in a comforting manner, she conveyed to him that she accepted his feelings. But what else happened? After much of this outburst, Jack became suddenly calm and began to suck on the bottle. I suspect that what took place at this point was that Jack became frightened by his own outburst, which went on with no evidence of any control and perhaps with encouragement from Axline, so that he then regressed to sucking on the bottle. It is likely that his direct display of anger had the primary effect of inducing guilt and fear in the child.

I believe Axline could have been more helpful if, instead of just giving permission or encouragement for the expression of anger, she had helped place it in context for him. For example, she might have said that she could see how that kind of treatment would make him very angry with them. It would also have been beneficial had she given some kind of limits that may have been comforting to the child. Perhaps it would have been constructive to say, "In here you can show how mad you are. You can say anything you like." This approach would have conveyed to the child that even though there are places and times when one cannot say what one feels in an unrestricted manner, the *feeling* is not to be prohibited. It is not a good idea simply to emphasize or encourage the expression of anger in the playroom because anger in itself can become addictive (Szalita 1968).

Nor does permission to spit without restraint or limits seem to me to be a good idea. In chapter 6, on limit setting, I discuss a child who spit regularly as a symptom of her pathology and suggest a manner of handling it. With Jack it would have been better if the spitting were somehow confined, perhaps to a sink or the water fountain or a toilet. Spitting involves other problems, such as cleaning up and socially unacceptable behavior. More importantly, the child might have been frightened to have been allowed such unrestricted behavior.

The nondirective approach assumed an underlying concept that might be considered as a corrective emotional experience. That is, those who favored this approach seemed to be operating from the standpoint that providing a child with a kind of treatment he had not received as part of his growing up would repair damage done by an emotional deficit. This concept of the corrective emotional experience did not correspond to Alexander and French's view (1946) that the therapy was somehow contrived to be different in corrective ways from the experience that the child had had with his parents, but rather to the sense that the therapeutic environment was fully accepting and nurturing. Although underlying dynamics may have been considered by the therapist, they were not effectively utilized in the treatment.

Interpretation Through Metaphor

I believe the most appropriate approach utilizes dynamic formulations for psychoanalytic theory while offering only very limited interpretation. I do not believe mere nurturance and complete acceptance is adequate.

If one accepts the concept that the therapeutic session is a kind of microcosm for life experience, then the therapy can be understood as affording an opportunity to work out new ways of dealing with the problems of living. The traditional psychoanalytic approach places strong emphasis on highly intellectualized verbal interpretation, which I feel is inappropriate for children. Interpretation through metaphor, however, is appropriate. One must convey a thought or feeling symbolically so that toxic aspects of the situation are omitted, and the child may be able to accept the meaning of the interpretation with little if any damage to his self-esteem. An example of such interpretation is as follows:

In the treatment of an encopretic 10-year-old an interesting problem arose that illustrates the principle of interpretation through metaphor. The child, Daniel, entered the playroom on about the tenth weekly session of therapy, having arrived directly from school. I distinctly smelled feces when he entered the room. To have ignored the odor and said nothing would have been a gross error: I would have been entering into a kind of conspiracy with the child not to talk about unpleasant things. That approach might also have carried the implication that the problem was so bad that even I was unwilling to talk about it. Since we both knew very well that soiling was his problem and a major reason for his entering therapy, I went beyond the obvious procedure of simply calling attention to the quite apparent odor. Feeling that any mention of it would be an accusation, which indeed it would be, but also believing that it could not be ignored, I worded my comment about the odor in a way that I thought would help him maintain his self esteem. I said, "It smells like you had an accident at school today." (The child was having a particularly difficult time with one teacher, whom he found very disagreeable, and it was in his class that he usually became so anxious that an "accident" might occur.)

"No," he said, "that doesn't happen any more," and he then went on to somewhat excessive additional denial. In spite of my attempt to make it easy for him to acknowledge the problem, he apparently still found it too humiliating. Of course, I let the matter drop at that point. We both knew I was right, and I am sure that he did not believe that his denial convinced me that he had not soiled himself.

A well-meaning "It's all right, you can tell me" kind of approach would likely have resulted in further humiliation and defensiveness. While my action may have been considered as collusive, one must note that I did not deny my perception; I simply did not pursue the matter. The child then proceeded to play with a car he had started constructing at his last session the week before. The car was made of small parts and designed to be powered by an inflated balloon in which the expelling air would propel it. It was extremely important to him that the car be very well balanced and exceptionally stable. I am sure needing it to be stable had a meaning of its own, perhaps representing some need to keep himself well balanced or referring to his concern about his mother, who was crippled and had difficulty walking unassisted. On some level the propulsion by air from the balloon could have represented flatulence or the expelling of feces. All of his behavior lent itself well to the potential for assistance through metaphor, even though I did not know what he had in mind and on what level he conceived of it. But it was not necessary for me to know its true significance; nor was it necessary for *him* to understand the symbolic significance of the car, and in fact such knowledge might have interfered with his constructing and using it in this symbolic maner. If, for example, the car represented him, he only needed to be concerned that it be well balanced and work. Though all of our behavior is colored by basic characterological and personality qualities—and the metaphorical implication in this instance seems clear—one must always be cognizant that, to paraphrase a founding analyst, sometimes a car is just a car.

In the course of constructing the car, Daniel had used small bits of clay as ballast. At one point he took a small chunk of clay and put it on the end of his nose. I do not know if a message was conveyed to me in an empathic way beyond my intellectual recognition, but, on a hunch and with no danger of injury to his self-esteem, I said in a questioning manner, "You look like Pinocchio?" To this he said an emphatic "yes" and went back to work on the car. I then said, "Pinocchio lied to Gippeto about school. Sometimes telling the truth is just too difficult or embarrassing." The child continued his play with no reference to what I had said, and I pursued the matter no further; my job was done. The important point was my expression of acceptance of his lying, without forcing him to acknowledge having done so and thus enabling him to protect his self-esteem. I do not know for certain that when Daniel placed the clay on his nose, he was consciously or even unconsciously aware of his wish to convey to me that he had in fact lied. I assume so because he acknowledged that he looked like Pinocchio, but it is conceivable that his behavior had another meaning. Perhaps he was calling attention to the odor.

A traditional Freudian might say that he felt inadequate under the circumstance and was making his nose, which represented a penis, longer to bolster his ego. Although I find that kind of interpretation too remote, the interpretation would not have mattered because by my way of dealing with it the effect could only have been to his benefit. The entire transaction could have taken place at any level of awareness, from complete awareness to complete unawareness. What is important is that I may have helped him realize that even well-meaning, acceptable people may lie under certain circumstances, that I accepted that fact, that I never called him a liar. Thus I helped him restore or maintain some of his self-esteem.

If I had said, "Listen, I know you lied to me, but it's all right to lie sometimes like Pinocchio did," in addition to possibly exposing something he may not have wanted to expose, I would also have insinuated that in a way I had read his mind. In such circumstances the right wording is important: one has to differentiate between empathic attunement and intrusive control (Kohut 1977:146–151). Very young children may accept what seems to be mind reading as a natural part of their connection with significant caretakers, especially if it conveys the kind of emotional attunement about which Stern (1985) writes. For instance, if a young child is bouncing around on one foot and his mother says, "Go to the bathroom," the comment may seem like mind reading to the child, who may not be aware of the cues he gave; the child may also hear the words as evidence of a caring rather than intrusive mother. However, for an older child who may have what he considers to be "forbidden" thoughts about death wishes, arson, or sex, having his mind read can be very frightening. If he were an adult, telling him what he feels might be somewhat more acceptable if it is clear that the cues the patient gave to the therapist were readily understandable, but it would still be an intrusion.

Metaphor may not always originate with the therapist. Patients frequently speak of situations symbolically, and the competent therapist, understanding the meaning of the metaphor, can continue with the metaphor that the patient is using without having to bring it to full intellectual awareness. To further illustrate what I mean by interpretation through metaphor I shall present another example. In this instance the use of metaphor was initiated by a child in a discussion about his goldfish.

A ten-year-old boy, Ethan, was referred for treatment by the analyst of the child's mother at the mother's request. The mother reported on the telephone that she was willing to come for an evaluative session with the child's father but that he could not come at any of the alternative times offered. Since she did not seem troubled by the father's unavailability and was anxious to see me herself, I arranged an appointment to see her without her husband; waiting until the father could come seemed like more than this mother could tolerate. The mother's attitude and the failure of the father to arrange an appointment time were in themselves indications of special problems in this family. She was an articulate woman whom I questioned at great length, but I was unable to get a clear answer about her reason for wanting Ethan to be in therapy other than that she thought the child was anxious. I agreed to see him for consultation.

Ethan seemed to be a healthy, good looking youngster with no immediately apparent problems. He talked readily about his school and described his family in general, but not uncomplimentary, terms. When discussing his pets, Ethan explained to me that he had goldfish, jointly owned with his brother, and that they took weekly turns with the responsibility for feeding the fish. I became curious about this arrangement and felt that questioning him about it might reveal significant information about the relationship between the brothers. While on the face of it, feeding goldfish may sound far removed from the real issues that one ought to be curious about, quite often a seemingly irrelevant comment may be central to the underlying major concerns of the patient, adult or child. The inquiry with Ethan was useful, but as so often is the case, not in the way I might have predicted.

What Ethan then revealed was that he did not always feed the fish on a regular basis. "I let them go a day or two without food sometimes." When I asked why he did this, Ethan said that it was good for them to get used to being without food for a while, that it did not hurt them, and that it "toughened them up." Further inquiry about the need to toughen them up, put together with the

hesitant way in which his mother had told me about her relationship with Ethan's father, suggested to me that Ethan was preparing
his fish for a "famine"; I suspected that he had similar anxieties
about himself. He expected a famine not in the sense of deprivation
of food but rather in the emotional sense.

Having completed my examination of Ethan, I arranged another
appointment with his mother and reported to her that although I
saw no evidence of serious pathology, I did detect some anxiety on
Ethan's part that might be considered more than normal for a child
of his age, but I was not clear about the origin of the anxiety. I
inquired further about the nature of the relationship between her
and her husband. Because of her hesitancy in answering me and
her indirect way of describing the situation, I suspected that she
was planning a separation. I asked her if it were true, and she replied with relief that it was, but she had not told anyone, including
Ethan's father, about her plan. Ethan apparently had sensed his
mother's intent from her words or actions with him and indeed was
trying to prepare himself for the possibility of parental separation.
This information might have been otherwise revealed to me, but
his discussion of the feeding of the fish was the metaphorical way
he expressed his concern.

Ethan's treatment was then oriented toward further discussion of
his anxiety about his fish. I first addressed myself to the thought
that the fish would feel awful if they did not know when they would
be fed again or, indeed, if they ever would be fed again. But then
I spoke reassuringly of the fishes' ability to deal with distress. I
told Ethan that even though I believed it may not be best for them
to do without food for a day, they had shown that they were able
to survive the ordeal. I said I was sure that neither he nor anyone
else would knowingly let them starve. I hoped that on a deeper
level I would reassure Ethan that he too could survive the ordeal
of a psychological "starvation" and that in fact if his parents did
separate, they would not deprive him of emotional support.

Several sessions later Ethan openly revealed his anxiety about
the possible separation of his parents. Had he not done so, I probably would have continued to deal with the issue on a metaphorical
level. However, since he chose to talk about it, the problem was
handled directly and effectively. We discussed his feelings about his

parents' separation and about how he might relate to each of his parents.

Other examples of this mode of communication and therapy are given throughout the rest of this book but particularly in chapter 4, and in chapter 6.

Regarding the matter of interpretation, I make no distinction between child therapy and child analysis, for, with children, differentiating analysis from therapy is primarily a matter of frequency of contact, and to some degree a case can be made for differentiating child analysis from child therapy by emphasizing that the goal in analysis is toward profound changes of character.

The concept that interpretation through metaphor is an appropriate avenue could also be applied to therapy with adults. Contemporary emphasis on transference and countertransference problems as central to analytic experience need not be accompanied by verbal explanations and interpretations. As Sullivan said, "The supply of interpretations, like that of advice, greatly exceeds the need for it" (1953a:187).

For example, a man of forty who had been in treatment for several months described his concern when his cat had escaped his city apartment. He emphasized most how this tough-looking cat was finally found cowering in the corner behind stairs. The patient's own "macho" concerns were of great significance to his dynamic structure, and the discussion of his cat's behavior was a ready metaphor for revealing his concerns about cowardice. However, it was some time before he could say to me that he really felt that he was basically a coward. Once I knew the cat was safe, which he told me early in his discourse, I might have become impatient and interrupted by saying that I wanted to hear how this story of his cat applied to his treatment. He might have heard this as an admonishment and felt that I wished to hear about something more significant. Had I done this, however, I would have missed some vital information that he may have been consciously unaware of or, because of his embarrassment, was unable to deal with directly.

Conditions for Change

Emotional attunement between the therapist and the patient is essential to successful therapy and includes the requirement that the patient feel understood. Attunement is more readily achieved by use of metaphor and the patient's own language than by forced "insight." In fact, forced insight is almost invariably damaging to the patient, no matter how accurate the logic of the interpretation may be. The most meaningful kind of changes come about when patients make their own discoveries, and insights are not hurried beyond the patients' capacity to integrate them. With both children and adults I seldom make interpretations as declarative statements; rather I pose them as questions so that the patient is free to reject them without having to deal with the effect on the therapist. In this manner the impact of the therapist's authority is diminished. "Could it be that . . .?" is always better than "The reason you do . . ."

Again, I wish to emphasize that early psychoanalytic techniques developed for working with children were compromises or adaptations of adult techniques. They were not specifically designed for working with the special problems of a growing, developing human being. Therapists who were first trained to work with adults are likely to feel that they are not doing their job adequately if they are not engaged in verbal discourse. For some, playing with a child doesn't seem like work, particularly if they are not oriented toward viewing play as diagnostically and therapeutically useful. Furthermore, many therapists have a basically obsessional nature and need careful delineation of what is going on; talking may falsely reassure them that not only are they doing their job, but they are also providing a comforting explanation about how it is being done.

Analysis of transference is the central feature of treatment with adults. The inability of adult patients to see people, including themselves, in an undistorted fashion is the essence of most psychopathology, and the goal of treatment is to enable them to see reality commensurate with concensual validation. With children, while the therapist must be cognizant of distortions that need to be untangled, the goal is to help them to develop normal adjustive mechanisms so that they are not defenseless in the face of certain harsh realities of life as they begin to refine their perceptions and minimize distortions. Attachments are made in early life; separation and individuation are ongoing processes throughout childhood and in effect throughout life. This process of separation and individuation requires the utilization of certain mechanisms such as projection and identification. Psychotherapy with adults often includes the untangling of distortions that are a result of this earlier process when such mechanisms became fixed or overused. To interfere with this process in an early stage is much like forcing an individual to grow up too soon. Insight, if it is to be labelled as such, should enable the child to be *aware* of his feelings, not to understand their dynamics and origin. To teach dynamics before they have fully developed would be like having an infant consider which leg goes first when he is learning to walk. If he does this, he is quite apt to fall on his bottom.

Schizophrenic Regression and Childhood Defenses

Distortions that are an indication of confusion because of transferential problems can be seen by comparing children to severely regressed and disturbed adults. While the early Freudian view was that schizophrenics were not analyzable because they are incapable of transference, the view of Sullivan (1953a) and most interpersonalists is that almost all schizophrenics view people in a manner that is highly colored by transference. With the schizophrenic, transferential distortions are ubiquitous. Schizophrenics have considerable difficulty differentiating their reactions to people and are constantly confusing all people with real or imagined early mothers, fathers, or significant others. Following the idea that schizophrenia is regression to early childhood development, we can assume that children in certain limited ways are like schizophrenics in that transference is ubiquitous and adequate defenses are not sufficiently developed. If one were to try to analyze the transference with a child, it would leave the child with no reliable concept of people because a child, like a schizophrenic, has not established a strong sense of self.

Further consideration of the plight of the schizophrenic can elucidate my view of defenses in children. One view of schizophrenia, which I find for the most part quite acceptable, is that schizophrenics are severely regressed, frequently in many areas of their life and for prolonged periods of time (Searles 1965c; Sullivan 1956, 1962; Will 1967; S. Freud 1900). The concept of regression assumes behavior that generally would be appropriate to an earlier (childhood) stage of development. It is understood that young children will have temper tantrums in the face of stress or that they might publicly manipulate their genitals or that they might defecate in their clothing. Strong prohibition against such behavior in a young child could well be traumatic and at the least would lead to confusion if not serious disorganization. Temper tantrums, publically manipulating genitals, and defecating in one's clothing in an adult are frequently indications of severe pathology. It is as if the schizophrenic has not adequately developed defenses or has returned to earlier ways of dealing with stress situations. Treatment orientation moves toward building appropriate defenses rather than further exploration of defenses that are too primitive and already too well exposed.

Another view of schizophrenia, which is somewhat dated and regrettably ignored, separates process schizophrenia from reactive schizophrenia. This model is intended to differentiate schizophrenics whose psychosis was precipitated by a known situation of stress from those whose psychotic behavior seems to have no known point of origin and appears to have been developing over a long period of time. According to this model, the degree of demonstrated pathology in reactive psychosis is related to the degree of stress and to the availability of defenses, with the severity of the pathology being dependent on the weakness or primitiveness of the defenses used. This model also suggests that with process schizophrenia the origin may have an organic basis. Of course, there is the possibility that with the process schizophrenic the basis is still one of reaction to stress, but the stress is an internal, emotional one not generally knowable either to the patient or other people. There is much evidence to suggest that the basis may be some combination of biology and psychology (Will 1983).

To elucidate further this model of schizophrenia as a form of regression to a level where mature responses are not available except under minimal stress, an example can be found in the response of a severely disturbed (and hospitalized) schizophrenic. If one greets him by saying, "Good morning," he may well be able to reply, "Good morning," but if one asks him how old he is, the question may contain more stress (for him) than he is equipped to handle, and his response might be a psychotic answer such as "God tells me I'm 1003 years old." This implies that perhaps a hallucination was necessary to protect the patient's self-esteem. With another patient, also quite disturbed but not so much so that hallucinations are necessary, the answer might be "406 years old." With a much less disturbed person who is, for whatever reason, also sensitive about revealing his age, the answer to the same question might be, "I forgot." This answer may be considered an indication of repression, still not a very good response, but it is less psychotic than "I am 406 years old." Another individual who is not schizophrenic and has no pathological condition but who is also sensitive about his age may simply say, "I don't like to talk about it." There are of course other mechanisms indicating varying degrees of pathology that might come into play. One might rationalize sensitivity to age by saying something like, "I'm 43, but I look older because of my grey hair." Or a defensive answer might be, "I'm 43, but I'm still younger than you." If a person is reasonably well adjusted and there is no sensitivity to age or if the person can tolerate some discomfort about revealing it, he might simply say, "I'm 43." This example indicates the range of responses that are related not only to the stress but also to the repertoire of responses available to the individual as well as to the internal security or self-esteem of the person.

Children can readily play that they are firefighters, police officers, or airplane pilots and at the time they are engaged in such play actually believe that their assumed identity is valid. In an adult this would be an indication of delusion or even a hallucination that would be characteristic of a severely disturbed individual.

In addition to developing sufficient self-esteem so that insults, failures, and rejections can be taken with relative equanimity, one must also acquire a repertoire of effective defenses on a gradient so that the injuries and vicissitudes of daily living can be met without resorting to poor or even psychotic defenses. Thus, for the emotional growth of the child through therapy direct interpretations are not made because they interfere with the development of the defenses, and, concomitantly, the process of child treatment must move toward adequate development of self-esteem.

Limitations on Interpretation

Another aspect of the problems related to providing too much information or analyzing transference too early is that it may engender in patients a tendency to overintellectualize. Such people can become quite expert at describing the origin of all of their behavior and their ways of relating, but they have incredible difficulty in solving problems of daily life or feeling anything.

The following is an illustration from my experience of the limits to be placed on interpretation with a young child:

A three-and-a-half-year-old girl, whom I had already seen some twelve or fifteen times, arrived in tears with her mother. She held onto her mother's leg and did not want to leave her. I removed the child from her mother (I do not think the need for therapy is a decision that a young child ought to make) and took her to the playroom. In the play room she continued to cry. She said, "You get out of here." and I said, "What will you do?" She answered, "I'll stay here and cry and when the time is up you knock on the door and I'll let you in." I told her that I couldn't leave the room but that I would be willing to go into the "hiding closet," a place that I had set off by the side of the room. She agreed to that. Then I said I would be lonely and asked if I could take a couple of puppets in with me to keep me company. She reluctantly agreed to that too.

The child continued to cry in the room, and I started a conversation between the puppets in voices that were familiar to her, since we had used the puppets before, and loud enough for her to hear. The puppets started a discussion about whether or not Grace was crying because she was mad or sad about leaving her mother. The discussion became more heated and turned into an argument. Finally, they knocked on the door and said they had a question for her. "Casper here says you were sad and I say you were mad at your mother leaving. Which was it?" Grace answered simply, but with remarkable insight about feelings, "It's like they are both mixed in together." (Spiegel 1973:170)

At this point I pursued the issue no further. It was my intention to help her clarify, and to put her in touch with her own feelings and to find them acceptable. I did not discuss her behavior toward me as an extension of her mother nor any other sort of transferential distortion. Had I done so, I probably would have confused her and most likely she would have ignored my intervention. In that way I would probably have done no harm. However, if she were a little older—seven or eight—she might have understood such an interpretation, and it would have been harder for her to ignore what I said. I believe this indeed would have been harmful; at the least it would have been an intrusion into the unconscious.

In the posthumously published book *The Piggle* Winnicott recorded his analysis of a $2^1/_2$-year-old child, making marginal notes to indicate what he believed was going on in the session. The following account appears:

Then she took a round object with a center piece that at one time belonged to the axle of a carriage and said: "Where did this come from?" I answered realistically, and then I said: "And where did the baby come from?" She replied: "De cot." At this point she took a little man figure and tried to push it into the driver's seat of a toy car. It wouldn't go in because it was too big; she tried putting it through the window and tried every way.

"It won't go in; it's stuck." Then she took a little stick and pushed it in the window and said: "Stick goes in." I said something about man putting something into woman to make a baby. She said: "I've got a cat. Next time I'll bring the pussycat, another day." (1977:10–11)

At the point at which the child says, "I've got a cat," Winnicott recorded in his marginal notation, "anxiety—change of subject." How does he know that is why the child changed the subject? Did he assume that the child was made anxious by an interpretation that he thought was too direct or premature? (He does not explain why he said to the child something about man putting something into woman to make a baby, and there is no indication in the book that those facts of life were ever explained to her or that she understood them.) Might not the explanation for the child's changing the subject simply be that she did not·know what he was talking about and this was her way of keeping the conversation going? Even if the child had been made anxious by Winnicott's intervention, her anxiety may not be related to the sexual content but rather to her believing that she ought to know what he was talking about and did not. In fact, her comment need not have been related to anxiety or even to what Winnicott said. Fortunately, as is perhaps illustrated by this case, children are very accepting of adults and are willing to tolerate not being understood or not understanding what the adult is trying to say to them. This is especially true if the adult conveys nonverbally that the child is liked and, like Winnicott, the adult is willing to sit on the floor and play with her. I do not doubt that the Piggle recovered and that Winnicott was instrumental in bringing about the change, but I seriously question his interpretation of what went on dynamically, both in his assessment of the problem and the interaction in the treatment.

Indirect Communication

Even with older children one cannot take questions at face value. Susan, a bright girl of nine, once asked me my age. What prompted a question of this sort? I did not hesitate to answer the question, for I saw no reason why she should not know how old I was. Some therapists might simply say, "Why do you want to know?" and not answer the question. There is nothing wrong in asking children why they want to know, but not providing an answer to children about something that ought not to be secret is rude. Adults probably would not ask such a question because they know that some people do not wish to discuss their age. If the therapist-child relationship is such that the therapist can respect the feelings of the child and say something like "I'll tell you in a minute, but I'm curious. How old do you think I am?" this might be a useful approach and provide interesting diagnostic information. My own inclination is to answer the question first and then attempt to find out what it means to the child. I believe this decreases the possibility for unnecessary anxiety. I told Susan my age, and while she continued to play with a doll in a carriage, the conversation proceeded as follows:

THERAPIST: How come you asked that question?
SUSAN: You're older than my father. (*At this point she lifted the doll out of the carriage and hugged it.*)

[I knew that her father was ill at the time. Was she fearful that her father would die? Was the hugging providing a kind of self-protection in the event of the loss of her father?]
T: How is your father now?
S: He has to stay in bed. Mommy says he'll be all right soon.
T: What do you think?

S: Jerry [Susan's older brother] said his teacher Mr. Adams died last Friday.

T: Are you afraid your father will die?

S: I'm afraid that I will die.

Here an apparently simple question about my age really represented a fear about death and led to an open conversation about dying. I could then reassure the child about how young people usually live a long time and at the same time discuss Susan's fears about death, dying, and her father's illness. Careful inquiry with cautious interpretation may lead to some rich and useful material.

Premature Interpretation

The problems and pitfalls of premature interpretations were recognized by such pioneers in child therapy as Axline who, in working with a child, essentially stayed with the play materials and reported the following:

A six-year-old boy was brought to the clinic for play therapy contacts because of his exaggerated feelings of fear and anxiety. He played with the family of dolls in the doll house. He took the boy doll out of the house and said to the therapist, "She is sending the boy out here where the quicksand is. The boy is afraid. He cries and tells his mother he is afraid, but she makes him go anyway.. And see! He is sinking down and down into the quicksand." The boy, showing much anxiety and fear, buries the doll in the sand. This child is certainly dramatizing his fear and his feeling of insecurity and lack of understanding. How should the therapist respond to this? It is very certain that this child is playing out the basic issue of his problem. If she follows the child she will say, "The *boy* is being sent out of the house and he is afraid. There is quicksand out there. The boy even cries. He tells his mother he is afraid, but she makes him go out anyway and he gets buried in the sand." The child is talking about "the boy" and the therapist talks about "the boy." She seems to be saying the child's words right back to him. Had the therapist said, "You are afraid and your mother does not pay any attention to your fears and that scares you still more," she is getting [sic] ahead of the child and interpreting his remarks. Perhaps the interpretation is correct, but there is the danger of thrusting something at the child before he is ready for the direct response, "you are afraid," etc. As long as he feels that it is necessary to use the doll as the medium, the therapist should use it too. (1964:262)

I fully concur with Axline's position in not making any interpretation to that child at that time. However, there is an implication in that account, as well as in much of her writing, that making the interpretation about the boy and his mother directly must be ultimately accomplished. By saying "before he is ready," Axline implies that at a later time the child will be ready and that "You are afraid" needs to be said. It may happen that the child will directly discuss such fears as being sent out to a dangerous world, or whatever he is indicating in his quicksand play, but it does not have to happen.

Given the conditions of the play that Axline describes, I would be unlikely to say to the child, "You are afraid," and so on. It is conceivable that under certain circumstances I might ask the child if he feels afraid, like the boy in the play, but even that would be unnecessary. If one were to make an interpretation or comment to this child, it would seem more appropriate to say something like "Quicksand is sure something to be afraid of." This might help the child by conveying to him that he has a right to be afraid of something as fearsome as quicksand. One might speculate about the meaning of quicksand to this child. Of course, we do not know what he has in mind, and as a metaphor it is likely to represent a general fear of catastrophe. While I do not subscribe to a concept of universal symbolism, I am impressed by dreams of water, drowning, or anything engulfing. Hence I might speculate that the quicksand here is something engulfing that might represent the child's being overwhelmed by some kind of parental overprotection even more easily than it could represent neglect or being out in a world that the child sees as threatening and engulfing. Only more complete knowledge about the history and current dynamics of the child would provide that information.

Verbal Interpretations versus Metaphor

In most circumstances I am reluctant to give verbal interpretations or label observed feelings. In the foregoing example Axline gave an extended "reflection" of the child's behavior with her verbal comments. It appears to me, however, that most children would be annoyed by such careful scrutiny of their behavior and would liken it to overprotection or to the "mind-reading" of an intrusive mother. In response to such a prolonged commentary many children would simply stop listening but would nevertheless react positively to the presence of the therapist because he or she was there with a warm and accepting attitude, perhaps much like Winnicott's as described in *The Piggle* (1977).

The actual work with children will now be discussed. Treatment starts from the very first contact, usually with the child's parents, and from an interpersonal vantage point the method of handling such contact requires very special care and consideration. The next chapter elaborates some of the issues involved from the beginning of treatment.

3

The Initial Contact

Children, even through adolescence, rarely request psychological assistance; for those who do there is every chance that the pathology is especially serious. Most children simply look to their parents for some kind of standard or guidance for their behavior. For adolescents, whose central dynamic is their concern with independence and the feeling that they need no one, to acknowledge that they cannot handle their own lives without the assistance of another person is an admission of a most serious nature. If they conceive of needing additional or outside assistance, it is an indication that they believe that there is something basically wrong with the way they think and feel.

There are, of course, possibilities other than the presence of serious pathology to explain the occasional child who requests help. If a family member already in therapy describes treatment to the child as a privilege and a pleasure or if being in therapy is seen as a status symbol, as might be the case among certain groups in major metropolitan areas, the child might seek it out. Nevertheless, most initial contacts are made by a parent.

A complex decision-making process is involved in initial consultation regarding children. One must decide if, in fact, the child is in need of treatment; the form the treatment ought to take, including alternatives to individual therapy; and the method of initiating treatment. These decisions may be made at the time of the original telephone call, at the time of consultation with the parents, or perhaps even after the child has been seen for one or more sessions. A thorough interview with the parents, the child, or both is most often vital to obtaining the necessary information to make these decisions.

When parents consider therapy for their child, they frequently face an immediate conflict. In my view psychopathology is primarily a result of difficulties in interpersonal relationships and most often a reflection of parenting. On some level the parents are likely to be aware of this, feel guilty or defensive, and therefore find it difficult to make the initial contact. Because dealing with this aspect of parental contact is complicated, difficult, and requires care and time, it is best that the initial telephone call be short and essentially directed toward setting up an appointment time. However, various questions must be considered before the appointment can be arranged.

The Initial Phone Call

There are many questions to be considered in deciding whether or not an appointment is called for. Obviously inappropriate requests for treatment include someone's calling about a neighbor's child or custody issues that require legal rather than psychological assistance. Once such cases are screened out, I ask for a brief statement of the nature of the problem. This will help determine the urgency of the situation and give some indication of the kind of treatment that might be indicated—or even whether I should be the therapist. For example, I might discover that the child is involved in serious antisocial behavior or is severely depressed. Such a child requires a great deal of attention and can be very taxing to the therapist. It is not wise to have more than one seriously acting-out or suicidal child in one's practice at a time.

The degree to which the child is aware that the parent is seeking outside assistance is also an important telephone question, not in deciding whether or not treatment is indicated but to give information about how the consultation is to proceed. This matter will be discussed shortly.

Age and Sex

If therapy by me seems feasible, I need to know the age and sex of the child, for these two factors may have a bearing on my ability to treat the child. With preadolescent children, the sex of the child is not usually significant. I believe, however, that it is usually inappropriate for a young adolescent to be seen by a therapist of the opposite sex. These youngsters frequently have concerns of a sexual nature that most adolescents would find especially embarrassing to discuss with an adult of the opposite sex. In addition, the seductive implications of the relationship might cause special problems. On the other hand, a same-sex therapist can serve as a positive role model.

There are, of course, exceptions to this rule. For example, a girl who relates significantly better with men than with women and who is reluctant to enter into treatment may find it easier to establish a therapeutic alliance with a male therapist than with a female one. Or a boy who is not only reluctant to go into therapy but also has obvious difficulty relating to men would have a much better chance of staying in therapy if he were to start with a woman.

Because the initial telephone call should be short, sufficient information might not yet be available for deciding to accept the patient. For this reason and because of other issues that might not be apparent at the outset, the therapist would do well not to make a commitment beyond an initial consultation.

If the problem is with an adolescent, for example, the decision may be made to see the teenager before seeing the parent. As a result of that interview, it may become evident that the teenager should see someone other than the therapist. That is, information might then be revealed that indicates that the youngster would do better with an older or younger therapist or one of the opposite sex. The adolescent can be told tactfully and carefully at that time that he is being referred to a colleague who would be better equipped to understand his problems.

It might be argued that such factors as age or sex of the therapist are not of vital importance, but it is my belief that although one might ignore such factors in patient selection and still be successful with the child, children, at best, are difficult to treat, and every effort ought to be made to provide an optimal chance of success. Reducing the chances of a negative transference based on the sex of the therapist increases the chance of therapeutic accomplishment.

Who Decides to Initiate Treatment

Many therapists give far too much responsibility to the child in deciding whether or not to go into treatment. An unfortunate precedent for giving children adult responsibility for treatment was established some time ago and was noted by Moustakas, who said, "It is especially important that the child himself decide whether or not he wishes to come to the playroom (1953:14)." Regrettably, many therapists still follow this dictum on the grounds of adherence to democratic principles. Children are not independent agents fully responsible for their own lives; to burden them with adult decisions would be in the same class as assuming they are capable of adult insight. Deciding whether or not treatment is necessary is no more the decision of the child than the decision to terminate treatment. (See chapter 9 for a full discussion of termination and chapter 6 for the special problems of dealing with children reluctant to enter into therapy.) These decisions rest with the adults—the therapists and the child's parents.

Who Should be Seen First

A significant issue to be decided is who is to be seen first, the parents or the child, or whether they should be seen together. Keeping in mind the likelihood of parental anxiety, the therapist must give special care to helping preserve parental self-esteem. For example, if it is decided that seeing the parents first would be best, the therapist may not know if the parents are part of an intact family and, if they are not, how the parent who calls feels about being a single parent. In that case it might be best to ask simply if the child's other parent is available for consultation. Answers may vary from "Yes" to "We are separated" to "He [or she] is not interested" to "His father [or mother] is dead." Even the last answer may be misleading. One mother who told me that the child's father was dead failed to tell me that she had been divorced for several years prior to his death.

With younger children deciding whom to see first is simple because a detailed history of the problem is necessary for competent treatment, and a young child is not expected to provide this information. With older children, who can tell something about their problem, it is often a distinct advantage to see the child first. The therapeutic relationship requires a high degree of confidentiality. Seeing the child first may convey respect for his privacy. With young children the question of confidentiality is more often purely academic, for if the therapy is provided as outlined in this book, they are not likely to feel that they have revealed any special confidence to the therapist. While children may have a right to privacy, it simply would not occur to them that there is anything that need be kept from their parents. Of course, there are times when even young children tell you things they do not wish to have you reveal to their parents, and usually, depending on the nature of the issue, this confidentiality can be fully honored. With all children it is hoped that the relationship formed with the therapist will be special, one different and separate from the relationship with the parents.

Seeing the Adolescent First.   Adolescents (usually those above 13, depending on their level of maturity) are frequently caught in issues of rebellion. For the teenager the transference to all adults is often negative since they see them as people with whom they do not wish to form alliances. Adolescents frequently see almost all adults as the enemy. Hence, adolescents usually view the therapist merely as a parent surrogate, substitute, or agent of the parents. If a relationship is to be formed in which the adolescent will be able to see the therapist as someone other than a parent, there is a better chance of achieving this if he is seen alone first.

If I do decide to see the adolescent first, I tell the parents that I will meet with them after I have seen the child for perhaps as many as three or four sessions but not until the youngster and I have had an opportunity to discuss my meeting with his parents. When I ask parents "if they can live with that," I seldom get a negative response. I then tell them to describe and explain openly to their child the nature of their contact with me and to arrange for the appointment—that is, to say that they spoke with me on the phone and to tell the child essentially what concerns them and why they arranged for the appointment. The parents might also tell the child that I chose to see him because I am not going to be working with them. This paves the way for a private relationship that the child will not have to share with the parents or anyone else. The issue of any future contact between the parents and me can be best left for me to explain.

Particularly with adolescents whom I will see prior to their parents and who have the mobility to attend therapy sessions alone, I may ask to have the teenagers call and arrange their own appointments. In this way they will feel consulted with and can weigh the relative importance of varying activities so that the schedule can be adapted to their own priorities; thus, their self-esteem is protected. Speaking to me on the telephone before seeing me allays some of the youngsters' anxiety about the pending appointment. With adolescents who oppose seeing me and deny any need for therapy or benefit they may gain from it, I frequently tell parents that they should insist that their child see me at least for one session and that the child will then be free to make a decision following this initial contact. Having one session with a reluctant child is often enough to establish the nature of the contact and for the therapist to provide sufficient encouragement for a return for further sessions.

Alternative Recommendations

Alternative recommendations that might be made on the basis of the information obtained from the original telephone call are to suggest that the parents wait and further observe what they assume to be aberrant behavior; that the children be referred to an appropriate clinic; that they be referred to another therapist, either by reason of schedule, fee, or, perhaps, the sex of the therapist; that they be referred to a pediatrician; or that they be referred to group therapy, although this is usually conducted in conjunction with individual therapy. Or they may be referred to a therapist of a different orientation—that is, behavior modification, family therapy, or learning therapy. (These alternative approaches are discussed in chapter 9, "Treatment Variations.") It may even be clear that therapy is not indicated.

An example of an instance in which I felt that therapy was not indicated was when a mother called to report that her husband, the father of her 13-year-old son, had died three days earlier. While the child acknowledged his father's death with sadness, the mother did not believe he was showing sufficient emotion about the loss. The mother felt that therapy was necessary to help the child recover from this sad event. It appeared from the telephone call that the child exhibited no remarkable symptoms. Obviously, there is a wide range of normal reactions to death. Failure to indicate extreme grief immediately after a death is certainly not an indication of pathology.

I suggested that the family wait "until the dust had settled" before assuming that therapy was indicated. I asked the mother to telephone in three or four weeks to report on the child's behavior during that time. She did call back as recommended, and it became apparent from that telephone call that no treatment was indicated.

Fees

The first telephone call might include an inquiry about fee. Some therapists are evasive about this matter for reasons that probably have more to do with their own attitudes about money than the efficacy of dealing with this issue. I believe it is inappropriate as well as unethical not to state the fee at the outset if it is requested. Failure to discuss fee may well imply some kind of conspiratorial agreement that such matters should not be talked about and that may not be valid, such as money is too gauche to discuss or the treatment really is worth more (or less).

If the therapist is willing to see some patients at a reduced fee, then this can also be clearly stated if relevant. For example, one might say, "My usual fee is x dollars, but if there are special financial limitations, I would be willing to see someone at a reduced fee." If even the reduced fee is prohibitive, the therapist might recommend someone whose fee is lower or an appropriate clinic facility. If the problem sounds especially complex and there are serious financial limitations, I sometimes find it useful to recommend that the patients see me for an evaluation at a substantially reduced fee. At that time it can be determined if therapy is in fact indicated or what other course of action might be taken, and a more precise referral can be made.

Fee issues with clinic patients may be quite different and depend largely on clinic policies. A clinic policy that is flexible, allowing for individual variations in circumstances, is optimal. I find the argument that all people should pay a fee regardless of financial circumstances because otherwise they will not value the treatment a fallacious one. Regardless of the fee they may or may not pay, there are those who place little value on treatment and those who value all treatment.

Recognizing this problem of individuality, Fromm-Reichman noted:

The old psychoanalytic concept that psychotherapy will not be successful with patients who do not make a financial sacrifice to obtain it, regardless of their economic status, is an unfortunate misconception engendered by misleading teachings of our modern culture. This does not mean to deny the desirability of nominal payments where possible, for the sake of the maintenance of the self-respect of the patient who does not wish to obtain something for nothing. (1950:67)

Seeing the Parent First

If it appears from the telephone call that the appropriate next step is to see the parents for the initial contact, the appointment can be scheduled and the parents should be instructed not to discuss the matter with the child until afterwards. Preparing the child for his meeting with the therapist can be taken up in the session with the parents.

Assuming, then, that one or both parents can appear for an initial interview, it is important to get a detailed history of the child's life as well as information about the background of the parents. Ideally, it is better to see both parents for this purpose, although this cannot always be arranged. If the parents are divorced and do not talk to each other or are unwilling to be in the same room at the same time, it is even more important to get a detailed history of the child's life as well as background about the lives of the parents. If the separated parents are unwilling to be seen together, it would be useful to arrange individual interviews with each parent. If one or both parents have been remarried or are involved in a significant relationship, I find it useful to see the parent with the present spouse or companion. Complex relationships involving children by previous marriages as well as children of the present marriage obviously pertain to significant aspects of the dynamics of the child's disorder. Varying alliances, both overt and covert, exist and need to be explored and understood.

Obtaining the History

When I see the parents first, my interview technique follows general principles not unlike those outlined by Sullivan in his description of the psychiatric interview (1970). However, the initial interview with the parents is geared to providing information about the child rather than the interviewee. Parents consult therapists because they are very much concerned about their child's welfare. Obviously, a complete description of the matter that brought them to therapy should be obtained before questions are asked about the history of the child and the family, the mother's pregnancy, the child's birth, and the like. Some overly anxious parents have children who are not in need of treatment. For example, enuresis that follows six months after the birth of a new sibling is not a remarkable occurrence. Of course, it probably represents some kind of envy of the new infant and perhaps an attempt to regress to such behavior as a way of obtaining the kind of attention the new child is getting. But only if the pattern continues for four or five weeks is it likely to be sufficiently serious to require psychological investigation. Normal reactions to stress are likely to cause some regressive behavior. This is a functional attempt at adjustment and in general is well within the range of normal behavior. Like enuresis, such symptoms as school phobias, temper tantrums, and lying do not always indicate pathology. Of course, they are to be noted, but there are times when the context indicates that therapeutic treatment is not immediately or at all in order.

Only after the parents have been able to describe the issues that concern them are they free to discuss some of the matters that seem less significant to them but that can be explained to them as having relevance. The underlying purpose of the initial interview is to obtain information pertinent to the problems of the child and many apparently irrelevant aspects of the history of the parents or of the child's upbringing may be significant. Therefore, the history taking should be painstaking, complete, and, above all, nonthreatening to the parents.

When I do get to the more detailed information about the history of the child and the family, which may require a second interview, I most often find it useful to ask the parents about the families they come from. This enables me to go back at least one generation and can reveal attitudes about child rearing that were conveyed by parents' parents and either adopted or protested against by the parents in raising the patient, their child. The presence of siblings in the families of the parents may have supplied or denied special experience for the parents with younger or older children, which is then reflected in the treatment of their own children. Often parents become so involved in their children's lives that they vicariously live their children's lives and contrive to have their children experience situations and events they were deprived of when they were young.

Relationships

Having relatively briefly explored the separate histories of both parents, I usually find out something about how the parents met and something of the courtship that led to marriage. History of the pregnancies follows, finally ending with the birth of the patient. Sometimes a simple question like, "How many pregnancies have you had?" reveals pregnancies that resulted in miscarriages or abortions. Surely one or several planned pregnancies that did not result in live births, particularly prior to the birth of the patient, are likely to have seriously affected treatment of the child and resulted in overprotection or rejection (as a way of not becoming too attached to a child who may die).

A question such as "What was Jennifer like as an infant?" is likely to reveal all sorts of information regarding sleeping and eating habits and, most significantly, how the parents reacted. Further questioning should explore such issues as separations from parents in camp, the first day at school, time the child spends away with friends or relatives. Information about baby sitters and relatives, in addition to providing information about the child's attachment to such persons, might reveal information about possibilities of child molestation experiences. Attitudes toward education, misbehavior, the display of affection, illness, and nudity can all be explored.

The importance of peer relationships is often understated and needs to be thoroughly investigated. The value of a period during which the child can correct perceptions by comparing his own family to those of his friends is emphasized by Sullivan (1953b) in his discussion of the juvenile era. A child deprived of experience with friends and their families may have a very limited view of humanity.

I find it quite useful to ask the parents to bring in family photographs for the initial interview. I ask particularly for pictures that show the patient together with other members of the family. Significant in these pictures is who stands next to whom; who has his or her arm around another person and whether the embrace is intimate; who is leaning toward or away from whom; who looks happy with some members and not with others. Of course placement might have been decided by the photographer, but that in itself might be revealing. Careful examination will reveal patterns that might not otherwise emerge in the initial interview. Knowing who is the designated family historian is an interesting and useful bit of information.

The Parents' Contribution to the Pathology

Throughout the interview one must keep in mind the vulnerability of the parents while balancing it with scientific curiosity. The interview should be most sympathetic and yet complete. While there are many factors that have affected the development of the child, interpersonal theory supports the view that it is primarily the influence of the parents that gave rise to the pathology in the child.

The parents are frequently painfully aware of this and likely to feel guilty and responsible for the difficulties that brought them to a therapist, even though their reasons for treating their child as they did are seldom a result of malevolence but rather of their own neurotic, psychotic, or simply misguided behavior. The matter must be handled with tact and delicacy. Some of the guilt might be reduced by noting that consideration must be given to the complex variable sources of pathology (Sullivan 1953:305). The therapist must point out that while knowing the basis of the child's problem is of interest, the major emphasis is on what ought to be done about it now. Adding to the parents' guilt and humiliation is neither humane nor effective in ultimately providing therapeutic assistance. A parent being interviewed in connection with the treatment of a child suffers the same kind of self-consciousness as an adult patient endures in an interview about himself. As Sullivan notes:

We find that from the psychiatrist's standpoint all of his contacts with any patient [or in this instance, the parent of the patient] are marked *by the patient's strange dependence for some kind of comfort on what the patient believes the psychiatrist thinks of what is being discussed.* It is hardly necessary to say that the patient's idea of what the therapist is thinking about the patient's remarks is often far from accurate. When it occurs to a patient that he does not have a fair idea as to what the therapist is thinking, his distress is often pathetic. The hesitancy—the attempt to cover two horns of a dilemma with one foot—is poignant, and is really distressing to the patient. (1970:93)

I often explain to parents that in the process of growing up children need to feel and act grown-up and that sometimes parents, overestimating the children's level of maturity, treat their youngsters as more grown-up than they really are. The children may then feel that they are frighteningly on their own and regress, acting babyishly. Trying to accommodate to this state, the parents then treat the child as much younger. This enables the child again to act more grown-up, and so the cycle is repeated in the process of growth. The parents can be sympathetically told that this is understandably quite frustrating—they can almost never feel they are treating their children in a manner that is appropriate to their children's actions—but that this circularity is an essential part of the growth pattern.

The Interview

The following extract is part of an initial interview with parents. It illustrates the method of the interview as well as some of the speculations regarding the dynamics that the therapist considered during the process. Special attention is paid to underlying qualities of speech which are frequently most revealing. As Sullivan stated:

Much attention may profitably be paid to the telltale aspects of intonation, rate of speech, difficulty in enunciation, and so on-factors which are conspicuous to any student of vocal communication. It is by alertness to the importance of these things as signs or indicators of meaning, rather than by preoccupation only with the words spoken, that the psychiatric interview becomes practical. (1970:5)

Prior to the session the mother telephoned to report that she wanted assistance for her three-year-old son, who three weeks earlier had suddenly refused to sleep in his room and insisted on going into his parents' bedroom at night. She could think of no reason for the change, but it was entirely disruptive to the family structure. Bringing him back to his room and staying with him failed to result in his staying alone. The telephone contact was relatively brief; a more complete evaluation was indicated.

MOTHER: Do we get the couch?
THERAPIST: Wherever you like, just leave me the chair by the phone. (*After the couple sat down, the therapist added*): Sometimes I record—it is part of a professional record and is treated as privileged communication—but of course if it makes you uncomfortable, I will not do so.
[The couple sit together on the couch, but leave space between them. Is this a statement of the relationship? An attempt to be close but still somewhat distant?]
FATHER: No, that's all right. (*mother nods in agreement*)
T: How can I help? (*no answer*)
T: You told me [on the phone] about his scratching at the door . . .
[It is important to pinpoint the specific reason for seeking help. A description of the current behavior as the first order of business is essential for the reasons just noted, is probably least anxiety provoking for the parents, and gives the therapist a framework for further inquiry.]
M: Well, that's stopped.

T: It did?

M: Ed got him to sleep on the floor, but in his room. He's not allowed out.

T: How did you do that?

F: I'm not exactly sure. We set out a blanket and pillow but it must be in his room. He does not want to stay in his bed. Even if we put him back in bed he moves back to the floor. He never gives us a clear answer if we ask him why he does not want to. He does not go into any details in discussing this. He says several different things. Sometimes he says there is something in the bed, sometimes he says he is fearful that something will get him, but he really gives us no clear definition of what is bothering him.

[These parents seem somewhat restrained and do not readily volunteer information. Ordinarily, as noted before, it would be appropriate to get information about the child's development next, but the therapist was beginning to feel uncomfortable because of their generally unrevealing and brief answers and felt he would do better to get information about the parents to give him a context about their attitudes and ideas and get a better sense of how to ask questions about the child, so he shifted to finding out more about them.]

T: All right, let me go back and get some history and then I may be able to get a better understanding of what is going on. I would find it helpful to know a little about you, the kind of family you come from, what your parents are like and things like that.

M: I don't know what to say.

[Is this a result of anxiety or lack of psychological sophistication? The question was addressed to both of them, but the mother chose to answer and yet she gives no information. How does this family operate? Are they essentially noncommunicative with a kind of pretense of communicating?]

T: Anything at all. Since I don't know you, whatever you tell me will be helpful.

M: O.K. I have an older brother, my mother is in Florida, my father is deceased.

T: How old is your brother?

M: Thirty-eight, I think.

T: And how old are you?

M: Thirty-four, I hate to talk about age.

T (*innocently*): Why?

M: I just don't like getting old, that's all.

[This seems to indicate a kind of magical thinking. If you don't talk about something it doesn't exist. What doesn't she like about getting older? Does watching her child grow up make her feel older? If that is true, it is possible that she needs to keep him a baby in order to feel young. These questions would be too anxiety provoking to ask at this time, but they are certainly to be taken into consideration by the therapist.]

M (*continuing*): That seems to be it. I have aunts and uncles and cousins.

T: When did your father die?

M: Thirteen years ago from a heart condition.

[She does seem to be getting a little more relaxed, but not to any substantial degree.]

T: Where were you living at the time?

M: In the county. X County.

[It is apparent that the mother resents being questioned, judging from her brief answers. To take up the issue of her probable resentment at this time would most likely make the problem worse. If resentment is the reason, why is she resentful?]

T: What were your parents like? [By asking what they were like, the therapist attempts to get some sense of the mother's childhood.]

M: Right now my mother and I are so-so. She chose another religion and that really bothers me, but other than that, all right.

[While the question addressed itself to the past, the mother chose to answer in the present. Is it because that is where she is now focused, or is she avoiding talking about the past?]

T: What was the change?

M: From Judaism to Catholicism. She says she does not like Jews.

T: How old is she?

M: Sixty-one or sixty-two.

[There seems to be no emotion connected with her response. Why the flatness? Is she depressed? Withdrawn? What is she like with her child? Neither she nor her husband seem to look at each other, even peripherally. What goes on between them?]

T [getting back to the issue of the mother's change of religion in an attempt to elicit some affect]: Does that strike you as remarkable?

M: Well, it's a very recent occurrence.

[Does this woman flatten all affect? What kind of signals is she giving to a child who may be too alive for her?]

M: It might be a fad . . . she has relatives down there who are Jewish who won't like it. [Does she mean that that's why she's doing it?] She works, she teaches.

T: What?

M: Dancing, singing. She's an entertainer. She lives in _____, but she's in the _____ Pops orchestra. But other than that we had our arguments while I was growing up.

[This woman seems to know perfectly well what the importance of the questions are: she'll get to it on her own terms as she feels more relaxed.]

T: Like what?

M: I can't remember, I've been out of the house.

[Again it is evident that this mother's attitude seems to be that if you don't talk about something, it doesn't exist. How hard it must be for her to come and talk about her child. I'll give it one more try.]

T: Well what kind of things would make your mother angry?

M: I honestly can't remember, I've been out of the house about thirteen or fourteen years . . . It's been a long time.

[This session is not for treatment of the mother; it is difficult to obtain information relevant to the child's difficulties. Note that she says, "I honestly can't remember." Is she frequently accused of being dishonest? Pushing further would only make her more anxious and not result in further information. Perhaps talking about her brother would be less anxiety provoking.]

T: What's your brother like?

M: He's a musician. Has a wife, two kids and lives in . . . He's O.K. [Note the judgment involved.]

T: What does he play?

M: Organ, piano. He produces also.

T: Are you musical?

M: I sit down at the piano once in a while. I'm a nurse.

T: Where do you work?

M: I'm not working right now.

T: How come?

M: I just graduated, I'm waiting for the boards.

T: How did you decide to go into nursing at this time?

[Who provided the mothering while she was in training?]

M: It's always something I wanted to do. I wanted to go into the medical field. I've been a medical assistant for seven years. I just wanted to go a little bit farther.

Clearly, the situation is complex. The interview went on for a long time. I usually allow more time for initial sessions than for regular sessions, and sometimes a second interview is necessary. In this instance the next area explored was that of the father's history and family. He seemed more willing to talk about his family than his wife was about hers, although he was not particularly conversant with feelings. Following this, there was some exploration of their courtship and marriage. Finally, and in greatest detail, a history of the child was given from his mother's pregnancy until his present age, tracing such issues as play, feeding, temperament, and physical health. It was only during the latter part of the interview that the information most significant to the present complaint came to light. This part of the interview went as follows:

T: Tell me what the child's room is like.
M: Well, the room is right next to ours. There is a bathroom in the hall just off to the side of his room.
T: Describe his room.
M: There is a dresser on one side of the room, a table in front of the window . . .
F: And a large toy box I made for him at the foot of the bed.
[There seems to be some pride in his accomplishment, and perhaps this is an indication of his affection toward his son.]
M: It used to be next to the table, but since we took the guard rails off the bed, we can keep it next to the bed and he can use it as a step to get out of bed.
T: Why? How high is the bed?
F: Average height, like most beds.
T: When did you remove the guard rails?
M: About a month ago.
T: How did that coincide with his unwillingness to stay in his bed?
M: It must have been the same week.

The reader will guess what happened at this point. Indeed, the removal of the guard rails was the basis of the child's new phobia. While all sorts of possibilities exist for the basis of this kind of phobic behavior—questions of separation from parents, events with playmates, nursery schools, siblings, and so on—it is only through this kind of complete interview that the appropriate information can be revealed. In this instance replacement of the guard rails resulted in complete success. It was recommended they be removed at a later date and that the child be given some option in deciding when. He was to be encouraged at that time to see removal of the guard rail as an indication of his own and his parents' recognition of his getting older and bigger. While there was evidence of other problems of development related to the particular style and characteristics of the parents, this is not why they consulted the therapist, and they were not seeking any other assistance. Foisting it on them would have been inappropriate, and the child himself was never seen by the therapist.

Further Notes on the Initial Interview. To return to the issue of how one might conduct initial interviews with parents, it is often useful to ask them to compare this child with other children of theirs or other children they have observed. Developmental lags—psychological, social, physical, and intellectual—are frequently best understood by them in this light.

Other issues need to be discussed as well as the method of presenting the issue of treatment to the child. It is not remarkable for three sessions with the parents to be necessary before the child is seen for evaluation. Often, particularly if the child is being referred for problems of unacceptable behavior, the initial interview with parents is so filled with complaints about the child that it is helpful to end the session on a more positive note by asking them to describe the things they like about their child. This enables them to leave the session thinking kindly of their child instead of being angry with him for causing them to have to consider the possibility of treatment. They may also contemplate the possibility that they might not be as good parents as they thought they were.

Scheduling

The issue of schedule deserves a good deal of attention for it has a significant effect on the course of the therapy. Children's schedules are frequently more complex than those of adults. Besides school, among the other things that occupy children are extra curricular activities such as sports, scout meetings, religious instruction, school tutoring, ballet lessons, dental and medical appointments, as well as regular visits with separated parents. Some schedule problems must be considered on an individual basis. There also may be problems of transportation to the therapist's office. Depending on the nature of the problem, any of the foregoing may take priority over therapy. Of course, even in the attempt to interfere with as few activities as possible, the therapist is still constrained by his own schedule; something in the patient's activities may have to be omitted.

Unless there are special circumstances, it is best not to interfere with a child's school day and not to remove him from actual school work. However, when the degree of pathology does make it necessary to remove a child from school for therapy, the problems that may result must be examined. Certainly missing instructional time is a significant disadvantage for educational reasons. On the other hand, if the child does not like school, providing a reason for missing some school time may seem at first to be an advantage to therapy because it will serve as partial motivation for being there. However, this motivation, which at first may be an advantage, can later become a disadvantage and be the equivalent of a compensation neurosis: by remaining distressed, the child can continue to miss school. Again, it is best to interfere with school only if absolutely essential.

Adults in therapy have varying arrangements to accommodate missed sessions and vacations, but the course of attendance is fairly regular and predictable. Schedule problems are more complex with children, and sometimes a basketball or hockey game may indeed be more important than the child's therapy appointment. In addition, children are more likely to "forget" sessions. While the underlying dissociated motivation for forgetting may be obvious to the therapist, most children are not able to accept the idea that there is a part of them operating separately from their conscious intention; pointing that out to them would deny them the process of the natural formation of a defense. Furthermore, telling the child that he forgot because he really didn't want to come might cause the child simply to assume that the therapist does not know what he is talking about and this would undermine the therapist's credibility. Or if he did feel that the therapist knew, then it would be another instance of the therapist's reading his mind. Knowing all this and recognizing its implications for the smooth continuation of therapy, most therapists are able to work out a satisfactory arrangement with parents for such missed sessions. Special notation of this problem and suggestions for dealing with it are made by Zaslow (1985), who suggests that therapists clearly tell parents that children, particularly adolescents, often miss appointments, and that they (the parents) are responsible for payment of all sessions whether or not they are kept.

Resistance

Collecting fees from parents can be difficult because parents sometimes protest their dissatisfaction with the way in which the treatment is progressing by withholding payment. This problem can frequently be avoided by coming to a clear agreement about fee arrangements at the time of the initial session with the parents. With some children, increased assertiveness is frequently one of the outcomes of therapy, and, while parents may approve of the child's being more assertive with playmates and other people, they often find it objectionable when the child starts to be assertive with them. (See chapter 8 for a lengthier discussion of ways in which parents express their resistance to the course of therapy.) If good contact with the parents is maintained throughout the child's treatment process and the course of the therapy is explained to them as it evolves, such problems can sometimes be avoided. With few exceptions, the goals the therapist has for the child are essentially those of the parents.

Preparing the Child for the Initial Interview

If the child is an adolescent and protests directly against coming to treatment, the parents can, as indicated earlier, insist that the child appear for at least one session.

With young children the problem is somewhat more complex. It is likely that there has been difficulty in the family prior to consulting a therapist, and such children may be misbehaving in school or at home. They can hardly view being told that they will see a doctor because of their misbehavior with other than fear and trepidation. They are likely to see the therapist as a person of authority, not unlike a teacher or school principal who will make them behave. I do not advocate lying to children, and so the question as to why they need to see this particular doctor must be handled somewhat delicately. Problems of self-esteem often come into play. Of course, with some young children it is not difficult for the parents to explain the coming appointment: they can simply be told that they have an appointment with Doctor X, and they may take it as readily as they would an appointment with a dentist or a physician. Explanations about the purpose of the visit are best kept brief and deferred so that most questions regarding the treatment can be addressed to the therapist. Parents can defer questions about frequency or length of visits by suggesting that they ask Doctor X.

Young children who are more inquisitive might be told by the parents that this doctor will help them have more fun because they seem not to be having much fun in life. To some parents, who complain that the child spends all of his time having fun and pays no attention to those things that need to be done, such as homework and cleaning his room, this may sound like a contradiction. Nevertheless, the explanation has a high degree of validity because children who are constantly bombarded about cleaning their room or doing their homework, even though they are doing something they see as more enjoyable at the time, are not really having fun.

It is also often useful for parents to explain that this is not the kind of doctor who checks children and gives painful examinations or shots but one who talks and plays with them. Accordingly, the parent should be reminded that the child should not be brought to play therapy in his best clothes but rather in play clothes. It is no more appropriate that the child be concerned about getting his clothes dirty than that the therapist be especially fastidious.

Although some therapists encourage the use of the term "talking doctor," I prefer to deemphasize the verbal aspect of the relationship, particularly with young children. While the role of doctor as someone who plays with them is somewhat hard to understand, it is certainly more palatable than the prospect of being prodded, probed, and physically exposed.

A word or two is necessary here about referring to therapists as

"Doctor" or "Mister" or "Miss," as opposed to calling them by their first names. Calling a child a child, rather than seeing him as a peer, is not demeaning or pejorative although some people may use the term that way. I disagree with the idea of having children address adults by their first names. I am aware that many "progressive" schools encourage this approach in the name of equality or democracy and that some parents encourage children to call them by their first names. I believe the benefits of maintaining the differences between children and adults far outweigh any advantages that might inhere in the "democratic" approach. Children need to realize that they are in fact different from adults and that adults recognize and respect this. It is not simply that there are certain privileges of independence bestowed on adults by virtue of their age, but that children must realize there are also privileges to being children.

Understanding the differences between children and adults, children then do not feel the burden of adult behavior and responsibility nor that it is expected of them. It is too threatening for most children to see themselves as peers of their parents and other adults. They must be permitted to enjoy the special advantages of child hood; if the distinction is blurred, they feel forced to act more "grown-up" than they are capable of or to behave in a manner they believe is expected of them but that is inappropriate for children and difficult for them to attain.

For example, a bright child of 11 was referred to me because of a reading disability. He had had special tutoring in reading but showed no substantial improvement. Although the underlying dynamics of his problem seemed to relate to certain exaggerated intellectual goals, values, and rivalries within the family, the course of treatment in play therapy rarely included direct discussion of these problems; metaphor through play was the essential tool used in the therapy. On completion of treatment some eleven months later the child announced that he was pleased that his reading was better and that he did not have the slightest idea of how playing with me had caused this, although he felt fairly confident that in some way it had. In fact, the underlying dynamics that interfered with his reading and enjoyment of life had been altered sufficiently to effect a substantial positive change. I did not see the patient's remark as an inquiry as to how this change had come about; had it been intended as such, it would have been appropriate for us to discuss the matter. As we ourselves have considerable difficulty in explaining the complexity and vicissitudes that bring about therapeutic cure, its explanation to the child can be of only minimal significance. The important consequence is that the child's view of himself had changed so that he became happier and more effective in his overall functioning.

Other Issues; Arranging for Parental Sessions

There are, of course, other orders of business with the parents that need to be attended to. One of these is defining and arranging further contact with the parents. The issue of privileged communication with a child will be discussed in chapter 8. Suffice to point out here that since therapists are responsible for the course of the treatment, regular communication with parents to hear about problems and to gauge progress is essential. They should be seen on a regular basis, with a schedule varying according to the nature of the problem and the course of the treatment. In general, I find it is helpful to see the parents about once every five or six weeks.

If, as with adolescents, the child has been seen for one or more sessions prior to seeing the parents, he must be given an explanation for the therapist's sessions with the parents. This will be discussed in chapter 7.

4

The Playroom: Equipment and Use

Because of space, equipment, and economic constraints, certain compromises may have to be made in constructing and equipping a playroom. The playroom, however, is *the* essential tool in working with children in a way that I consider to be the most effective form of child therapy. Therefore, if severe restrictions must be imposed, it is best that one does not do therapy with children.

Ideally, the playroom should be a separate room. It should be arranged in a way that is effectively different from the schoolroom or most parts of the child's home. A playroom that allows for the most freedom, the least restriction, is likely to be the most conducive to effective therapy. If by the very nature of the construction rules and regulations need not be invoked, the therapist is free to establish his role as therapist rather than disciplinarian. The playroom should be free of breakable equipment. It is not a place for lamps that can be easily tipped over, objects of art, plants, breakable clocks, or delicate crockery. In the same way the person or clothes of the therapist should not be easily damaged. As you will see in the chapter on limit setting, I do not believe in physical encounters with children, but accidents happen. Thus, if the therapist is not dressed so that he or she must protect clothing against the ravages of finger paints or Play-Doh, it is easier to attend to therapy.

If a part of one's office is simply sectioned off to be used as a playroom, then one raises issues of limit setting and discipline that might not otherwise arise. Enough of these issues occur naturally in the course of play therapy, and there is no need to increase those problems and concerns. Essentially, play therapy should be a process enjoyed by the child. However, in some metropolitan areas where space is at a premium therapists may have no choice but to set aside parts of their offices for play purposes. If this is necessary, the divided area should be clearly delineated so that the child can feel comfortable in it, and the therapist can refer to it as the play area. The therapist might even say to the child, "Play is for the play area. We will use the other area for talking." This can be especially helpful for children who genuinely prefer to talk.

Because some older children may use a chair in the office instead of confining themselves to the playroom or play areas and especially if one treats adolescents, be wary of the chair that swivels a full 360 degrees—the therapist might end up seeing the child about a third of the time. As for the couch, I feel it is a completely inappropriate tool for either child or adolescent therapy. Of course, one cannot be rigid about rules, as the following illustrates:

Mark, a 14-year-old youngster, once entered the office having just completed a difficult tennis match. Instead of proceeding to the playroom where he generally spent his time in therapy, he sat in a comfortable chair in the office and indicated how tired he was after the tennis game. In an attempt to be sympathetic and hospitable I invited him to lie on the couch. He accepted the invitation readily. His eyes wandered up to the bookcase where he could read the book titles. A book on sex therapy caught his eye, and he asked what the book was about. In a short time he was talking about some of his concerns and fears regarding masturbation and sexual growth in general. Had he not been in a position where he could readily avoid looking at me directly, I doubt that he could have discussed such difficult matters at that time, or perhaps ever.

In general, however, using a couch with a child—and especially encouraging free association—might cause considerable damage. The child's connection with reality is not all that secure, and he might "float away." In some ways, as with a schizophrenic, powerful fantasies and thoughts in the presence of another person in a situation where it is emphasized that they have great psychological meaning could be most frightening.

The degree to which the therapist gets involved in the play depends primarily on the demands of the situation. There are some therapists who maintain a stance of distance and "objectivity," while others expect to become involved and are very much a part of the play activities. The determining factor ought to be the needs of the child rather than the personal predilections of the therapist, a concern for cleanliness, say, or other matters that may be of a countertransferential origin.

There are two kinds of therapists who can work with children in a participatory manner: those who are themselves immature in some way and essentially operate on a childlike level; and those who are sufficiently mature that they do not feel threatened if the situation calls for them to operate on a childlike level. Obviously, the latter make better child therapists. Another point of view was indicated by Ginott, who took the position of not playing with the child: "The writer believes that the therapy is retarded when the therapist participates with the child in play activities, either as 'parent' or 'playmate'" (1964:128). This is certainly possible if the therapist is not vigilant about the effect of his degree of participation. Of course, there are situations where participation, such as picking up darts for the child and returning them, can result in exploitation of the therapist, but a therapist need not permit this, for it is certainly appropriate to state that he does not like to have to chase after darts and prefers for the child to do his own retrieving. There is a line between courteous assistance and being exploited, and this is one of those instances where the therapist should be quite aware of his countertransferential feelings so that they do not interfere with his work.

To return to the playroom: while one cannot arrange an entire playroom for each child, there are certain objects that ought to be present for some children and not for others. Therefore, some rearranging ought to be done prior to each child's entry into the room. With certain older children, for example, I might permit the use of pointed darts.

Listed below are first the objects that I feel are essential in a playroom, then those important to have, and finally those that are also helpful. Of course, they must be considered in terms of the particular child in treatment. Clearly, some of these items cannot be included in every playroom, nor should they be there for every child.

Essential Items

1. A variety of easily manipulated hand puppets. It is preferable that these be people rather than animal puppets. If only animal puppets are available, then they should be easily identified to represent male and female, adult and child.
2. A "hiding closet" where the child can go to be by himself. If this cannot be provided, it is useful to have a large (paper) tablecloth over the play table, which hangs well over the side so that the child can crawl under there for privacy.
3. A table and chair appropriate to the height of a young child. A removable cushion might be additionally helpful.
4. Balloons that can be easily inflated by a young child. If such are not available, a hand pump may be quite useful so that the child need not struggle to inflate them, nor will he have to ask the therapist for assistance.
5. Watercolors, paper for them, and construction paper, crayons and magic markers.
6. Dolls scaled to a dollhouse. If a dollhouse cannot be included, it would still be quite useful to have dolls. In addition, larger dolls should be available.
7. Construction materials including such items as string, rubber bands, paper clips, glue, a small magnet or two, and round-tipped scissors.

Useful Items

8. Blocks and other construction equipment such as tinkertoys or an erector set.
9. Small toy cars and trucks.

10. Clay or Play-Doh.
11. Suction tipped darts and gun.
12. Play telephones or walkie talkies.

Also Helpful

13. A sink, preferably equipped so that the water supply can be turned off, ideally from a location outside of the playroom.
14. A blackboard, with colored chalk.
15. A dollhouse.
16. Finger paints.
17. Masks and dress up clothes.
18. Carefully selected games.
19. A sandbox.
20. Equipment requiring physical prowess or skill such as a basketball hoop with a styrofoam ball, a ring-toss, and rubber horseshoes.
21. Miscellaneous.

I shall discuss these in the order in which they are outlined. I wish, however, to emphasize that their importance is relative to the particular needs of the child.

Puppets

These are probably the most useful items in the playroom. They are barely more than one step removed from reality; allowing not only for projection, they also allow for complete denial of personal meaning in the same way that the Thematic Apperception Test (Murray 1943) cards do. A relatively extensive example of their use is shown in the chapter on limit setting. The obvious use of puppets to express and discuss significant feelings and events need not be discussed here: their use will be illustrated by later therapeutic accounts.

The therapist is free to select and use puppets himself or ask the child to use them freely. In a special kind of group arrangement puppets can be a most effective method of enabling a large group of children to deal with significant psychological issues (Spiegel 1959b; Woltmann 1964). This method (which has obvious adaptation possibilities for an individual child) involves presenting to a group of children a puppet play in which the children are encouraged to interrupt the puppet play and their advice is solicited by the puppets (see chapter 9 for an example).

Another aspect of the value of using puppets and other toy figures representing people is indicated by the following:

Ronald, a small ten-year-old who lived in ghettolike conditions, reported to the therapist about a fight in his house during which the police were called by a neighbor because of the noise. The intensity of his feelings and the rapidity with which he wanted to recount the information made it a difficult task for him to report this without adding to his distress. To assist him the therapist suggested that he use the puppets to illustrate and explain the event. Statements such as, "Okay, now here is the couch and here is the chair, right? Now show me where you were sitting. And your mother?" etc. created a comfortable environment. Projection was unnecessary since the child was relating to a real event, and for this reason the tools he was encouraged to use were toys because they were most familiar to him, effectively in his vernacular, and therefore provided additional comfort.

Scary-looking puppets may pose a problem for very young children, about 3 or 4 years of age, who may have considerable difficulty differentiating fantasy from reality. These very young children have an insufficiently developed sense of self to distinguish "other" from themselves. The same problem might arise with children with severe pathology, arrested development, or regression.

The best puppets are those easily manipulated, such as "glove puppets," as opposed to marionettes, which can be rather complex, difficult to operate, and easily entangled. Simple knitted puppets are relatively inexpensive; other materials can be readily utilized. One creative 11-year-old girl taught me to make hand puppets with small pieces of cloth and styrofoam balls that were slightly hollowed out.

A Hiding Closet

Children need to go off to a secret place. Having such a place in the playroom gives them the privacy they seek, and at the same time they know they still have the protection of the therapist and the playroom. A closet is best (of course without a lock, which might result in special problems). However, just a long tablecloth that hangs over the end of the table can be quite useful. In keeping with the make-believe world of the child, the hiding place allows for much pretending. It could be a spaceship, a deep cave, another planet, or a haunted house. In the case of any of these the hiding place can represent even more on a deeper psychological level. Keeping within the metaphor, the therapist can make optimal use of multiple meanings.

To illustrate, Albert, a 6-year-old who was quite frightened of being alone, frequently checked to see where his mother was even if she were only in the next room. He denied his fear and always covered up by asking something of his mother. The arrival of a new sibling some three months earlier was probably at the root of his concern, and his activity made this underlying issue fairly clear to the therapist.

In the playroom he was often involved with watercolor paints, and, had such paint books been present, he would have been most comfortable painting "by the numbers." He drew simple pictures of cars and planes and then filled them in with paints. At one point when he drew a spaceship, the therapist suggested that the boy pretend he was in one by going into the protected area under the table. With some reluctance but genuine interest he agreed to do this and crawled under the table, taking a kind of pegboard with him to use as spaceship controls. He communicated with the therapist with walkie-talkies.

The therapist suggested and assisted in the pretense of a long voyage to another planet. Albert frequently checked back with the "mission control" base, mostly to report that the mission was proceeding as planned. His questions about the state of things back at the home base led the therapist to suppose that the child was, in addition to other things, concerned about the welfare of the therapist. When the therapist pretended that he was often too busy with other matters having to do with instruments and the success of the mission even to talk with the "astronaut," Albert was forced to repeat his calls to "mission control." Through this play the therapist was able to encourage Albert to express his anger for apparently having been abandoned as well as his fear of being alone, and at the same time he could reassure Albert about several things.

By telling Albert he wasn't surprised at his anger over the apparent neglect, he was able to provide reassurance that Albert's feeling of anger was not only appropriate but also not so powerful as to destroy the therapist. In addition, he provided Albert with the reassurance that even though he wasn't with him all the time, he was very much concerned and cared about his welfare.

If the therapist had attempted to work out this dynamic more directly by talking about the child's relationship with his new brother, he might have missed the central dynamic of Albert's anger with his mother. Albert was not angry with his brother, whom he could understand as genuinely needing attention. Albert was concerned about the consequence of his anger. Could it in fact hurt his mother? At his age Albert was not capable of accepting, let alone directly admitting, his powerful hostility. By dealing with all of this through metaphor, the therapist allowed Albert to maintain his private thoughts without feeling that adults could read his mind and at the same time to be reassured that "thoughts don't kill." If Albert had been consciously aware of his concerns and had wished to discuss them, the therapist would of course have done so, but awareness is a matter of varying degrees of dissociation on a continuum and should not be relegated to a simple category of conscious or unconscious.

Furniture Geared to the Height of the Child

By virtue of obvious evidence, such as relative size, it is quite apparent to all but the most disturbed child that the therapist is an adult and that he or she, the patient, is a child. I do not wish to interfere with this concept; indeed, it is appropriate. The playroom, however, represents the world of the child, and the furniture in it should be keyed to that world. It is difficult enough for children to have to look people directly in the navel when standing up, so some attempt at equality ought to be made when sitting down. If a table is to be used by a child it ought to be geared to his height. There is a built in inferiority to being a child, and it is not healthy for the child's self-image to overemphasize this fact. Some therapists are fearful that they will blur the boundary between adult and child if they themselves are able to enjoy childlike behavior, but this apprehension is more likely to be in the psyche of the therapist than in that of the child.

Easily Inflated Balloons

Balloons offer a tremendous range of possibilities for the playroom. To avoid unnecessary involvement in a limits issue, it is a good idea to regulate the number of balloons that appear in the playroom for any one child. Five is an arbitrary but convenient and workable number.

If a balloon is inflated and the air let out slowly by stretching the neck, a variety of noises can be reproduced, ranging from that of a crying baby to flatulence. Balloons can also be inflated and then allowed to fly into the air by suddenly letting the air out. This phenomenon can be representative in the same way that dreams of flying suggest a need for freedom, a relatively common dream in this culture.

Balloons are easily broken: children can puncture them with a pencil or sit or jump on them, and they can be used for some kind of target practice representing effigies of various sorts. Children can be encouraged to draw faces on balloons with magic markers so that they represent different people in the child's life whom the child can symbolically destroy.

To investigate the degree to which the child is conscious of the anger he feels and the wish to destroy, a dialogue might be as follows:

THERAPIST: You made that look like a person.
CHILD: Yeah, it's a girl.
T: A girl you know?
C: Yeah.
T: Somebody you see every day?

At this point we might look at some of the possibilities of how the child can maintain his privacy or reveal it. In effect, the device offers the child an opportunity to indicate some of the feelings he has that he might ordinarily find quite unacceptable. With enough questions from a therapist who does not force interpretation, the child might, for example, reveal his intense dislike for his sister.

On the other hand, he might easily divert the inquiry away from the psychologically sensitive material by saying, "No, it's no one I know." At this point it would be most therapeutic to avoid probing and to obtain information and expression of feeling by allowing the child to utilize the balloons as projective material. If clinical judgment indicates that the child is ready to deal with such information directly, he could be asked, "Is that the way you feel about your sister?" The child is free to say no, and no harm is likely to be done. Or the dialogue might continue as follows:

C: Yeah, every day.
T: Someone in your own house?
C: Yeah, my sister.

There are obviously many possibilities in this kind of approach, and, as in therapy with adults, one can get optimal mileage out of a metaphorical dialogue without destroying the transference. If an adult is talking about his feelings toward a supervisor where he works and this appears to represent feelings he has toward the therapist but does not feel free to express, allowing him to continue to discuss it in terms of his supervisor will provide more information and a more cathartic release. If an interpretation is to be made and is worded as a question, such as "Is that the way you feel about me?" the patient has an opportunity to reject the interpretation without feeling he has to confront and oppose the therapist directly; thus there is no risk to his self-esteem. Questions should always be geared to opening dialogue and inquiry, never cutting it off.

In the same way it is not useful to ask a patient how he feels about something or someone. It is too easy to answer "good" or "bad." If the question is "*What* do you feel?" the answer is likely to be expanded and more elaborate. It is part of the purpose of the therapy for the patient to learn about himself and at the same time maintain his self-esteem. He might learn from a therapist who simply interprets his behavior, but he might then also have the feeling that while he has a smart therapist, he himself must be pretty stupid not to have made the discovery himself. In general, learning is more effective if the patient achieves it through self-discovery rather than by being told.

Watercolors, Crayons, Magic Markers, and Paper

Even the most restrained and timid child usually takes well to drawing or painting materials. While one need not follow the dictates of using them as a diagnostic projective technique, such as in the Draw a Person test, if the child does not draw freely on his own various suggestions can be made about things the child might draw.

With these materials, constructions with clay, and construction sets, the issue arises about preserving objects or pictures for the child. The literature is filled with a number of approaches to this problem (Axline 1947; Klein 1932; Moustakis 1953; Allen 1942). Probably the most troublesome aspect of preserving and displaying art work is the constant reminder to the current patient that the therapist sees other children. Of course, all children know that the therapist sees other children, but it is important that each one feel special when he is with the therapist; reminding them that there are others is not useful when this is already all too apparent. If artwork is retained and placed where other children can see and otherwise have access to it, there is the possibility of the work being damaged in addition to emphasizing the competitive aspect of sibling relationships.

Of course, work can be stored where it is not readily visible or accessible, but then practical problems arise. The therapist must find an appropriate place to store the material and then bring it out before each session. If the child gets his own material from a drawer or shelf, there might be considerable curiosity about what is in other drawers or on other shelves. Some therapists advocate this practice as a reminder to children that they are not alone in having problems or seeing the therapist, but I am inclined to limit such reminders. Undoubtedly, there are many such reminders in most children's lives, and additional ones are not helpful.

When the issue of the therapist's seeing other children comes up directly in treatment, it is important to emphasize to the child that, even though the therapist sees other children, the time he spends with each one is special and individual. In a similar way I recommend to parents of large families that they not try to see and be with all of their children at the same time (although of course there ought to be some time for this) but that they should spend special time with each child individually.

Again, then, in general I do not recommend placing the child's paintings or drawings on a wall where they can be viewed by other children. Having a drawer for each child is sometimes helpful and is recommended by a number of child therapists, but I believe it is better to assume that playroom equipment is community property to be used by all the children while they are there. Drawings and paintings can of course be taken home, but other kinds of constructions usually should not be because the practice tends to use up materials and cause special problems with children who are oriented toward being possessive and materialistic. For example, the therapist frequently gets caught in limit-setting issues in that he can permit some things to be taken out of the playroom but not others. If he lends the child a doll, will the child then ask for doll furniture or the doll house? What if the child does not bring the item back as agreed on? Some therapists say that such problems created by taking home material or damaging or destroying some other child's productions is "grist for the mill," but I believe that in the process too many useful principles are bypassed. There is enough opportunity for handling problems in the natural course of play therapy without that kind of rigging.

The issue, like many in child therapy, cannot be dealt with in a black or white manner. An example of the flexibility sometimes required of therapists is a situation in which Gloria, a rather needy 9-year-old, asked me to post a picture that she had painted. She knew this was not my practice and telling her so only increased her disappointment, so much of which she already had in her life. I therefore told her that although I would not post it on the wall, I would place it inside the door of my clothes closet so that I would see it every time I entered the office and hung up or removed my coat.

Consistency on the part of the therapist need not become rigidity. Of course, if the child's parents are pushovers for any pleading the child may do, it is not a good idea to give in too readily to the child's wish. But if children feel they have very little to say about what happens to them, the therapist can contribute to their self-esteem by letting them see that the therapist can be influenced by what they say.

Dolls

The playroom should be equipped with several dolls scaled to the size of a dollhouse and representing enough ages and sexes at least to denote the average family, including grandparents and even pets. The dolls can be used together with a dollhouse, if one is provided, in addition to conveniently serving as targets for rubber tipped darts.

Other useful dolls include those with easily changeable clothing. Baby dolls that can be diapered and given nursing bottles, even those that "urinate" can be quite useful with some children. The issue of anatomically correct dolls is relevant here. It is of course artificial and misleading to have dolls that have no genitals, and so in general I prefer to use dolls that do have them. However, their absence is not a serious omission, for children can discuss this matter, and the conversation might well include the idea that these are private parts that people don't usually display publicly. The specific problems and the age of the child in treatment may dictate whether or not such dolls are present in the playroom.

There are extremely realistic dolls with extensive vaginal parts or with penises that can be made erect, but these can be frightening to small children. They are useful, however, as a means of helping children to describe sexual molestation that they have experienced. That is of course a special use and not a typical part of play therapy except with those children whose sexual history or problems apply. (For further discussion of this matter see chapter 8).

Varying degrees of regression can be enacted with dolls, in addition to revealing problems and attitudes about parents and siblings. For some children dolls may resemble humans too closely to enable them to express some of their feelings. For them it might be useful to include small plush animals as well as miniature animals, both domestic and wild. The inclusion of soldiers, farm ani-

mals, and equipment or whatever is pertinent and locally familiar
has much to be said for it.

Miscellaneous Construction Materials

Under this general heading many kinds of items might be included, much as the contents of the pockets of a small boy, and
would be limited mostly by the imagination of the therapist. Strings,
rubber bands, paper clips, magnets, and round tipped scissors all
lend themselves well to play therapy. Imagine the possible meanings that can be expressed with magnets that repel or attract each
other. And in addition to their usual uses, particularly in the construction of models, rubber bands can be used as make-believe
weapons.

Regular Construction Materials

Blocks, tinkertoys, erector sets, and other fit-together materials
are most useful in the playroom. Some of the materials, such as
blocks, are simple, and some construction sets are rather sophisticated. It is good to have both, so that more advanced or older children can use the higher level material. The important factor is that
the material can be readily manipulated by the child, easily put
together, and as easily taken apart. With blocks a child can have a
sense of mastery over his environment that greatly contributes to
a satisfying self-image. For the child the world is constantly filled
with situations that require the assistance or direction of an adult.
On some level, towers might represent houses, big people, schools,
or even genitals; competence in dealing with all of these represented situations is an essential part of development.

One particularly useful technique used by Louis Gilbert (1964)
is to have the child construct a house of blocks—assumedly he will
represent his own—in which problems can be acted out. This has
the special advantage of not requiring a dollhouse and, better than
a dollhouse, has no prearrangement of room locations. The conversation might go something like this:

THERAPIST: Say, I have an idea, why don't we build a house?
CHILD: Yeah, but how?

T: Well, let's make this the living room. (*Places the blocks on the floor on a single level to outline a room, much like an architectural drawing, and leaves an opening.*) Let's have the door here. Or should we have two doors?

C: Yeah, let's put another door here.

T: Now where should we put the bedroom? Any more bedrooms?

This dialogue can continue until the essential floor plan of the house is laid out. Then, using dollhouse-size equipment, the therapist can suggest adding furniture—chairs, beds, tables, lamps, etc.— and finally people, all at the child's direction as to where and how many there should be. It is highly unlikely that the arrangement will be other than a representation of the child's own house. When the layout is complete and populated, the therapist might say, "Hey, let's make believe the dog knocked over the lamp in the middle of the night. Who gets up to see what the noise was? What happens next?"

If the therapist is well enough aware of the family dynamics, he might inject a statement such as "It sounds like two people are arguing. What's going on there?" or "Let's pretend there's a noise at the front door." Various scenarios can be played out in this way. The therapist should be cognizant of the dynamics of the youngster and the family and readily tailor the situations to deal with feelings and issues of great importance to the child. An imaginative therapist can make excellent use of this technique.

Small Toy Cars and Trucks

There is every likelihood that in the manipulation of small cars and trucks the child will identify with the smallest (depending on his own family position) and use other vehicles to represent other family members. This is seldom explicitly stated by the child, although such terms as "baby car" might be used. The possibility for a family configuration allows the therapist to take full advantage of views he would like to convey without having to deal directly with the child's family and their dynamics.

Through the use of toy cars and trucks children can readily indicate concerns they may have about self-control. These concerns may be on a level sufficiently dissociated so that the child cannot easily articulate them but must show them through play, much as an older person might through a dream. While at times it may be appropriate to encourage conscious awareness of this aspect of the self, it must be done cautiously, for full revelation of such an aspect of the self might be frightening or even terrifying for a young child. If appropriate to the child's use of the car in this fashion, it might be helpful for the therapist to indicate that in fact the car does show control and does not damage other cars or objects as badly as the child seems to think it might. If toy cars and other inanimate objects are used judiciously in this manner, much can be done to strengthen the self-concept.

In an incident I described elsewhere (1973:169) a child frequently made a truck ram into a car of almost equal size and another, smaller car. The dynamics of this child's family and his fear of involvement made it likely that he was enacting arguments in the family as well as representing his fear of becoming directly involved and possibly being hurt. The first task in this kind of situation is to provide some evidence that the feelings that ensued can be understood and accepted. By keeping within the metaphor, the therapist is in no danger of intrusiveness, of "mind reading." An appropriate reaction by the therapist at this point would be to indicate the potential danger to a small car should there be an accident with a large one. "Small cars can get pretty smashed up in a collision." Without having to spell out the child's feeling about his family, but with an additional comment, the therapist was able to convey possible actions by saying, "Perhaps if the little car stayed over here in the corner and out of the way it wouldn't get damaged." Regardless of the validity of the position of individual family members in a family argument, it is extremely difficult for a small child to be critical of his parents, particularly his mother. We all have a part of our mothers in us and to "kill off" that part is tantamount to self-injury. Even with adults, where the separation is more complete and there is generally less need to maintain a good relationship with one's mother because maternal care is no longer required, it is important to allow for protection and retention of at least parts of the maternal figure (Searles 1965b). As for fear of the father, an explanation of dread by virtue of sheer size and apparent physical strength is sufficient for a child's fear. To my way of thinking, while the concept at times may have validity, one need not get into the ramifications and the complex dynamics of an "Oedipus complex."

Clay or Play-Doh

I generally prefer Play-Doh to clay, although it tends to dry up easily if not placed back in its covered container following use. However, it is especially pliable and easily cleaned up as well as being nontoxic but not very palatable. Children can build all kinds of figures with the substance and convert their constructions to other objects with relative ease. They can add, remove, or exaggerate parts of bodies, or readily destroy them, all within the safety and privacy of their own minds. Whether or not the therapist participates in the play is somewhat controversial (as noted earlier in this chapter) and depends on the situation, the inclination of the therapist, and the needs of the child in treatment. In general, I prefer to be more of an observer than a participant. Since I am of a somewhat restless temperament, if a child is constructing with clay I find it valuable to participate in a kind of parallel play, constructing something while sitting opposite the child. It is important not to be competitive by becoming a better sculptor.

Here is an example of the use of Play-Doh that is particularly interesting because the theoretical orientation of the therapist did not determine how she conducted the session.

A young child constructed a long, cylindrical object, and the therapist, being quite traditional in her Freudian orientation, was convinced that the clay represented a penis. When the child said, "Guess what this is?" she did not interpret but simply said, "What is it?" The child then said, "It is a snake," and proceeded to break it into pieces. Although she still believed she was dealing with a representation of a penis, the thoughtful therapist then said, "And if you put the pieces back together, it is a snake again." With this interpretation or commentary on the part of the therapist, she did not have to spell out her understanding of the dynamics and whatever she believed the clay represented to the child. Her indication that it could be reconstructed to its former shape was likely to be comforting to the child, and her theoretical orientation, however correct or incorrect, was essentially irrelevant.

Suction Tipped Darts and Guns

The basic tenet of not introducing weapons as toys for children in order to minimize the teaching of violence as a solution to problems is indeed an important one; there are many parents who will not allow such toys into their homes, a position that certainly has considerable merit but will not be debated here. In the playroom weapon toys can be quite valuable when the underlying idea to be conveyed is that thoughts and play violence do not kill. If all people who had been wished dead were in fact dead, there would be few people left on this planet. For children whose hold on reality is flimsy, however, the use of play guns might be too real. Most children are, however, able to distinguish play from reality, and, even if they can actually express in detail the meaning of their symbolic gun play, they know it is not in fact dangerous. The message "Do not even think such things" is not a sound one because it contributes to the concept of magic and omnipotence. This is as inappropriate as contributing to a feeling that one cannot be playful or giving a feeling of complete impotence.

In fact, proper use of play weapons can help a child to learn to control his impulses and to express them in a socially approved manner. If a child says something as openly as "I want to kill my baby brother," it is appropriate to say "Of course you can't do that, but you can *pretend* that doll is your baby brother and shoot him with the dart gun." It is also hoped that the anger will be dissipated when accepted and better understood.

A child can shoot at a target, balloons, or dollhouse dolls, depending on his degree of awareness of his feelings and relative willingness to express them. As noted earlier, child therapists ought not get into the position of having to pick up and return darts for the child. This is not a suitable role for an adult and will likely result in some countertransference problems on the part of the therapist, if not realistic resentment.

Play Telephones or Walkie Talkies

Remote communication allows the child to talk with the therapist and yet be far enough away from him to encourage some pretense and projection and thus to be able to say something on the telephone that he could not say face to face. The child is also able to have imaginary conversations with parents or other significant figures. In general, the child should not be encouraged to use the real telephone in the office; children who have special difficulties in control may use real telephones to act out unacceptable behavior.

A very creative 12-year-old delighted in calling me when I was not in the office and leaving messages on my answering machine. I did not discourage this practice, because often the messages gave him an opportunity to relate things he was embarrassed to say to me directly. One day I found an unidentified message on my machine in a voice that was obviously his, in a language he would not ever use to me directly. The message was "Shit, shit, shit, shit, shit . . . shit, tune in tomorrow for fuck." In a subsequent session he identified himself as the caller, and we discussed his parent's restrictions on obscene language.

A Sink

A sink with running water is not for everyone. If one is included in the playroom, it is almost essential that the water supply to the sink can be turned off so that for certain children it is simply inoperative. An inoperative faucet may be somewhat frustrating to some children, but because it is not a good idea to allow children to leave the playroom during the therapeutic session, it would be no more frustrating than to be prohibited from removing toys from the playroom and taking them to the washroom. For those children with whom the use of water is permissible, the therapeutic possibilities are remarkably wide. Various dolls—and thus the persons they represent—can be drowned or rescued from drowning. With some children who show an obsessional bent, the cleaning of hands and toys can be conveniently performed and its meaning explored in therapy. The possible problems that can result from having a sink are unfortunately quite numerous. They include having water all over the playroom, water balloons that can be dropped fròm windows, and the filling of water pistols, which, even if they are not part of the regular playroom equipment, may be brought in surreptitiously by some children who own them.

A particularly disastrous outcome as a result of having water in the playroom is noted in the work of Bixler and referred to in chapter 6.

A Blackboard with Colored Chalk

Like paint and crayons, the blackboard offers possibilities for eliminating, destroying, or easily correcting figures and constructions in addition to providing possibilities for the drawing of pictures.

One 9-year-old girl entered the playroom and, on seeing the blackboard, promptly reached for a piece of chalk. She wrote the letters "D-A-G" on the board and then said "dog." This was a child of above average intelligence with no learning disorder; surely she must have known how to spell "dog." What was the meaning of this behavior, and what should the action of the therapist have been?

This child seems to have been testing in some way, perhaps even being provocative. To ask why she spelled "dog" that way would not have been inappropriate, but such a question would not have been nearly as fruitful as saying, "In here you can spell things any way you like." In this way the therapist acknowledged the child's misspelling and at the same time set the limits of the playroom and defined its function. Perhaps the child thought of the playroom as a classroom or was asking if indeed it was one (and in some instances with school psychologists it may have been). The therapist's answer made the difference clear in addition to conveying that he did not see his job as a teacher or in any sense as a disciplinarian.

What does one do if the child writes obscene words on the board, something clearly not permitted at home? Again, the answer could indicate that the playroom is a special place where the therapist has no objection to the child's using or displaying such language. The child might be asking about the meaning of such words. When children ask directly, they probably already know what the word means and are just checking or even bragging.

A blackboard is a good place to play Winnicott's "squiggle" game

(1971b). In this game single lines, curved or straight, are chalked on the board, and the other person can use these lines as the beginning of a picture to complete. In the hands of someone with even a little of Winnicott's skill and imagination this is a most valuable therapeutic and diagnostic tool.

Dollhouse

A dollhouse has obvious value in enabling a child to enact a number of family situations, as the chapter on limit setting explains more specifically. Dollhouses tend to be somewhat delicate, however, and since they are usually too large to be removed or replaced for individual children, the problems of protecting them from being broken do arise. Nevertheless, I find it far more useful to have one in the playroom than to omit it.

A dollhouse placed on a table with wheels, much like a typing table, can be moved out of the way or out of the room when not in use. Obviously, it should not be a collector's doll house with delicate, carefully scaled items but one that lends itself easily to the changing of furniture, space, and placement of dolls.

While some boys may relegate dollhouses to the exclusive play of girls, dollhouses can be particularly helpful in encouraging boys to take on caretaking and housekeeping roles without feeling that their masculinity is threatened. It is important that children (and some adults) learn not to confuse tenderness with passivity. In the contemporary vernacular, to be kind to babies and animals or to love flowers doesn't make one a "wimp."

A boy of 13 whose problems resulted in an emphasis on "macho" qualities was helped to accept his more tender feelings by constructing from kits furniture for the playroom dollhouse. He went through great effort to inform me that he felt that dolls, dollhouses, and anything that had to do with kitchens, dishes, or cooking was "sissy stuff," and he became primarily engaged in model construction. After a number of sessions at this activity I informed him that the dollhouse was in need of new furniture and that I understood that such furniture was available in kit form. I noted his competence in model making and asked if he would help me construct some pieces of furniture. Soon he was assembling a chair, and to be sure that the chair was the right size, I suggested that he could put one of the dolls on it. It was not too long before he was setting the new furniture in the house and arranging dolls to "see how they looked." Our conversation included a discussion about who ought to be in which room, and in talking about the kitchen, I was able to convey to him that cooking might indeed be fun and that such activities are not the basis for a definition of manliness.

Finger Paints

This is a most useful but very special item because of the complications involved. The paints come in small cups, and it is difficult to keep from contaminating the colors unless the child is fastidious enough to wipe his hands before he scoops out another color. The use of tongue depressor sticks can be helpful. However, if a child is fastidious, there is an implication of pathology of an obsessive compulsive nature, and the treatment ought to include "loosening up." Obsessive children often have difficulty accepting the fact that they can put their hands in the substance and be "messy." Children who have such restriction can be encouraged to be untidy by such statements as "Sometimes it's fun just to be messy."

Use of finger paints may engender concern with economy of materials and thus encourage behavior on the part of the therapist that is contrary to what is in the best therapeutic interest of the child. In the less technical sense countertransference problems (I mean all feelings the therapist has toward the child rather than just his own unconscious ones) might significantly interfere with optimal use of this medium. In addition, while the material is easily removable with water, one must protect clothing and room equipment. One solution is to buy finger paints in large quantities (somewhat hard to find) and then to provide the child with smaller amounts in small paper cups. The time required for preparation might be somewhat annoying but for most people probably less annoying than contaminating the whole supply each time they are used. Additionally useful items are smocks for the therapist and the child.

Masks and Dress-Up Clothing

By taking different roles, children can experiment with different kinds of interactions and get the feel of being another kind of person without having to accept that style as an integral part of themselves. In addition, young children in particular do like to pretend they are athletes, astronauts, chefs, doctors, truck drivers, vampires, ghosts, and parents. Equipment to help them in their fantasies can be most useful. Of course, one must never impose the materials on the child, only suggest them. Children whose sense of self is poorly established might be threatened by makeup items such as masks that would appear too real. While attending to the psychological significance of the part the child might play, one must consider the readiness of the child to deal with it. Some children may use the playroom opportunity to regress and play baby, and for this reason nursing bottles as well as a blanket might be especially appropriate. Costumes, masks, blankets and nursing bottles are particularly useful for group therapy with children, as explained in chapter 8.

Carefully Selected Games

It is my opinion that games should be used only to a limited degree and then in a carefully prescribed manner. In a comprehensive book on game play (Schaefer and Reid 1986) a multitude of games, including card games, checkers, and games that are especially designed for therapeutic purposes are discussed with emphasis on their therapeutic use. Other games specifically designed for therapeutic purposes are suggested by Kritzberg (1975), Jernberg (1979), and Gardner (1973a). The major function of games seems to be teaching such issues as rules, word usage, coordination, and mathematics. These are worthy goals, more or less related to psychotherapy but more appropriate to education per se. This is not true of games specifically designed for therapy, but those games also have serious limitations.

Perhaps my major objection to games is that they are too limiting in their therapeutic application even with the most imaginative therapists. One can of course deal with competition, rules, cheating, and to some degree other issues, but materials that are not so confined by rules lend themselves better to projective metaphorical behavior.

There are nevertheless specific instances where games are especially useful. Ekstein (1983) made imaginative use of chess, seeing a child's protection of the queen as analogous to his protection of his mother, and Gardner (1986), who himself objects to checkers in general as being "low in therapeutic efficiency," discusses ways in which the game may be somewhat therapeutic. Therapeutic use with resistant children is indicated by Loomis (1964). Games that require skill more than chance pose special problems for therapists. By virtue of age and experience it is assumed that the therapist is more skilled at chess or checkers than the average 9-year-old and, since competition is indeed part of the game, a game in which the therapist always wins and the child always loses does not contribute to the child's self-esteem.

Some therapists—for example, Gardner (1986)—advocate cheating to allow the child to win. In addition to the complications caused by the basic dishonesty introduced into the relationship, however skilled the therapist is at rigging the game so that children do not know they are being allowed to win, children generally expect adults to be better at games that require experience and training. To have the therapist lose under such circumstances may contribute to a false sense of omnipotence and a distorted view of the benefits of experience and growth.

I tend not to have such competitive games in the playroom, especially with young children, but they are sometimes there for special purposes (as will be shown in my use of them with adolescents). I am more comfortable with those games that are intended to be therapeutic rather than games that at best have educational value. Such games as Operation, Clue, and Bingo do not do well in a playroom.

If a child with whom I do not feel it is appropriate to play games suggests playing checkers, for example, I might reply by saying simply that I prefer not to:

CHILD: Let's play checkers.
THERAPIST: I prefer not to.

C: Come on, let's play.

T: You play for me. You play both sides.

Sometimes this approach has especially useful results. Children can play both sides and can then rig it for you to win or lose or have either of you cheat. Obviously, a discussion of these events has therapeutic value. However, if the child is not satisfied with the suggestion to play both sides, the conversation might continue as follows:

C: No, I want to play with you! Why won't you play with me?

T: Because I've been playing for many years so I play pretty well and probably better than you, so you would end up losing most of the time, and losing most of the time is no fun.

If the child still insists, perhaps because he is unrealistic and believes that he can win, then I will play. The child is likely to lose and probably will soon give up the game. This experience, if handled with gentleness, is not a bad way for him to learn to deal with reality. "I told you so" is not a good phrase for the therapist to use; it is better to let the problem fade away and suggest some other material for the child. Of course, if one does not have checkers in the playroom, this difficulty can be avoided.

There are a number of games that I consider more therapeutic because they do not force obvious self-revelation but rather work more through metaphor. While there is some chance and reward involved in the games, they are essentially designed to explore feelings and thus are frequently quite useful.

Gardner's Talking, Feeling, Doing game (1973a) encourages the child to deal with imagined situations in which he is to tell how the boy felt, what he should do, and so on.

Examples of the kinds of statements Gardner includes in his cards are as follows:

What do you think of a girl who does something disgusting in class?

A big boy picks on you, show what you would do to him.

What do you think of a boy who hates his sister?

What should you say to a younger brother who takes your things?

Useful discussions can be started through this game, which requires fairly active participation by the therapist. The rules allow players to refuse to deal with any particular item and simply lose a chip for not doing so. This is a kind of built-in safeguard against probing too deeply. I find this also works well for the therapist who may feel that the question requires too much personal revelation or physical activity, such as hopping across the room on one foot.

Although I see little about it in the literature these days, Schneidman's Make a Picture Story (MAPS) test (1949) has similar possibilities when used projectively. In the MAPS test figures are set up against backgrounds by the child and he then invents a story to go with the picture. There are obvious variations of ways in which that material could be utilized. The Thematic Apperception Test (TAT; Murray 1943) and the Children's Apperception Test (CAT; Bellak 1949) can be used in this way therapeutically as well as diagnostically.

Gardner (1969) also has a story completion game, similar to one children sometimes play in camp or in the Boy or Girl Scouts, in which each child stops the story at a crucial point and the next child must continue it. As a therapeutic device this game can easily give rise to a kind of adversarial mode in which the therapist attempts to probe sensitive areas and the child is able to defeat him by staying with nonsensitive issues. In storytelling games, a tape recorder is often a useful item. One youngster of 12 used this with the therapist, inventing a kind of TV talk show in which various people with different accents and voices were interviewed. The therapist was able to take part in this activity by being either the interviewer or one of those interviewed and ask relatively personal questions while still maintaining the fiction of a TV talk show.

I have heard experienced child therapists say that all they need to do therapy with a child is a deck of cards. I suppose this is true to a certain degree, but I find a very limited use for card games. They can too easily be used as ways of not doing therapy by some therapists and some children. Their presence in the playroom requires considerable discretion, although, again, with some adolescents they do have a place as a way for them to be relieved of more direct discussion and at the same time allow them to shift back and forth between concentrating on talking and on play.

A Sandbox

In general, a sandbox cannot be considered for most playrooms. The problems such equipment engenders makes its presence almost prohibitive. In addition to space requirements, there are considerations of cleanliness, the possibility that in the hands of an overly aggressive and relatively uncontrolled child sand may serve as a formidable weapon, and that portability for its presence or absence for particular children is not easy to arrange. However, assuming one has the appropriate space or that it can be kept outside of the building, the sandbox can have considerable value for some children. Sifting of sand, with all of its tactile and visual qualities, can be most satisfying to very young or severely regressed youngsters. Children can write in sand, draw pictures, and readily disguise or erase their productions. The sandbox is a luxury to be carefully considered.

Equipment Requiring Physical Prowess and Skill

This category includes such items as a ring toss, rubber horseshoes, and a basketball hoop. Hyperactive and some overly anxious children need some kind of physical activity and do best if the activity is permitted while they are in the playroom because the room provides physical boundaries at the same time. These items are not very useful as projective devices, although some children do well setting up a score-keeping system and playing against themselves to establish new records. In this regard they may get into issues of competence and cheating. If their self-esteem depends on coordination and skill of this sort, the therapist can be quite helpful in enabling them to deal with failures.

These kinds of activities as well as dart throwing or shooting can be dangerous to occupants and furniture. Useful safeguards are such items as Nerf balls of varying sizes and outdoor play, which will be discussed in the chapter on limit setting.

Miscellaneous

Included in this category are doctor and nurse kits, scientific toys, and magic tricks that assist children in feeling that they have mastery over some parts of their environment. Doctor and nurse kits can be used to handle anxieties about health, issues of death, and sexual concerns and are effectively used in conjunction with a variety of dolls that are somewhat bigger than dollhouse size. One might also consider such items as a small cradle, play dishes, and cooking equipment. Play-Doh cookies, while unpalatable, are most useful for dealing with issues that revolve around food and eating. Woodworking and other tools are useful but of course do have space limitations. Play money can be quite useful for such play as "store keeping" and "shopping trips."

An Etch-a-Sketch or a magic slate has the potential for a sense of mastery: with them a child can make things appear or disappear just as magic tricks do.

Odd objects can sometimes become quite helpful in therapy sessions and are limited only by the imagination of the therapist. For example, with Arthur, a child who had threatened suicide, I used a room as a playroom in a section of my house, and therapy often included the presence of the family cat. At one point Arthur announced that he could talk cat talk. I encouraged this and asked him to converse with the animal. The boy made a series of meow sounds to which the cat sometimes replied. By asking Arthur to translate for me, I was able to perform some worthwhile therapeutic work. At times it became useful for me to say something like, "I thought he [the cat] said he would rather be outside" or "with his father" or "with his mother" or any number of things that were pertinent at the time. As long as his conversation was with the cat, a conversation from which I was virtually excluded, the child could convey much useful information, and in talking about the cat, I was able to get important information back to the child on a level he could understand, with little intellectualization and with significant impact.

Summary

The above playroom equipment has been classified here according to its relative importance in the playroom in general. While some note was made of the significance of different items for different children, it is useful to have certain items in the playroom for children with specific needs and necessary to eliminate certain items for individual children. With this in mind, an alternative way of classifying materials was thoughtfully devised nearly thirty years ago by Ginott. His classificatory system, which placed emphasis on diagnostic categories, was as follows:

Tools for the therapeutic relationship
Toys for catharsis
Materials for insight
Tools for reality testing
Media for sublimation (1960:243–246)

Having provided an outline of the equipment and structure of the playroom, I will consider next the initial session with the child, contact that takes place primarily in the playroom.

5

The Initial Session with the Child

The first contact between the child and therapist is usually in the waiting room, where the child is ordinarily accompanied by one parent, most frequently the mother. If the parent does not introduce the child to the therapist, then the therapist must introduce himself: "Billy, I am Doctor Smith." Then the child is invited into the playroom. Occasionally, one encounters a child who cannot separate easily from the parent in the waiting room. If reluctance is detected, it is recommended that beyond the initial invitation the child not be asked to come alone. Instead, the invitation can be followed by, "Your mother [father] will come along with us to see where we are." Both can then be led into the playroom.

If the parents were seen prior to the initial session with the child, then the parents have been properly prepared for this initial session and some problems will thus be avoided. Ginott wrote:

It is advisable to tell mothers in detail what to expect and how to react during the child's first playroom visit. Thus from the beginning, they are given an opportunity to help the child to assume more independence. The mothers are told that the child may hold on to them, cry copiously, and refuse to follow a strange therapist to an unfamiliar room. They are told about the child's great fear of abandonment and are instructed what to say to the child and especially what not to say at the moment of separation.

When the therapist first meets mother and child and says, "Good morning, Johnny and I are now going to the playroom," mother should respond, "Fine, I'll wait here." She should not hold on to the child desperately, nor should she wave a heartbreaking good-by, as though he were going overseas. She should not give him lessons in etiquette or last-minute advice, such as, "Stop crying. Look at the man when he talks to you. You better go with this nice man or he won't like you. I am so ashamed of you; you promised to behave. Now be a good boy," and the like (1961a: 76)

The next step in separation is to reassure the child that the parent will be in the waiting room while he is with the therapist. If such reassurance is not sufficient to persuade the child to leave the parent, one can suggest that the door will be left open, and if separation is still too anxiety provoking, the child can be told that the parent will be permitted to remain in the playroom as long as the child feels it is necessary. Conducting therapy with the parent in the room is advisable only when the separation is simply more than the child can handle.

Another point of view about parental presence is advocated by Gardner (1975), who believes that all therapy with children should be conducted in the presence of the parent. He believes that in addition to having the mother as a therapeutic assistant, the process includes "training" the mother in healthier methods of child rearing. I see this approach as more educational than therapeutic. If one deals with problems of transference and the underlying dynamics between the therapist and the child, having a third person in the room can cause serious difficulties. For one thing, as noted in the discussion of family therapy, it is difficult enough to understand what goes on between two people; the presence of a parent seriously complicates this dyadic arrangement. While the parent may be taught in the treatment situation to make appropriate comments and interventions, the transmission of more subtle, nonverbal, highly significant, and frequently confusing messages cannot be easily regulated with a parent who has serious conflicting feelings toward the child and toward the therapist. Furthermore, the child can get caught in rivalries between the therapist and the parent. Even with adults, groups of three are least successful for productive meetings or enjoyable social occasions.

Beginning the Session

Most children, even those who are quite insecure, can tolerate being alone with a therapist, particularly in a room that is obviously equipped for play. Some children may head straight for toys; others may sit and readily engage in conversation. Many therapists begin the conversation by asking the child if he knows why he is there. While I believe it is important for the child to have some concept of the meaning of his sessions, that kind of question seldom leads to directly useful answers and often brings about an initial defensiveness. Children frequently answer the question with the truthful, not necessarily evasive, statement that they are there because their parent brought them there. I am speaking primarily of younger children. With adolescents, the initiating procedure is somewhat different (see chapter 7). With younger children a simple invitation to play with the toys will usually suffice.

The ways in which a session with a child can begin are as varied as the children themselves. A few examples are given here to show the course a session opening might take. The initial session with a child is usually a diagnostic one and proceeds somewhat differently from a later session, when it has been established that the child is in fact in therapy.

While adults make conversation with strangers by discussing such things as the weather and local geography or perhaps some item of dress such as "I like the necklace you're wearing," children have less sophisticated ways of starting conversations, but they are essentially not too different. Because one of the early tasks of growth is to identify the world around them, young children, or those psychologically younger than their chronological peers, might well enter the playroom and identify the toys that they see. Simple confirmation of the correctness of identifications might be sufficient. Other children might ask about everything in the playroom: "What is this?" and "What is that?" even though it is clear that they know what the item is.

Richard, a child of 6 who came to treatment because of problems at home and at school, quickly spotted a broken toy during his first visit to the playroom. "Who broke this toy?" he asked. What was the meaning of this question? Did Richard really want to know *who* had broken the toy? More likely his question was about something else. He might have wanted to know if I see other children, an assumption he had probably already made but wished to check; or, as later exploration revealed was actually the case, he might have been questioning what happens to a child who breaks a toy in the playroom. What is my attitude toward children who break toys? One does not, especially with a child, take such a question at face value. In addition to being a violation of confidence, disclosing who had broken the toy would have been of little use to Richard. Rather, what I deemed more appropriate, particularly with Richard, was to say, "It was an accident." Such a reply was more likely to convey my accepting attitude and to suggest that I was understanding of Richard's behavior. At best, the answer was what Richard needed to hear; at worst, it was gratuitous but designed to do no harm.

If Richard had really wanted to know who had broken it or perhaps even wished to know if a particular friend of his also came to see me, he would have probably followed with, "Yes, but *who* broke it?" The following dialogues demonstrates a probable procedure with such a child.

RICHARD: Yes, but *who* broke it?
THERAPIST: [Somewhat arbitrarily, but knowing Richard felt his sister got away with more misbehavior than he did]: A girl.
R: What's her name.
T: Susan [a fictitious name clearly not the same of Richard's sister].
R: Is she in the fourth grade?
T: No, she's no one you know.

In a later session in this case, I might have asked: "What do you think of girls who break toys?" or "Do you know any girls who break things?" or "What would your mother [or father] do if you broke something?" The information might have been retained to use in future play. For example, in a constructed playhouse, a pretend lamp could be broken, and a discussion about the subject of broken objects and parental reactions might ensue.

In a diagnostic interview it is of course important to discover how the child relates, with minimal intervention by the therapist, to the therapist and the playroom. However, because there are specific questions that one needs to answer to determine the future course of action, spontaneous, undirected play may not be sufficiently revealing. A child who settles down to moving a car back and forth across the room or repeatedly throws a Nerf ball through a basketball hoop or bangs away at a toy xylophone does not reveal much information other than perhaps some fear or timidity. It is helpful in an initial session to steer children toward the more projective materials, perhaps even to present them with crayons and paper and ask them to draw. Suggesting that the children draw a person or a family might give information about how they conceive of themselves and their families. Draw a Person techniques remain a diagnostic means of assessing children; while I object to some of the precise and rigid interpretations that some diagnosticians provide on the basis of these techniques, they do provide useful information. (The general use of diagnostic tests will be discussed later in this chapter.) Since crayons and pencils are readily familiar material even to young children, they rarely pose a threat when children are asked to draw. Some children might become defensive about their drawing skills, in which case it is of course inappropriate to insist that they draw, but their defensiveness in itself is quite useful information.

If children are sufficiently free to use different materials and explore the playroom on their own without prompting in the initial session, then careful observation of the materials they choose and the ways in which they use them provides a good deal of information. Does the child move toward guns? Or away from them? Is he quick to construct something? What if the child goes to the dolls and or a dollhouse? Of course all of this can be quite telling, but the revelations must be carefully considered in terms of the specific child and in the context of his total behavior. A child may move toward guns, for example, not because he is particularly hostile or aggressive, but rather because guns are not permitted in his house.

Or perhaps something of the events he experienced on that particular day is being acted out.

If dolls and a dollhouse are more appropriate for a specific child than crayons and paper, he or she can be encouraged to arrange figures and furniture. A useful method of initiating therapy is through hand puppets. If the therapist places them on his own hand, he might encourage the child to do the same, or the therapist could simply start a conversation of his own between puppets. As long as the material is kept projective, such issues as why the child is there or how people feel in a strange room or with a strange person can be easily explored.

In the initial session one is evaluating such dimensions as timidity, aggressiveness, anxiety, intellect, self-image and self-confidence, suppression and repression. If the child reveals sufficient information about these dimensions with only minimal prompting, so much the better. The therapist is a catalyst, not the dominant or primary figure in the playroom.

One young child of 3 was reluctant to touch or use any materials in the initial session. I soon reached for some of the puppets and had them playing with each other. One puppet, somewhat grotesque in its appearance, brought about a frightened look on the child's face. I replaced the puppet in the box and remarked that some children thought that puppet was scary. I did not specifically say, "I can see you're frightened"; he might have heard that as an accusation, for he was trying to appear brave. I conveyed that being afraid was not remarkable and was a feeling I respected. Important information was thus elicited: this child was timid and easily frightened—at least by some puppets.

During the initial session some children who at first are able to separate from the parent become concerned during the session and wish to go back to their parent. The exact nature of their concern may not be known to either therapist or child. Possibly they are frightened and feel they need the protection of their parent, or it is even possible that they are angry with their parent for having brought them there and need the reassurance that in some magical way their anger has not done the parent harm. Difficulty in separating from the parent often can be handled by telling the child that the therapist will go with him just to see if the parent is all right. While this may or may not be addressing the concern the child has, it generally proves to be comforting. If the reason for the child's fear is his concern over the force of his own anger, such material is bound to be so out of awareness that in this instance he does not see "checking on mother" as a mind-reading act. I then take the child by the hand, go back and see the mother, and then gently guide the child back to the playroom.

While the passage of time is a difficult concept for children to understand, reassuring them that there are only five minutes left might be helpful. Returning to the parent, one has an opportunity to note not only the child's attitude toward the apparent safety of the parent, but also the parent's attitude toward separation from the child. Much in the writing of Stern (1985) indicates the various cues that parents can give about the safety of leaving them. Anxiety in itself is certainly communicated from mother to child, as indicated by Sullivan (1953a) and Stern. Often the verbal message the parent gives may not be the same as the "real" message conveyed, and even a well-trained and sensitive therapist might miss the private communication that is being transmitted (Levenson 1972).

In an example of misattunement, Jane, a 10-year-old in the fourth grade, was brought to treatment because she was reported to be quite upset about her parents separation eight months previously. She was having considerable difficulty in attending to her work at school and difficulty in sleeping at night, sometimes going to her mother's bed. When she arrived for her session accompanied by her mother, she carried a large doll wrapped in a blanket. Jane had been told that she was coming to see me to play, and her mother reported that for this reason she brought her own things to play with. Jane shyly carried her armload with her into the playroom, and I asked her what she brought. She proceeded to unwrap the blanket from the doll and revealed a number of small dolls that she said were the playthings of her doll. At my request, she proceeded to show me the dolls one at a time. The first doll she revealed was a homely "cabbage patch" doll. I reached for a hand puppet of a dog and started a conversation between the puppet and the doll.

The conversation revealed that the doll's name was Joan and that she was 3 years old; when Jane gave the puppet a voice, she sounded like a 3-year-old. She said that Joan was in nursery school, and further exchanges reinforced the idea that Jane would have much preferred to be 3 years old and in nursery school than 10 years old and in the fourth grade.

When Jane left the playroom to go home, she cuddled up next to her mother on a couch in the waiting room. At this her mother announced to Jane that pretty soon Jane would be bigger than she was. Jane then moved even closer to her mother, almost sitting on her lap. Her mother then said, "Pretty soon I'll be able to sit in your lap."

In this situation Jane's mother was having a difficult time being a single mother and raising her child essentially by herself. Jane's father made infrequent visits and was unreliable about appointments with the child. Jane had to contend with her father's unreliability and her mother's consternation about being a single parent who had been left by her husband who was now with another woman. She certainly had good reasons for being upset and wanting to be 3 years old and back in nursery school. At the same time her mother felt burdened in having to raise the child by herself and wished she were grown up. When Jane acted like a baby it probably frightened her mother, who then reflected her need to see Jane grown. Announcing to Jane that she *was* grown was frightening to the child, who then acted more childishly. Obviously, they both had different agendas, and the interaction reenforced their misattunement.

Psychodiagnostic Testing

There are instances where psychodiagnostic testing is in order. In regard to this procedure two questions need to be considered. The first and primary one is to consider the purpose of the tests. What information is needed to be provided in this manner? The second is should the therapist be the one who does the testing?

What is the function of psychodiagnostic test procedures? Twenty to thirty years ago it was routine to test all children prior to entering them into treatment. In hospital settings this routine was even extended to adults. Now, for the most part, tests are infrequently used, and some graduate schools in psychology provide little if any instruction in psychodiagnostic test procedures. In educational settings tests are used somewhat more frequently, but they are usually achievement and intelligence tests, with relatively little attention being paid to projective techniques. Much of the personality information that psychological tests provide can be obtained from interview and observation in the playroom. There are, however, certain advantages to psychological testing. The most important is that it provides information in a relatively short period of time. In addition, there is more precision in tests of intelligence and achievement. Psychological tests can provide an extensive description of underlying dynamics in addition to answering some very important questions, such as what are the possibilities of suicide, organic involvement, or psychotic processes? In terms of underlying dynamics they can provide such information as ego strength and weaknesses, obsessional thoughts and underlying attitudes about self and others.

For the most part I believe the use of such tests is essentially optional. However, there are instances where significant information is needed quickly. If there is potential for suicide, obviously it is of vital importance that it be known quickly. As to further use of psychological tests, if one is dealing with the possibility of an organic disorder such as a brain tumor, psychological tests might reveal the presence of such pathology even prior to a neurological examination. It would be most unfortunate to start on a course of psychotherapy aimed at curing headaches assumed to be psychogenic in origin and then to discover that the cause was a progressing carcinoma. In addition, prolonged or excessive use of drugs can have serious effects on one's ability to conceptualize and organize thinking. Such confusion and deleterious effects can often be competently detected through psychological tests; these would be more appropriate to adolescents and adults than to children.

At times tests are requested for the wrong reasons. In school situations teachers sometimes request tests "to see if the child is working up to his level." If such a request is made and one is taking the role of diagnostician, it is important to inquire further before complying with the request. Often the real issue is not whether the child is working up to his "level" or not. What if he is not performing at his assumed capacity? What does this mean in terms of the teaching situation? Asking the teacher how possible underperformance would effect the situation often brings the response that the teacher wants to know if he is sufficiently challenging to the child—whether, in effect, the teacher should demand more.

The fact is that most learning is essentially sequential. Children cannot learn language until they can vocalize, no matter how smart they are or whatever their potential is. Spelling requires a prior recognition of letters, and writing sentences requires a knowledge of words. Children cannot learn higher levels of mathematics until they know simple arithmetic. Potential is not something that can be measured; it can only be speculated about. Often additional questioning of the teacher indicates that the real reason for wanting the child's intelligence checked is that the child does not seem to be learning and the teacher may be insecure about his own competence as a teacher. A report that the child has a low I.Q. can be comforting to teachers who are insecure about their skills and can reassure them that they are good teachers. However, as far as teaching a child is concerned, good pedogogical methods require that the child be taught whatever is the next step in the sequence of the subject matter he is learning regardless of I.Q. For the teacher to be able to answer the question "Is it he or is it I?" (who is at fault?) does not seem to me to be an adequate reason to subject the child to a series of psychological tests.

There are times when parents request psychological tests. Most often they think of tests as relating to intelligence rather than adjustment and may also be questioning their own adequacy as parents or have suspicions about their child's intellect. If they have other children older than the child brought for treatment, an inquiry comparing the two (or more) children can usually be quite revealing in regard to this matter. Parents are far better at judging the competence and level of adjustment than they usually permit themselves to believe.

If the therapist decides that tests are indicated, deciding who is to do the testing is not a simple matter. Of course, if the therapist is not qualified to make psychodiagnostic evaluations, it is a simple matter—someone else must. However, if the therapist *is* competent to perform tests, there is the question of defining his role. As a therapist he is an accepting presence and not an obvious authority. As a tester he is not quite so accepting and is more clearly an authority. Moreover, a sophisticated child might feel that the therapist can in some kind of arcane way obtain information about him that he does not wish him to have. This certainly could seriously effect the course of the therapy. Ideally, the child should feel that all the therapist knows about him is that which the child has told him. There are times when the therapist might do the testing himself and deal with the consequences accordingly, but if testing is indicated and one has the option of having someone else provide the examination, in most instances that is the preferable path.

Having initiated treatment with the child, the therapist is then faced with the problems of ongoing therapy. Many therapists have difficulty in differentiating between permissiveness, structure, rules, and freedom. The next chapter is devoted to setting of limits in child therapy.

6

Limit Setting

The important issue of limit setting in child therapy does not get the attention it deserves from therapists or in the psychological literature. Many therapists seem to assume a method of dealing with the setting of limits (mostly as it applies to behavior) in child treatment as if it were not controversial or even worthy of further discussion. I believe the how and why of dealing with the setting of limits are of vital importance in providing effective therapy with children, and the rationale for specific choices needs careful examination.

In the history of child therapy the earliest trend seems to have been toward a minimal attempt to establish limits. Melanie Klein apparently felt that acting out would arouse guilt, which could then be constructively interpreted. She said, "Often a toy is broken or when a child is more aggressive, attacks are made with a knife or scissors on the table or piece of wood; water or paint is splashed about; and the room generally becomes a battlefield. It is essential to enable the child to bring out his aggressiveness" (1964:120). Anna Freud (1946) said that the first principle of child therapy was total acceptance of the patient and all his impulses.

Some pioneers in child therapy, such as Axline (1947), Allen (1942), Moustakis (1953), and Slavson (1952), were greatly influenced by the work of Rogers (1942) and the nondirective school. Their underlying assumption was that, given a proper nurturing, noncritical, and reflective environment, people would grow and neurosis would disappear. When nondirective therapy was transformed from an essentially verbal medium to one of play as required with children, it led to nonlimiting, extreme permissiveness. It is one thing to permit any kind of verbal behavior, as is expected and agreed on with adult patients, and another to transfer that permissiveness to play behavior. Adults have many built-in controls, and although they too may test out a therapist's permissiveness, it is seldom in the form of throwing things or being physically destructive. If one conveys to children that they are free to do as they wish, their testing of limits is quite likely to lead to physical acting out; by allowing for complete permissiveness, acting out is effectively encouraged.

Most therapists in the 1940s and 1950s permitted so much freedom that it could readily lead to the breaking of toys and equipment; the only real prohibition against destructiveness was actual injury to the child or the therapist. They placed no limits on language other than loudness, which might be distracting to others in the building, and allowed without protest all sorts of verbal abuse. In fact, Slavson (1952) even suggested that young children be permitted to strike the therapist, so long as the therapist was not injured.

Following Rogers (1942), therapists emphasized that the only important message to be conveyed to the child was that his feelings were understood, reflected, and accepted. Hence the reflection of feelings was the central ingredient of nondirective child therapy, and therapists showed little regard for the setting of limits. Only insofar as the lack of limits impinged on the therapy was the issue of limits given serious consideration.

After some time therapists became more sophisticated or perhaps simply less tolerant of destructiveness, and limits became tighter and a matter of increasing attention. An indication of this change is found in the writing of Bixler, who listed five items to the setting of limits: "A child is not supposed to: (1) destroy any property or facilities in the room other than play equipment; (2) attack the therapist in any physical sense; (3) stay beyond the time limit of the interview; (4) remove toys from the playroom; (5) throw toys or other material out of the window" (1964:136).

While Bixler advocated clear limits, protocols of his therapy sessions indicated a somewhat more arbitrary position in the actual setting of limits. An example of this discrepancy and the problems it caused for Bixler is as follows:

At this point he came over and hit me. The time was about up and I told him it was time to clean up the water on the floor, and he asked me what I would do if he didn't. I told him, "nothing." He said, "Who would clean it up?" I said, "I would." He threw the rag on the floor. I mentioned that it was a lot of fun to think I would be the one who would have to clean up any mess that he left. He was pleased by this and then gradually became more angry again. Apparently because I didn't get angry. (1964:138)

A more natural and appropriate response for the therapist would have been for him to get angry, to express this anger verbally, and to set limits. It is difficult to see the therapeutic value of such permissiveness, assuming the therapist was angry and exercised control of it, or to understand the value of such remarkable control on the part of the therapist. The expression of anger by the therapist is not prohibited. Children need to know that therapists are as human as themselves and other people. The therapist's never showing anger is just as much an error as his becoming angry at everything. On the other hand, extreme permissiveness is usually quite unrealistic and may be seen as a challenge to the child, who as a result may become quite provocative. Thus, permissiveness is an aspect of child treatment that needs to be addressed in terms of a host of variables.

In a session with this same child three days later, Bixler reported: "He tried to destroy the doll and was unable to. He poured water on the floor from the nursing bottle and when he began to fill it up the second time to throw it on the floor, I told him that he could throw two bottles of water on the floor but no more" (p. 141).

The child then proceeded to empty the second bottle on the

floor, followed by a third, by which time Bixler had him leave the room. It is not clear why Bixler established two as an arbitrary number of bottles to be spilled; it appears that he should never have allowed the child to get to that point. As for Bixler's final solution, few therapists would terminate a session solely because they disapproved of the child's behavior: to terminate the session in this manner is a statement of complete defeat and rejection. Bixler's termination corresponds to his overall handling of this water event. His approach to limits was arbitrary and constituted a failure of the particular approach used. Impulse regulation, acting out, termination of a session, and the therapist's response to his own anger clearly are part of the entire morphology of setting limits.

Another example of the kind of problems therapists faced regarding limits when they assumed a very permissive attitude can be seen in the writing of Wolf:

His behavior in the playroom became not only messy but destructive. He proposed tearing up all the other children's pictures on the wall and he hurled some wet sand about everywhere. The psychiatrist [Wolf] said that she did not mind the mess; that could be cleaned up, but that she would not allow him to destroy other children's paintings just as she would preserve his own. At one point she actually held on to stop him from daubing paint all over a picture on the wall (1969:232).

Some therapists began to question the efficacy of a laissez-faire attitude in child therapy, and the scene began to change. Limits became of real concern, and practical matters having to do with the possibility of the breakage of materials and physical injury to the child or the therapist were given more careful consideration, not only as problems of treatment, but as an integral part of the treatment process. Therapists began to recognize that complete freedom in the playroom was not always in the best interest of treatment.

Therapists' rights were proclaimed by some as early as 1950. A pioneer in regard to limit setting, Woltmann (1964), reported a child who asked him his given name in the first session. When Woltmann said his name was Gus, the child said, "Well I'm going to call you shit." To which Woltmann replied, "If you call me shit, I'm going to call you shit." To which the child said, "All right, Gus, what kind of toys do you have to play with?" I do not recommend the procedure that Woltmann followed, but it is reported here because it illustrates an early setting of limits. I would have replied to this child by saying, "I don't like to be called shit, but in here you can use whatever words you like." This would have placed the emphasis on the obscene word and implied permissiveness without encouraging the use of a disparaging term for the therapist.

With further consideration of matters such as the value of time and the cost of materials therapists were led to establish more severe limits. For example, Ginott (1963) prohibited the breaking of toys with a statement like, "Toys are not for breaking." He devised the unique solution of keeping a box of toys that had been accidentally broken. When a child wished to break a toy, he would direct the child to the box labeled "toys for breaking."

The cleaning of the playroom was a debated issue. Although Ginott was relatively strict in his limit setting, he did not require the child to clean up after his session. It is interesting and somewhat amusing to note that he emphasized that this was not the job of the therapist but of a maid. He said,

The playroom is a miniature world to the child, and the neatly arranged playroom symbolizes that the world can be orderly. The playroom must be neat in the beginning of each session, with the floor swept, broken toys removed, paints and clay in working order, and the nursing bottles sterilized and refilled. This job requires the services of a professional maid. The therapist should be able to rest in the interlude between sessions and meditate about life outside of the playroom. (1964:130)

Few therapists have the luxury of following that prescription, and most therapists would probably make cleaning up the playroom at the end of the session a joint project.

As more therapists advocated stricter limits, some took to reciting limits at the beginning of the first session, and many started the session with a little speech:

"This is a playroom. In here you can play with these toys in any way you like. You may not hurt me or yourself, and you may not destroy any equipment. This is your time every week and we will have fifty minutes each time. You may not remove anything from the playroom."

Some therapists added additional rules, such as not bringing guests, food, or toys from home and not leaving the playroom until the end of the session. The latter ruling was interpreted by some children as an almost instant challenge, and they immediately announced that they had to go to the bathroom. The variations of the speech ranged from therapists who said, in effect, that children could do almost anything they wished to others who were quite strict and figuratively read children the riot act. Some children were traumatized by such speeches and could hardly move in the playroom; others devoted much of their behavior to testing limits. If the therapist was lucky, the children listened selectively and hardly heard the speech.

Limits should be considered and stated as the need arises. But the guiding principle—to maintain and enhance self-esteem—requires limiting behavior and not feelings. Today, few therapists are as permissive as therapists once were, and there is less of a dichotomy between "hard" and "soft" therapists. For the most part, the question of where to set limits is not very controversial. In this chapter, minimal attention is given to where limits are set: the focus is on how and why limits are set. A simple statement of how I view development will be helpful in furthering an understanding of my approach to the setting of limits.

Limits and Maturation

Patterns of growth and development have a vital influence on the learning of limits. In the process of growth and development attachments between the child and significant others are made and broken. For a detailed discussion of attachment theory, see the writings of Mahler, Furer, and Settladge (1959), Schachtel (1959), Guntrip (1969), and Winnicott (1971). The more recent work of Stern (1985) will probably result in revision of some of the generally accepted attachment theory (Spiegel 1987). Some of the controversial implications of Stern's work are indicated in Katz (1987) and Kaplan (1987). For the purpose of discussion here, the focus is on dependence and independence (I will avoid the more precise but more technical words such as "individuation," "bonding," and "fusion").

By virtue of physical, emotional, and intellectual limitations, infants cannot be anything but dependent and consequently vulnerable. This is the natural state of infancy. Adults have options; they can be dependent or independent or combinations of the two. Since the word "dependency" as applied to adults is often considered to be pejorative, many adults cannot admit this state and develop various ways, frequently quite subtle, indirect, and even ingenious, of getting other people to make their decisions for them. Simply stated, the problems of adults who are still very dependent are quite complicated and disabling.

Feelings of dependency are not completely noxious, as is often assumed, and a certain amount of need for people adds to the richness and enjoyment of relationships. On the other hand, people who are almost completely independent—for example, some children who were raised under certain kibbutz community conditions (Rabin and Beit-Hallahmi 1982; Paves 1986)—can be lonely, cold, detached, and show a pervasive quality of depression. Therefore, we hope that with adults the major basis of relationships is not dependency. We like to see relationships based on intimacy (a feeling that cannot be experienced by one person), mutual respect, love, affection, admiration, warmth, desire, and wish. The terms that should be least applicable to mature relationships are "need" and "demand."

The question for child therapy is how children, who are basically dependent, are supposed to become adults, who are basically independent. Accomplishing this is the job of parents as well as therapists. It appears to me that the process of growth occurs in jumps with partial regressions. With the increased development of the child, society and parents grant more privileges and rely more on the child's own inner sense of responsibility and control with fewer prohibitions. In other words, in some way external limits are reduced, and internal limits are increased. Children grow by tentatively trying out what they consider to be adult behavior. Not only do children alternate between mature and immature behavior, they often show both at the same time. For instance, a teenager once came to a therapy session smoking a pipe. I commented on the shape and style of the pipe, and he explained to me that he had had two dollars and bought the pipe for $1.95. "What did you do with the change?" I asked. "I bought bubble gum," he said.

Since adult and childlike forces operate at the same time, the question arises of how child therapy (which I believe requires of the therapists not so much the relation of insight as the ability to create a special kind of relationship and experience with the child) facilitates the developmental process. A primary curative value of therapy is ·to provide a corrective emotional (growth) experience. Insight becomes part of the process of providing this relationship with adults, but the content of the insight in itself is frequently not of major significance. If it were, therapists could simply perform a complete psychodiagnostic test evaluation and provide the patient with the results of the test. If a therapist were foolish enough to do this, he would discover that in most cases the patient simply accepts the findings they find ego syntonic and deny anything they find ego alien. If the authority of the therapist is so well established (as it might be with children) that it is difficult to deny some of the findings, other mechanisms, such as selective inattention, projection, or even psychotic behavior, may be required and utilized to maintain self-esteem.

Insight, if defined as the awareness of dynamics, etiology, and transferential distortions, is inappropriate with children. What the therapist seeks out is awareness of feelings, so that these are not dissociated. How, then, does limit setting enter into this process that leads to greater independence? Children must try out behavior before they can master it. If a child is too young to ride a two-wheeled bicycle, one does not permit him to attempt it. If he is old enough to try, one can expect him to fall at first, but, most important, one stands by to catch the child if he falls (Ekstein 1983). Similarly, if a child of five in therapy shoots suction-tipped darts at a target and some adhere to the wall beyond his reach, the child may use a chair to retrieve them. The therapist stands by, allows him to use the chair, and catches him if he loses his balance.

Suppose a young child wishes to use a knife to cut rope on some project he is making in the playroom, and use of a knife by a small child is prohibited. Does the therapist then say, "You are too young to use a knife"? What is it the therapist wishes to convey to the child in addition to the fact that he wants to protect the child's life? Since the child is in the process of achieving independence and forming his self-image (Sullivan 1953b), the task is to help him maintain or even enhance his self-esteem and at the same time to prohibit behavior in which he is not equipped to engage. In this case, rather than telling the child he is too young to use the knife or even simply that knives are for older people, it would be more therapeutic to say, "I can see you are almost ready to use a knife by yourself. Let me help you. Here, you hold the rope, and I'll cut it."

It is important that therapists weigh carefully each communication having to do with limits so that they can provide help and encouragement appropriate to the unique situation at the same time as they set limits.

Ann, a 9-year-old, came into therapy because she compulsively spit every four or five minutes. In situations where she was being watched and she tried not show that she was spitting, she spit into a tissue. But if she thought no one was observing her, she would spit on the floor. This unappealing symptom posed a special problem. If the child confined herself to a tissue, it was more injurious to her self-esteem than spitting on the floor because it required some restriction; spitting on the floor obviously created other problems. Spitting was the primary, almost characterological, symptom that brought the child to treatment; and simply prohibiting spitting would not have solved the problem, on the contrary, it would have conveyed to her an unwillingness to accept her as she was.

The solution arrived at was to set paper cups around the playroom. On each cup, marked in large letters, were the words "FOR SPITTING." While this device also posed a restriction, as would confining her to a tissue, it carried with it the recognition of the act as more than something to be hidden. It was a statement that her behavior was recognized and effectively accepted. Perhaps primarily because of this acceptance, the spitting diminished in frequency and soon stopped altogether.

The Use of Puppets

In the following clinical illustration I examine in some detail an incident with Martin, an 8-year-old boy who was referred primarily because he had few friends and was bullying and hitting smaller children.

After twelve weeks of treatment with me the conversation during a session was as follows:

MARTIN: I am going to take these tops home with me.

THERAPIST: I can see you would like to have them, but toys in the playroom must stay here.

M: Please may I take them? I'll bring them back next time.

T: I'm sorry Martin, but the rule is that you can't take them out of the playroom even if you bring them back next time.

M: I don't like the rule and I don't like you. I'm going to hit you with this stick.

T: You can't hit me, but you can write my name on Bobo [an inflatable clown] and hit him.

M: You always say that. I want to hit the real you.

I restrained Martin as he started to swing the stick. Martin silently walked aside and started to shoot the dart gun at some toy figures set up on a shelf, but dangerously close to me. At this point, I picked up two hand puppets that were familiar to the child and started a conversation between them.

PUPPET CHARLIE: Did you see what Martin just did?

PUPPET MARTHA: I sure did. He almost got him, didn't he? Boy, was he mad.

C: Why was he so mad?

M: Because Dr. Spiegel wouldn't let him take the tops home, stupid!

C: Don't call me stupid.

M: I'll call you anything I want to call you, and I'll hit you, too!

C: No you won't!

M: Why won't I?

C: Look, Martha, you can be as mad at me as you want, but you can't hit me because you shouldn't hurt people and because I'm bigger than you.

M: Sometimes it's tough to be little.

C: Yeah, I know, I was little once, myself.

In expressing his intent to take the tops home, Martin was making several statements. He had developed a fondness for me, and taking the tops home would be a symbolic way of taking me with him. Martin was also testing a limit. A child cannot be sure a limit or a rule exists unless he tries to go beyond the limit or break the rule. Martin probably thought, "This man is sort of nice. He seems to let me do most anything I want in the playroom, but is he really so nice? Can I really do anything I want?" and so Martin engaged in the preceding dialogue. He tested limits first by declaring his intent to take the tops home and then by trying to hit me. His limit-pushing followed much the same pattern as it did at home. Knowing the underlying dynamics of Martin's pathology, particularly that his grandmother often took care of him and allowed him complete freedom to do whatever he liked so long as he said "please," enabled me to avoid reinforcing this kind of relationship. Obviously, I did not say, "I'm not like your grandmother, so saying 'please' won't work."

First of all, as I have noted throughout this book, it would not be suitable for the child to be informed about the transference phenomenon. Moreover, as a therapist I would have been engaged in a dialogue avoiding the real issues, which were those of taking the toys and hitting me.

When Martin tried to hit me, I followed a typical therapeutic formula; as a way of trying to teach displacement, I directed Martin to hit Bobo. In fact, Martin's going to the dart gun and shooting at figures dangerously close to me was displacement, but Martin displaced his anger on his own terms.

By restraining Martin and preventing him from hitting me with a stick in addition to protecting myself, I reassured Martin that I would not permit him to lose control over his hostile impulses.

Parenthetically, as far as the issue of fighting is concerned, in working with groups of children I have often stopped fights by asking each child if he is playing or fighting. When the answer was "I'm playing, but he's fighting" or if it was obvious that someone might get hurt, I stopped the fight, of course. If they were truly playing and it was evident that no injury would be incurred, there was no need to discontinue the behavior. For reassurance, children need to know that a responsible adult will keep them from being hurt or from completely losing control over their impulses. It is likely that for this reason children who arrange to fight after school choose their locations carefully. If it is somewhere behind a building where they are not likely to be seen by an adult, they fully intend to fight. On the other hand, if they select a place such as the front of the school or in a school hall, they probably expect to be rescued by an adult.

With Martin, if I had merely put up my hands, allowing Martin to hit me but protecting myself from serious injury, the child would have been quite frightened; he would have been likely to feel that his impulses were indeed out of control and much too dangerous. Preventing Martin from hitting me, as I did, might have been sufficient. The subject could have been dropped, especially since Martin went to a displacement kind of activity. However, the situation had really been humiliating to Martin who had to retreat in the face of superior strength. Here was an opportunity, first, to be sure that Martin was aware of and accepted his feelings and, second, to undo or make the humiliating aspect of the situation more palatable, thereby protecting his self-esteem.

I could have engaged Martin in a dialogue to explain to him the residual anger, but at best the dialogue would probably have turned into a monologue and Martin would have stopped listening. Long explanations should be avoided, even in therapy with adults. It is apparent that people do not learn well that way, particularly if their history includes lectures by overly intellectualized parents.

Use of the puppets here maintained a projected imagery for Martin so that while I hoped he would identify with Martha, he was also free to say, at least to himself, "That's her" or "These are just puppets. That's not me." Puppets permit projection and denial. I chose Martha, a female, with a name something like "Martin," to permit Martin either to identify or to further reject the ideas postulated.

In the dialogue between the puppets Martha said, "It's tough to be little." Now in a way, I was telling Martin that I knew what he was feeling, even though it is seldom advisable to tell anyone, child or adult, what one assumes he feels. This is not respectful of the autonomy of the individual. Again, reading minds can be frightening as well as rude and intrusive. Such mind-reading is reminiscent of a mother's knowing when her infant is hungry or angry or ready to have a bowel movement. Telling someone what he feels is therefore a way of encouraging regression. I believe that in good therapy one should not encourage regression, which causes infantilization; rather the therapist should permit regression, which encourages growth. This is in concordance with Principle 7. People are not free to change until they are free to be what they are. If one finds that regression is permitted rather than prohibited or promoted, there is freedom to examine the alternatives without pressures of one sort or the other and the defense can be more readily discarded. Therefore, it is important that any interpretation of an adult's or child's feeling be presented in such a way that the patient can safely reject the interpretation. Using puppets provides children with a structure in which this is fairly easy. To allow adults these alternatives, interpretations should be presented as easily rejected questions. One does not enter the psyche of another without the utmost respect and consideration for the other's autonomy, especially if the other is a child and has doubts about his independence.

In the use of puppets with Martin, note that Charlie said, "Yes, I know. I was little once myself." This conveyed to the child that I was accepting and forgiving of Martin's hostile behavior, for Charlie obviously represented me. But, as in a dream, all characters can represent projections of the dreamer as well as other significant figures, and Charlie can also represent the part of Martin that forgives himself.

In a related comment about dreams and play, Ekstein said, "The play of the child has been likened to the dream of the adult, and the opportunity for play action bears many similarities to, and many differences from, the opportunity for free association in relation to various dream elements" (1983:173).

I also implied a significant point when I noted the discrepancy in size as a reason for Martin's not hitting. Indicating the realities of the world is part of the job of the good therapist.

In this incident, knowing Martin's history, I might have continued the puppet dialogue and included a statement by Charlie and Martha about bullying or perhaps just further elaborations about other themes discussed, but this would have been just as undesirable as overexplaining a point with an adult in therapy. Therapy should be a way of encouraging natural growth processes with minimal tampering.

Puppetry in general is an excellent therapeutic device with much potential for teaching limits and controls with groups as well as individuals (Woltmann 1964; Spiegel 1959). In chapter 9, "Treatment Variations," I give an example of how this method is used in groups.

Guests in the Playroom

One issue that frequently arises in child therapy is the bringing of guests into the play session. In general I find this unacceptable in child treatment, but the reasons for the child's wishing to do so need to be explored (probably through metaphor) and the issue and method of denying the child his wish must be handled with care. There are a multitude of reasons for any of this behavior, and some of them will be examined here.

For instance, if a child wants to bring a friend into treatment with him, he may be testing to find out if the session is really exclusively his. In this case telling him that he cannot bring a friend may be very comforting. If the requested guest is a sibling, the child in treatment may be trying to find out if the therapist prefers one to the other. If the child were to risk asking such a question of the therapist, he might anticipate the answer that many well-meaning parents are inclined to give: that both are liked equally. Children are not easily fooled by such evasive answers, which, if used as a model for their own communications, leads to patterns of hypocrisy. Parents would be well instructed to answer such questions by saying, for example, "Right now I like you, but if you don't clean up the mess you made, it won't last too long." Children's concepts of like and love do not have the sophistication most adults have, and such statements as "I love you, but I don't like what you're doing" frequently result only in the children's becoming confused. Evasions and duplicitous answers that do not correspond with what children perceive emotionally prompt them to test out such issues.

Another reason children might have for wanting to bring guests is to dilute the therapy. Therapists who ask too many direct questions and make children uncomfortable may be faced with such a reaction. Children might also feel guilty because another child they know is not included, or they may wish to "show off" their friendship and special privilege connected with being in therapy. The reason is not always apparent; curiosity and exploration are necessary to discover the purpose and to utilize it in therapy.

Toys and Food

Children may bring toys to the playroom as a way of diverting the therapy, to display their skills with the toys, or just to enable them to brag about their possessions. If a child asks if he can bring a toy from home, one can answer by saying he can only play with the toys that are in the playroom. A discussion may ensue about what the child really likes to do and how the playroom is not equipped for such play. The therapist and child might arrive at a way in which something might be provided in the playroom that would come close to what the child likes to do. If he brings the toy without asking, it would probably be too injurious to self-esteem to prohibit the child from bringing it into the playroom for that session, but he could be told not to bring it again.

As to food, children may bring it to satisfy some emotional hunger that cannot be fully supplied by the treatment or because the session may provide an opportunity to eat foods that are prohibited at home, or even in an attempt to feed the therapist. Obviously, other possibilities can explain such behavior, and the matter should be explored.

Some therapists supply food, cookies, or candy in the playroom. In general, I find this an objectionable practice, but with genuinely needy children it may sometimes be appropriate. If a therapist chooses to offer food, it is best to limit the quantity not by saying "You may have three cookies" (or two lemon drops) but rather by having only the amount he is willing to give in the playroom for that session.

When the Child Wants to Terminate the Session

An important example of behavior that requires limit setting is that of a child who decides to terminate a treatment session. Here the position of child therapists varies from Gardner (1973b), who is inclined to discontinue the session if the child so chooses, to the extreme of Ginott (1966b), who advocates sitting with your back to the door to keep the child in the playroom. In general, it is my inclination to try to determine the reason for the child's wishing to leave so that specific action can be taken. For example, if the child is concerned because of the separation from his parent, I might invite the child to go to check on his mother or father, or perhaps I might simply invite the parent into the playroom and then have the child help determine when it would be safe for his parent to go back to the waiting room.

It is a common phenomenon for children to express a desire to discontinue not just a session but all treatment after two or three months. This may be puzzling to inexperienced therapists, who find it difficult to understand why a child would wish to discontinue treatment just when a good relationship has been established. Asking the child why he wishes to stop coming usually evokes responses such as "I like to come here, but I have to have time to do my homework" or "I'm taking dance lessons on Thursdays" or any number of excuses. Most often it is precisely because a good relationship with the therapist has been established that the child wishes to discontinue treatment.

The explanation for this frequent phenomenon may be connected to the fact that in most families where children are in treatment there is overt or covert animosity or disagreement between the parents, and their disagreement is often focused on the child. As a result, the child feels that to be loyal or close to one parent is to betray the other. This is especially evident with children of divorced or separated parents because often the child feels that in some way he himself is responsible for the separation. Perhaps this same problem of divided loyalty can be attributed to an Oedipal conflict, but I believe that using that explanation would violate the principle of "Occam's razor": it is a more elaborate and complex hypothesis than is necessary to explain the situation. Regardless of the explanation, the discord between parents often causes children to feel unable to maintain a close relationship with either parent.

Given such a familial situation and with the reasonable assumption that after two or three months of treatment the child's relationship with the therapist is an essentially transferential one, the therapist becomes a surrogate parent, and the child is faced with the same problem of divided loyalty and so wishes to withdraw from therapy rather than make a choice. Usually he is not consciously aware of the reason, so that the reasons he gives for wanting to terminate treatment seem to be the real reasons to him. Unless the real parents are actually malevolent rather than misguided or neurotic, the child, believing he is forced to make a choice between parent and therapist, invariably chooses in favor of the parent.

If parents are alerted at the beginning of treatment that their child is likely to desire to terminate after two or three months, they can feel comforted when the child expresses his desire to leave, knowing the change in attitude fits some kind of psychotherapeutic schedule. They can be helpful by doing all they can to unite in encouraging the child to stay in treatment.

Clinical Illustration. Lisa, a timid, almost withdrawn child of 7 who was mildly asthmatic and occasionally enuretic, spent most of her time in the playroom arranging people and figures in a dollhouse. She seldom spoke, but her play clearly conveyed feelings of rejection, loneliness, and an attempt to substitute fantasy for reality so that she did not have to face the problems involved in forming and maintaining relationships. The therapist, also using minimal verbalization, cooperated in play, helping to manipulate objects and people in the dollhouse, and in this way encouraged Lisa to consider new solutions to old problems.

At one point, when Lisa arranged her symbolic world so that all family members, including the dog, were in their own rooms watching their own television sets, the therapist obtained Lisa's permission to arrange some objects in an unused room of the dollhouse. He placed a cat sitting alone and looking out of a window. Given the opportunity to add dialogue, the therapist had the cat invite a dog in from outside to play. After the dog first said that he hated cats and after some further discussion, to the cat's surprise, the dog agreed to come into the house, and they played together.

Lisa continued with her dollhouse play for about two months and then occasionally ventured to play with other objects in the room. Whenever she became anxious, however, she returned to her dollhouse play. Eventually, she spent more time in other play and less in the silent dollhouse manipulation. At about this time Lisa started to test limits by informing her parents that she did not wish to return for therapy. She explained that she liked the doctor but was too busy with her school work and piano lessons. With their encouragement she was able to tell the therapist of her desire to terminate treatment. While some improvement had been shown—her enuresis had diminished and her asthma attacks were not as frequent or severe as they had been—therapy was still clearly indicated.

Lisa was far from able to try out and test limits at home or in treatment. This testing is necessary before treatment can be completed with most children for they must test their strength to know its limits and parameters and this was especially true with Lisa.

The therapist told Lisa that he was glad that she was able to tell him of her objections to continuing and that while he did not wish to make her unhappy, he believed that she was still not able to have enough fun in her life and that therapy would be continued. Lisa's parents concurred in this position and treatment went on for eight months more. Had Lisa been able to protest more strongly her desire to discontinue, that in itself would have been an indication of greater improvement.

Broader Implications of Limit Setting

It is apparent that society poses many problems related to the issues of limits. What are the factors that determine behavior that we consider to be lawful, ethical, and moral? I expect no quarrel in stating that while we do not wish to discourage uniqueness and individuality, we hope to assist our child patients to obey the rules and laws of society. If they object to other laws, we would like them to work to change them legally rather than disobey them.

There is a bipolar but not dichotomized distribution of people who obey laws: those who do so because they believe in them and those who are afraid of the consequences should they disobey them. Obviously, we prefer to see people obey laws because they believe in them. In the earlier discussion of Ann, the therapist wanted her to confine her spitting to an appropriate place not because she was being watched but because she had come to think it was more appropriate behavior and she was in charge of it. Following rules should become a self-generated superego function; decisions about behavior should be grounded in internalized values and standards.

Making a clear, simple statement about what children can or cannot do is helpful, but it is more helpful if they make their own statements about what they can or cannot do. For example, to say "You are not permitted to throw toys out of the window" will probably prevent a child from throwing toys out of the window, but it will probably not help him internalize the information as a statement that requires him to consider the matter and come to the same conclusion himself. It would be better to say to him, "When toys are thrown out of the window, they may hit someone." The child must then think, "I do not want to hurt anyone, so I better not throw toys out of the window."

The prohibition might even be worded as a question, if it can be done without irony or sarcasm. The therapist might say, "Why do you suppose it is wrong to throw toys out of the window?" If a matter has to be considered carefully and does not come as an intimidating order, it is more likely to be incorporated into the child's superego.

Limit setting, as it relates to play therapy, has implications that go far beyond the microcosm of the playroom setting. Teaching and applying such limits in child therapy must be done with very special care and thoughtfulness.

As children grow older, not all therapy with them takes place in the playroom. Older children require an opportunity to try out more adult behavior such as talking in a consultation room as well as having the freedom to go outside of the therapist's office. The approach to the adolescent years presents many special aspects of treatment unique to that period in life. The next chapter is devoted to that subject.

7

Adolescence

Only the most courageous, or perhaps the most foolish, therapists are willing to treat adolescents, for they are the most difficult group of children with whom to work. Still, successes can be very rewarding in spite of the difficulties one encounters in working with them.

Some clinicians limit their explanation of the difficulties of the adolescent period to factors of changes in biology. While indeed there are biological changes, including the awakening of sexual urges, which partly account for some of the turmoil of this period of development, stating the problem as the fear of the breakthrough of "id" drives according to some orthodox Freudian explanation hardly accounts for all of the special problems that adolescents must face. Moreover, this view considers drives in too negative a light. The word "id," as defined by Freud (1949), was conceived as a kind of militant, unfriendly force quite different from its original meaning as used by Groddeck (1979), who saw it as an amiable drive. In adolescence children become more aware of and begin to interact with the opposite sex differently from the ways they did in the past. Contrary to the Freudian view that sexual drives are terrifying forces threatening to break through, it is my impression that these early sexual urges accompanying certain hormonal changes in adolescents involve possibilities for going beyond fantasy to expression and enjoyment and need not be accompanied by terror.

Adolescent difficulties might be seen in comparison to schizophrenia. There was a period when I did a great many psychodiagnostic test evaluations. A principle test used in these evaluations was the Rorschach. Responses of adolescents on this test tended to include confabulations, poor form level, and other indications that are frequently considered pathonomic of schizophrenia. Other projective tests also showed indications of serious pathology, and I concluded that the only apparent difference between adolescents and schizophrenics, or at least borderlines, was that the adolescents usually recovered from their seeming schizophrenic or borderline condition with the passing of a few years, while spontaneous recovery from true schizophrenia is quite rare.

People must use their best defenses to face the stresses of life. During adolescence the defenses are not yet well developed but the stresses are monumental. It is during this period of teenage growth that most children are given new and substantial freedom in making choices. For example, their mobility is no longer limited to the times when parents can escort them to their activities. They usually are able to use bicycles or other public transportation. Therefore, they are faced with the possibility of more choices in their activities and in choosing the friends they wish to be with. They can be away from home more frequently and for longer periods of time. Their career choices are no longer as simple as saying "I will be a computer scientist . . . or an astronaut . . . or a police officer . . . or a teacher when I grow up." They now have a reality to contend with in that they have some concept of the educational and other requirements of commitment connected with vocational goals. There is some feeling of urgency in that they will have to start directing themselves toward some occupational objective.

At this age children must also make important decisions not only about the friends whom they choose but also about their moral and ethical values. They become more critical of the values they have already incorporated from family and friends regarding theft, cheating, capital punishment, and so on. In this process of evaluation and refinement they formulate new views that become more firmly established in their character structure.

Adolescents usually discover with both relief and trepidation that their parents are not as knowledgeable and wise as they had previously thought. It is at this age that youngsters do not know if they are adults or children and, as noted in the example of the teenager with the pipe in the chapter on limit setting, they often feel that they are simultaneously child and adult. Is it any wonder then that they may resemble those with thought disorders?

Therapists, like parents, are constantly faced with children who, as a result of the protection and support they have been receiving, feel strong and competent and suddenly declare that they are now fully grown (usually at about age 12 to 14) and that they should no longer be treated like babies. Parents whose children now suddenly appear to be young adults start treating them as if they were in fact more mature in an attempt to do the best for their children. Consequently, the youngsters become frightened of being on their own. They regress and act again like young children. Feeling they were wrong to think their children were so mature, parents start to baby their children, and the cycle begins again. This is a most useful cycle, for it enables the child to titrate the experiences of acting like an adult, but it is generally frustrating and sometimes baffling to most parents.

In therapy the process is similar, but manifested somewhat differently. The very idea of going to someone for help of some sort is already the equivalent of a red flag for adolescents. No matter how carefully worded, the suggestion that they see a therapist is a statement to them that they cannot deal with life without someone else's assistance. For this reason it is especially important to do all one can to convey to teenagers that the function of the therapy is not to tell them how to live their lives but rather to help them to see all the alternatives to the problems they face so that they can make their own decisions from a more informed vantage point.

Missed Sessions and the Pursuit of Independence

One of the major difficulties of working with adolescents, as opposed to adults or young children, is their missing sessions. This is acknowledged with embarassement by some therapists who see it as being a result of some technical error they have made and/or a treatment failure. Of course, such explanations may at times be appropriate, but more often it is the very nature of the dynamics of treating adolescents that results in this frustrating aspect of treating them. Sometimes they forget or get involved in a ball game or have trouble getting transportation or have to stay after school. Because most adolescents are not ready to accept the idea that there can be unconscious motivation to their behavior, analyzing the "selective inattention" required to forget is at best a useless endeavor and at worst a way of incurring anger and interfering with the formation of a useful therapeutic alliance. It is difficult enough for most adolescents to sort out their own behavior and motivation; to add the concept of dissociated materials can only confuse them.

It is not that selective inattention is not operating; the process of growth in adolescents requires it. This is not merely a ramification of treatment with adolescents—something that one must put up with. Missing sessions as an assertive act is the most probable way for teenagers to express their independence in therapy. It is essential to growth because missing sessions is a way of testing their strength (a more positive way of wording it as opposed to saying "testing limits"). Likewise, being able to return to treatment is a way of asking for help without feeling a sense of humiliation. Such vacillating behavior may be an indication of the success of the therapy, not of its inadequacies or failure, as is frequently assumed. All of the ramifications of this testing behavior at the time it occurs must be fully understood. In the growth process where the central connection with parents and significant others is dependency, to be grown up means to be independent; but for adolescents it is lonely and frightening to feel apart and unsupported.

For adolescents, more than for adults, being in therapy is more of a reminder of their dependent state than they often can tolerate. The following is an account of therapy in which a 16-year-old appeared for only one session and then decided against entering treat-

ment. While in similar situations therapists may be filled with mis-
givings and consider better ways in which they might have handled
the session, instances of such aborted treatment following initial
sessions is not infrequent.

Clinical Case.   Allan, whose parents are both in the mental health
field, was referred by the therapist of one of his parents. Allan telephoned within a week to arrange his own interview and left a message on the therapist's answering machine: "This is Allan, and I
need to make an appointment with you. My number is
_____." He did not say that he wished to make an appointment
with the therapist but that he *needed* to. When the therapist, not
sure at first who Allan was, called him back, Allan assumed that
the therapist already knew him and some brief discussion concern-
ing why he had called this therapist to arrange an appointment was
required. The therapist had been given some minimal information
about Allan when he was originally consulted by another therapist
so that, when he realized who the boy was, he was able to say to
Allan that Dr. X had told him he might be calling and the appointment was made.

Often when people start talking to others on the telephone and
do not identify themselves very well, it is because there is such
self-involvement or threads of grandiosity that it does not occur to
them that someone does not know who they are. Obviously, there
are also other explanations for this behavior, such as timidity, conflict, lack of social experience, or the transference of a symbiotic
relationship whereby they expect the other person as "parent" to
be able to read their minds. However, adolescents are so involved
in their own images and problems that it is certainly likely that they
will not state their identity in a telephone conversation because it
simply has not occurred to them that someone does not know who
they are. This most likely is a reflection of the special circumstances
of adolescence rather than an indication of major pathology.

To reassure Allan that he was interested in him at least enough
to remember the school he attended, the therapist said that he
understood Allan's schedule and that he went to X school. This also
served the function of providing information useful in arranging a
mutually satisfactory time. The appointment was arranged for two

days later. While this required the therapist to juggle his schedule a little, it is generally not a good idea to keep adolescents waiting as long as a week. For them the thought of initiating therapy is likely to be quite anxiety provoking, and if prolonged anxiety can be avoided at this stage, it certainly should be.

Allan arrived for his scheduled appointment some three or four minutes late. He was an attractive youngster who appeared somewhat anxious. After inviting him in and pointing to a seat where Allan might be comfortable, the therapist excused himself to go to the bathroom and returned shortly. The trip to the bathroom could have been postponed, but in this instance with this apparently anxious adolescent, the therapist believed that it might give Allan an opportunity to familiarize himself with the surroundings, noting the therapist's books, furniture and plants, so that he might be more comfortable when the session began. The fact that the therapist showed evidence of having the same biological functions common to the teenager as well as to all humans might have been additionally beneficial to the child's demeanor. Because of the dishonesty it involves, I do not recommend this as a ploy, for that kind of contrivance might backfire as the child could easily feel he is being manipulated. In this instance the therapist's need was fortuitous and seemed to have that extra utility for this boy. It might be argued that the additional wait in the office until the therapist returned would add to the anxiety rather than ease it, but because of his "reading" of the situation, the therapist's inclination was to the action he followed.

Allan's first statement was that he did not wish to be there, but that he came because his parents had been urging him for several weeks and that he thought that by coming he would get them "off his back." Allan then went on to protest that he did not need any help with his problems, that he was perfectly capable of solving them himself, and that relying on anyone else was an indication of immaturity and weakness. With some minimal explanation from the therapist that his function was not to make decisions for Allan but perhaps to be of some assistance in enabling Allan to examine the problems, Allan agreed to go ahead and describe his family.

Allan then launched into a long series of complaints about his mother's inefficiency, her failure to show concern for him and his siblings (a sister four years younger and a brother nine years younger), her neglect of cooking and household duties, including her unwill-ingness to lend him her car, and in general her unwillingness to accommodate to their needs. He expressed a fear that she would damage his younger brother by "spoiling" him with oversolicitous-ness so that he would be demanding and complaining (in effect, that he would probably become very much like Allan). At the same time he said he was concerned that he and his sister would be neglected. Allan's complaints continued to tumble forth in a tor-rent. He hardly spoke of his father other than to suggest that his father was overly tolerant of his mother's outrageous behavior. The therapist became fearful that this outpouring might result in Allan's feeling guilty for having complained so much about his mother, es-pecially since Allan had not inquired and did not know what, if any, relationship existed between the therapist and his parents. At the same time the therapist did not want to convey that Allan was not free to say and complain however he wished.

When Allan commented that he was really "spilling his guts" and seemed to indicate that he was not comfortable in doing so, the therapist said that Allan was free to say whatever he wished and that privileged communiction was assured. However, knowing little about him, the therapist said it might be useful if Allan told him about other parts of his life (and at the same time provide some diversive relief). Allan then readily talked about school and other less toxic areas of his life.

Allan arranged a time for a next appointment but clearly indi-cated his ambivalence by stating again that he did not need any help. He reiterated that at 16 he was perfectly capable of solving his own problems. When Allan asked about telephone numbers where the therapist could be reached, the therapist told him that he could contact him whenever he wished. Allan replied with some sarcasm, some humor, and obvious conflict by saying, "And you can call me anytime you like."

Allan called the therapist's office the following Sunday, a day when he would most likely be able to avoid direct conversation with the therapist and instead leave a message on the answering machine. The message he left was that he did not wish to start therapy at this time. He thanked the therapist for his interest and said that if he changed his mind at a later date, he would telephone.

The ambivalence that was so apparent from the beginning had crystalized and Allan had made a clear decision. The therapist certainly could not know the reason for it from this single contact. It is, however, possible to speculate about reasons. While they could be completely independent of the actual transaction and could as readily relate to some incident or attitude resulting from subsequent conversations Allan had with his parents or with friends, his decision may well have been a reaction to his initial session. Perhaps he felt he had revealed too much in his complaining or possibly that the therapist did not want to hear him complain. He may have reacted to the therapist in some transferential way, the identification between his parents and the therapist being all too easily made by virtue of all three being in the same profession. Perhaps there were other negative factors that had transferential implications, such as the appearance of the therapist or of his office or even the building or the neighborhood. It may be that the therapist was too oversolicitous in inviting Allan to call whenever he wished: Allan may have seen this as a potential trap in which his neediness might take over and he would be caught in a dependent relationship. It may have been any combination of those reasons or even something else. Most likely, the real reason will never be known.

Allan had made the initial contact by himself. In fact, the therapist did not even talk with either parent prior to Allan's session. In view of the prominence of the dependency problems assumed to be involved in adolescence as well as the fact that Allan himself had treated the initial contact as if he were an adult, the therapist decided not to contact the parents either before or after the session. He believed that Allan would inform his parents of his decision not to continue in therapy and that the parents would contact the therapist if they felt a need to do so. What seemed appropriate, and what the therapist did, was to write to Allan. There are times when writing is the preferred way of dealing with situations of this sort if for no other reason than, unlike the telephone, a note gives the patient an opportunity to consider the matter without having to respond immediately. The therapist wrote:

Dear Allan,

I am sorry that you decided not to start therapy at this time.
I believe it would be helpful to you. If you decide that you
wish to see me at a later date, I shall be pleased to arrange
an appointment, or I can assist you in finding someone else
if you think you might be more comfortable with another
therapist.

Cordially yours,

It was important to convey to Allan that such decisions are not
remarkable and are certainly acceptable. It is unlikely that Allan
would call the therapist to ask his assistance in finding someone
else, but the statement was included to indicate to the boy that his
feelings were to be respected and even relied on.

Vacillations in Growth

Just as the adolescents vacillate in their development between being
young adults and being children, their behavior in therapy shows
the same vacillation. As noted earlier, adolescents are at the stage
when they are frequently considered too young to talk and too old
to play. However, with their mercurial nature there are times when
they are too young to talk but can play and other times when they
are too old to play but can talk about their problems and feelings.
The therapist must show considerable flexibility in being able to
adapt to the changing status of adolescents and in making teenagers
comfortable with these fluctuations. If the youngster is at a point
where he sometimes prefers to sit in a chair rather than play, it is
helpful to have the room arranged so that the adolescent can choose
between entering the playroom or the office, or if the rooms are
connected, he can go from one to the other at any time during the
session. If an important issue needs to be discussed, such as a recent telephone call from a parent, the therapist can make the choice
instead of allowing the child to do so. It is certainly appropriate for
the therapist to say that he received the call and believes they ought
to sit down and talk about it. In this way the therapist is saying in
an indirect way that he believes this is a matter that requires consideration by the child as well as the therapist, and that he wishes
to connect with the adult qualities of the child.

The reluctance of adolescents to talk about their problems and feelings directly can be considered, by definition, resistance, which carries a pejorative implication. To my way of thinking, resistance has a useful, protective quality that helps adolescents to maintain integrity of self-image. For an interesting discussion of this matter, see Schaefer and Reid (1986). A feeling of safety and growth enables them to talk about difficult issues, so the therapist need not be concerned that significant issues are not being openly considered. Many of the issues should never be dealt with directly but instead through metaphor. In this way they will nevertheless be resolved. The assumption I am making is that if one learns to deal with issues of self discipline, for example, it does not matter if these are dealt with by the therapist and patient's talking about doing homework or parental nagging or completing the construction of a model or teaching one's dog to lie down on command; if the concept is thought through and mastered in any one of these areas, its effect will reach far into other areas of life.

Game Playing

The equipment and activity with adolescents are frequently quite different from what they are with younger children. As I indicated in chapter 4, I am not a strong adherent of the use of games with children, even those specifically designed for therapeutic purposes, but I do find games sometimes useful with adolescents. I am always alert to the possibility of the use of metaphor in my therapeutic work with children, and even games can sometimes provide that opportunity.

For the most part, I see games as an appropriate and useful way for adolescents to escape from toxic issues when they are talking about them and become too anxious. Adults, who are more facile with language, can change the subject with skill and fluidity or even declare that they find the subject too anxiety-provoking and that they wish to escape it. My response to adults in this situation often is to remind them that they are free to talk about whatever they wish, but that if they do not tell me about something, I cannot help them with it. Adolescents cannot so easily change the subject; instead, they can escape from conversation that is anxiety-provoking by discussing the game they are engaged in, thereby receiving relief from the more significant issues of concern. Of course, there is the possibility that youngsters can use this diversion as a habitual method of avoiding anxiety and manage never to deal with significant issues. However, it then becomes the responsibility of the therapist to help these young patients to make optimal use of therapy by switching to some other, more revealing activity or, with some adolescents who are more inclined to talk about problems, by reminding them that they are there for more significant reasons than learning to play card games.

The distinction between activities appropriate for adolescents and for younger children should be quite clear. It is only with older children who are aware of and generally willing to discuss significant issues that I find game play most useful as an occasional way of shifting away from anxiety-provoking issues. With youngsters who are too young to talk—too young in terms of their level of development and regardless of their chronological age—or even with older children who are regressed in a specific session, I do not encourage the use of games. If children wish or need to "regress" to the point of playing with toys that are generally considered more appropriate for younger children, then the play objects should be used as outlined in the chapter on play equipment.

In the same way that some teenagers use games as a diversion to escape the anxiety of having to deal continuously with difficult issues, some do well to construct models such as trains, airplanes, cars, trucks, or boats. While constructing the model, they are free to talk about significant issues or to keep the conversation confined to the immediate project. For one 15-year-old girl who was competent at and enjoyed painting, I provided a set of quality crayons and a sketch pad that I always placed on the table prior to each of her sessions. When she needed the diversion, she worked on a drawing; at other times she would simply talk and not draw. While the drawings were frequently suggestive of underlying dynamics as well as reflecting her immediate mood, I never interpreted the drawings or shared my impressions, although I was always alert to what I felt might be communicated by her art. Had I provided interpretations, particularly if they were accurate, I would have deprived her of the escape from my psychoanalytic eye, and she probably would have diminished her use of drawings, which effectively diverted anxiety and enabled her to feel comfortable. On occasion she herself speculated about how she was feeling and how it was expressed in her drawings. When she did so, I sometimes cautiously offered suggestions about meaning, but I did not encourage such activity for fear of eliminating the use of the drawings as a diversion. It is my impression that too much effort is expended in therapy in an attempt to overcome resistance. All patients know why they are there and need the opportunity to titrate the work at their own pace.

Many child therapists get caught in a kind of "game" or maneuver with teenagers or even young children in using these diversionary activities; the therapists are so intent on discussing meaningful material that they judge their success as therapists by the amount of talking they are able to elicit from the youngsters. Children through adolescence easily catch on to this, as indeed they should, and see their part in the game as doing as little talking about meaningful material as they can. Of course, the discussion of meaningful material is useful in therapy but forcing it can only result in disaster. For many teenagers, particularly those whose problems led them to psychotherapy, there are few places they can be free to work on a project without being nagged or otherwise pressured by an adult. In what I consider to be good psychotherapy, providing a place where one can show genuine respect for a patient's privacy and allowing adolescents to do things in their own way and at their own pace can be most therapeutic. With a responsive, thoughtful, and competent therapist, adolescents will seek the help they know they need. Sessions that go by with little apparent movement are not to be discounted as indications of failure on the part of the therapist nor as unproductive sessions.

Communication Through Metaphor

There are other methods of treatment with adolescents that I find quite useful and in keeping with effective therapy as outlined by my principles. For example, as I noted elsewhere:

An adolescent who was concerned about his small size walked with me in the street in the area of my office. Noting the varying cars I asked what kind of car he would like to have. When he stated his interest in large cars, Cadillacs, Rolls Royces, etc., I pointed out to him that small cars could be just as powerful. While I would have talked to him directly about his height if he had chosen to, the car metaphor message was clearer and more appropriate to an adolescent. (1987:12)

It might also have been helpful if I had included some empathic statement about the unfortunate aspects of being small such as, "Even though small cars are likely to get more damaged in an accident, by being powerful they might avoid accidents more easily than large cars." This kind of communication through metaphor can be the avenue of therapy with adolescents, especially with those who have a high level of anxiety and a consequent need for physical activity. With these teenagers, treatment need not be confined to the office or playroom; walks or other outdoor activity can be quite effective. I have found this to be true occasionally with severely disturbed adults as well, for whom the intensity of anxiety is sometimes so great that motor activity is helpful as a partial release, enabling them to talk without so much discomfort. By being alert to the content and underlying communication of the conversation and by directing it on occasion, the therapist can deal with issues that are significant for the patient, adult or child. The size and relative power of automobiles, as in the example just noted, is just one kind of metaphor that can be used. Many other conversations also lend themselves well to therapeutic metaphors with adolescents.

Relating Film Plots. Most adolescents, especially younger ones, are frequent moviegoers or TV-watchers and can spend a significant amount of time relating *ad nauseum* plots and actions of films. Rather than considering it a waste of time, the therapist can make excellent use of this recounting by asking appropriate questions about the feelings of the film characters with whom the children empathize and about other characters they may dislike. Do they know any people like that? And so on. For example, a 14-year-old boy, who was very much concerned with the attention of girls and who felt he was rejected because he was not considered sufficiently masculine, described a movie in which two teenaged boys fought over the attention of a girl. In encouraging a discussion about the attitude of the girl in the movie toward the boys' fighting, the therapist emphasized that there are qualities other than macho ones that are quite attractive to many girls.

Sometimes a conversation about a movie can lead to a direct discussion of significant issues. The following is an excerpt from a session with Billy, a 13-year-old boy whom I had seen five times prior to this session:

BILLY: [discussing a movie he didn't like] . . . and they like come down the river and they all come back to the boat and then we walked out and there was a whole line of people waiting to get in the movie and we said, "that movie sucked" out loud talking among ourselves and the bellhop [presumably the usher] like must have been embarrassed when he saw us walking out and the people were waiting to get in and he said "no, the movie is not over," we were saying "the movie sucks," and it was funny and people saying like "really?" and we said like "yeah," but it was true though the movie was terrible.

THERAPIST: You could write a better one yourself.

B: Sure, about my life. It would be a classy movie.

T: All right, let's hear it.

B: I don't know.

T: What's the title?

B: The Life and Times of Billy Andrews. I'll just put in all the good stuff in my life.

T: All right, what's that?

B: I don't know. Stuff. I couldn't write a movie. I could direct a movie like that.

T: O.K. What incidents would you put in it?

B: The good ones.

T: Like what?

B: Like when I was at camp and getting into mischief.

T: Yeah? What kind?

B: My dad was worse than me. Like when my grandmother had this new kitchen table with a glass top . . .

Billy went on to discuss some of the mischief his father had gotten into when he was child. After hearing a number of these incidents and then some of the minor mischief Billy himself had gotten into, I asked him to tell me about some of the bad things that would go into the movie, since he considered the incidents he had just related to be good. Billy said he didn't like to think of bad things such as when his parents punished him or when someone did something he didn't like; he was beginning to learn to use dissociation to deal with issues he found unpleasant. Here was an opportunity to alter an essentially unhealthy mechanism at its inception. The conversation continued with Billy telling me about some of the things he felt to be bad, and we considered alternative ways of dealing with such incidents.

The Use of Animals as Metaphor. Conversations about animals, those the youngster owns or perhaps those he sees on the street during a "walking" session, can be most fruitful. It is easy to project feelings onto animals, and through metaphor the discussion of the feelings of the animals as they relate to different circumstances can be skewed toward issues the therapist knows are significant. It is frequently easy for an adolescent to talk about lonely dogs or angry cats; within these conversations the therapist can make helpful suggestions.

For example, with a child who speaks of his dog, whom he believes to be lonely waiting all day in a city apartment for the child to come home, the therapist might point out that it is too bad that, unlike children, when the dog is alone, there are few things he can play with, for if he had the freedom to get about by himself, he could visit other dogs. If the adolescent is relatively naive and the therapist is aware that the adolescent is much too timid or unassertive, the therapist can point out that it is too bad that the dog can't speak because, if he could, he would surely ask to be taken to visit friends. Here the therapist is suggesting a possible solution for the child's loneliness. Depending on the specific issues involved, this conversation could include a discussion of the dog's feelings about being with other dogs, big or small, smart or stupid, pretty or ugly, or with cats or with people. The issues of feeling deserted or angry for being neglected or envious of other children who live in different neighborhoods or have different kinds of parents could be explored. With sufficient patience and imagination, conversations about almost anything can be turned to useful therapeutic purposes.

Stories About Other People. Most children, even those emphatically resistant to talking about themselves, will talk about their friends and their friends' parents and about their own siblings. Much can be gained in these conversations if the therapist is always alert to the underlying attitudes and concerns that the child conveys. One can never be sure where one will find "pay dirt"—one must always be curious.

On some level, much of what all patients reveal in their discussion is their underlying dynamics and attitudes. Unfortunately, many therapists are tempted to convert the conversation quickly to a personal one by saying such things as "And is that the way you feel about your brother?" If a youngster wishes to tell you about his attitude toward his brother directly, he will do so.

However sympathetically a personal question is asked, the result is often contrary to the aims of the therapist, and the adolescent is likely to discontinue the conversation or enter into some kind of denial system. If the child is talking metaphorically, destroying the metaphor so that he must reveal his real feelings and bring it closer to home is likely to defeat the aim of encouraging the revelation of genuine feelings. In the same way, if the youngster is talking metaphorically about his attitude toward the therapist, interpreting that would be defeating. For example, if the adolescent is talking about a teacher whom he likes but toward whom he is reluctant to express his feelings and the therapist believes that the patient is talking about his attitude toward him, much more "mileage" could be obtained by asking what he would like to say to the teacher or what he feels he would like the teacher to say to him, than by asking him if he feels the same way toward the therapist.

The therapist might ask the child what he feels the teacher would say if he told him he liked the way he talked to teenagers or just that he was a good teacher. This might open the way to discussion of such issues as the possibility of rejection or perhaps even the idea that something said in reply might be embarrassing. Obviously, the dialogue might take a variety of directions.

Lateness as Metaphor.   Susan, a girl of 15, who was usually on time for her therapy sessions, arrived fifteen minutes late. Her therapist asked curiously but not in any chastising manner why she was late. To this question Susan responded by saying she had been late for many things the last couple of days. "How do you suppose that happened?" the therapist asked. Susan said she didn't know but felt that her attitude was changing and was sure that if she were late to class, she would catch up later. The therapist became even more curious and, suspecting that Susan might be talking metaphorically about the therapy, inquired for other examples of when she had been late.

Susan explained that she had missed her first period class the day before, but she said, "Missing one period doesn't mean any- thing." Susan was a girl who had always been prompt and relatively precise. Why the sudden change? "What if you missed a second period?" the therapist almost intuitively asked. Susan said that would be serious unless she got a medical excuse. Susan was usually quite healthy. Why would that come up? "How has your health been these days?" the therapist asked. Susan answered that she was a little worried because she cut herself the other day while slicing bread and noticed that it took a long time for the bleeding to stop. Susan was not particularly phobic, nor did she usually worry about what was normally considered of minor significance. "How long did it take?" the therapist asked. "About a half hour," the girl said. "How long does it usually take for a cut like that to stop bleeding?" the therapist asked. "Not long at all. As a matter of fact, usually quite quickly," she replied. "Speaking of bleeding," she noted that she hadn't had her period. "How late was it?" the therapist asked. "Oh, just about two days," Susan said, but added she didn't think it meant anything. Now the therapist caught on to the whole issue of lateness and missing a period in school. With encouragement and understanding she inquired about a recent sexual encounter they had discussed briefly and learned that Susan was very concerned about her late period but in her effort to appear "grown up" was reluctant to admit her apprehension. Further inquiry revealed that Susan's uneasiness was unfounded and based on sexual misinfor- mation. Explanation and reassurance were most helpful in this incident.

The Broad Extent of Analogy. There is a strong case to be made for considering the entire therapeutic session as a statement of transference (Gill 1982). While I am not in agreement that all sessions are always a statement of transference to the therapist, one must be alert to the possibility that a particular session contains that transference. If the child or adolescent reports a significant event, such as a fight with another youngster, or describes a new toy or something he recently observed, there may be transferential implications involved, but there are also times when the information should be simply taken at face value. This can be determined by the manner in which it is revealed. Nevertheless, if one is always aware of the possible metaphorical significance of all transactions in therapy, much effective work can be done in a short period of time. Again, my strong advice is to be aware of the possible analogy but not to interpret it. By staying within the metaphor, much more information can be conveyed to the patient in a way that is palatable and reaches the level of an internalized conceptualization rather than just intellectualization. The major goal of therapy is change in self-image and functioning. Intellectual awareness about the roots of the behavior may be only a fringe benefit.

Resistant Adolescents

In chapter 3 I suggested that unwilling adolescents be told that they should appear for at least one session. Much like Allan in the case illustration earlier in this chapter, such children are likely to announce in this initial session that they are not interested in therapy, that they have no need for help, that they can solve their own problems, that they do not wish to be there and are only there because their parents insisted they come for one session. As noted in the chapter on limit setting, with young children who do not wish to be there, the approach may range from the therapist's sitting with his back to the door to discontinuing therapy. Certainly prohibition or force cannot keep adolescents in therapy, particularly if the adolescent is bigger than the therapist. If the statement the adolescent is so desperately trying to make is that he needs the help of no one, the very fact of being in treatment is a glaring contradiction of that avowed position.

The Therapeutic Alliance. Reluctant adolescents can sometimes be engaged by therapist's making it clear at the outset that their job is not to run their lives for them but to understand some of the problems that exist between them and their parents as well as others and that they may be able to assist by getting their parents to be more sensitive to their needs and problems. It may also be helpful to point out at the outset that since they are in therapy, their parents are likely to feel something is being done about what they consider to be their shortcomings and thus would be less likely to pressure them.

Teenagers frequently initiate therapy by stating that it is not they who need to come to therapy but that it is their parents who ought to straighten out their lives. The truth in this statement is not to be ignored. With some encouragement, such as asking them just what is wrong with their parents, the children may become engaged in treatment. As is often my practice with adolescents, when I see the youngster, I have had only minimal contact with the parents and that was on the telephone. Being told of this and reassuring them of the confidentiality of the arrangement can encourage a continuing relationship.

As to confidentiality, the situation is well stated by Schimel:

The adolescent is also informed of this double standard: His interviews are confidential; those of his parents are not. He is usually delighted with the arrangement. In addition, he is asked what he would like his parents to be told and what he would *not* like them to be told. The response is frequently revealing and may open numerous possibilities for subsequent therapeutic interactions. Generally, the issue of confidentiality is smoothly resolved in this way, and the trust usually present in adolescents which needs to be expressed and reciprocated, even with grownups, is fostered. (1979:368)

Treatment on Demand. Allowing treatment to be provided on a demand basis, so that the youngster is allowed to arrange the appointment or see the therapist when he or she wishes to do so, may sometimes solve the problem of reluctance. However, because of the general reluctance of adolescents to be involved in treatment, this should be considered only in those instances when it is clear that treatment is desirable but not essential.

An interesting approach to utilization of treatment on demand is indicated by an elaborate study in Boston (Stumphauser 1973). Unwilling adolescents were first paid for coming and talking about anything into a tape recorder. When they came with a high degree of regularity, they were then required to come at specific times and, finally, when they followed the schedule, instead of talking to a tape recorder, they spoke to a therapist and became good therapy patients.

Joining the Resistance. Much in contrast to the general approach I express, a unique and effective solution is suggested by Marshall. He joins the resistance of the child and explains that he is equally a captive of the therapeutic arrangement. His approach is highly dependent on the concept of mirroring and projective identification. The following is an account of his experience with an "antisocial" girl:

A teen-age girl, who had functioned as the scapegoat of the family and had been diagnosed as sociopathic and untreatable, had been hospitalized because of her running away and her thoroughly defiant behavior. Released from the hospital with dire warnings about her need for treatment, as well as her untreatability, she appeared for her first interview under threat of rehospitalization. She had no conception of the proper use of the session and said she might read and the therapist might do paper work. He asked her whether she had any objection to just coming to the sessions on time and bringing the fee at the end of the month, but there would be no therapy. She laughed and insisted that he was crazy. He asked her if she had any objection to his being crazy, which brought more laughter. He told her that under his plan everyone would be happy: her parents, because she was coming to a psychotherapist; she, because she would not be incarcerated; and he, because he would collect his fee and could use the time to do his own work. She asked if she could smoke. He said that he did not allow his patients to smoke during therapy sessions, but since she was not in therapy, she could smoke. The upshot of this arrangement was that, with virtually no exceptions, she was prompt in arriving for her sessions, arranged to bring the fee, spent her time talking about her life, and during a whole year, functioned in an integrated and socially appropriate manner so that her parents felt she no longer needed psychotherapy. (1979:539)

Marshall goes on to say, "In this situation, the therapist appeared to the patient to be as detached, manipulative, 'crazy' and selfish as she. The 'mirroring' by the therapist of the patient's character defenses induces the patient to unconsciously feel 'If he is like me, he must like me' " (p. 539).

In another instance Marshall (1979) joins the resistance by asking the child to teach him to be as indifferent and worry-free as he is; and with one youngster who ran away from home and was picked up by the police he suggested working on a plan to enable him to run away more effectively.

This approach, while quite successful, is obviously not for everyone. Marshall's scholarly book is highly readable and hence may be misleading, for readers might think that by merely following it they can be successful with resistant adolescents. His technique requires an ability to say things to the child that, if taken literally, appear paradoxical and contrary to what a therapist would be expected to say and to do this with a perfectly straight face. I cannot use this technique successfully myself, and I suspect that not many therapists can, but in the hands of Marshall, with his own special personality qualities, which clearly include warmth and caring, the approach, well grounded in theory, can be highly successful.

Therapy with Adolescents

The Traditional Approach. In contrast to Marshall's and as an example of a treatment approach also quite different from mine, I shall describe what I believe to be the traditionally classic psychoanalytic approach. Because of the prevalence of this approach, I discuss it critically and in some detail.

Pearson describes the analysis of an adolescent who was seen from age 12 to about age 16. It is not clear how frequently the child was seen, but, since the approach seemed traditionally and classically psychoanalytic, it was probably four or five times a week. At several points in his discussion Pearson deals with difficult questions having to do with limits, parent contact, and ethical questions. Pearson describes his action in these instances but does not provide the rational for his decisions. For example, in reporting the second session with this adolescent, he notes:

At Mark's request, the appointment times were again reviewed and he indicated his wish not to miss school for appointments, and wondered if another after-school appointment could be scheduled. If this were possible he would have to miss Sunday Hebrew School, which he abhorred. It was possible to make this shift in appointment times. (1968:178)

We can assume, then, that Pearson made the change as requested. Did he make it to give the child an indication of his support or respect for the child's wishes? Does this give the child a feeling that Pearson joins him in his negative views of his father, since there is an implication that going to Hebrew school is a result of his father's wish? I do not know if there was further discussion about matters of missing appointments, but the next session with the child is a telling one and probably an outcome of the interaction that took place in the second session. Pearson reports:

Soon the youngster asked if he could miss appointments during the Christmas holidays; when questioned, he said he didn't want his free time interrupted. The analyst was curious to know why he was asking at this time. Mark said it was because his mother was marking his appointment times on the calendar, and he wanted to let the analyst know well in advance. The analyst sympathized with the request but wondered if so much free time would really be missed. This proved to be a mistake because it impugned Mark's motives. It might have been better simply to have added to the sympathetic statement already made by commenting that it was unfortunate but treatment took precedence because of the severity of his suffering; otherwise the analyst could have simply agreed to his request without comment at this early point in the analysis. In general, youngsters don't tolerate analytic appointments well during holidays and it is better from the standpoint of rapport not to schedule them. Mark's response to the question was to whine and say he didn't want any interruptions of holiday time. He insisted on having the time off. This was then agreed upon. (1968:179)

One must ask what real message Pearson was giving to Mark in this exchange. In the second session he agreed on a regular appointment change to miss Hebrew school, and while presumably this did not decrease the number of times a week Mark saw Pearson, Pearson did acquiesce to the child's request. Was Mark then testing limits in the third session as a result of his prior encounter? What effect did it have on the child for Pearson to change his mind after the child whined? Did this indicate to the child that Pearson was a "softie," "wishy-washy"? Or did it simply reinforce whining as a method of obtaining what he wanted?

The point I wish to emphasize here is that there are many factors that underlie such issues as schedule changes, and these must seriously effect the transference to the analyst as well as the course of treatment. Pearson's discussion suggests that he does not consider these factors central to the analysis and does not attend to them as important theoretical issues.

A reading of an account of the analysis reveals that what Pearson attends to in most detail are the child's sexual thoughts and fantasies. I wonder if the preponderance of sexual material that is brought into the analysis as it progresses is not a result of Pearson's encouragement of presentation of this material. That this is so is suggested by noting Pearson reports at one point that "The analyst said, 'So, in this sense you think that I led you to be a sex fiend?' Mark smiled and agreed, but said he never really thought it quite that way" (p. 256).

Because Pearson's theory of development is strongly dependent on a Freudian approach to sexuality, it is difficult to trace through the analysis from another point of view. His orientation causes him to select those aspects of dynamics and behavior that fit best with his theoretical position. Pearson's preconceived notion is indicated in part by the following:

The reader will recall that the adolescent is dreadfully afraid of his sexual development and fantasies about his parents because he has the physical capacity to carry out his fantasies of intercourse and impregnation, and thus must make himself distant from his parents. This accounts for so much of the storming and quarreling that occurs during adolescence. To be tempted by a parent would only make the struggle more acute, as occurred in Mark. (1968:273)

Fitting the concept of the action of the child into an established theory based on Oedipal problems limits the consideration of alternative explanations that might account for the distance an adolescent might keep from his parents. How, following this theory, does one allow for all of the ramifications of an adolescent's being overly attached to his parents? Reducing it all to a matter of drive theory, of sexual rivalries and attraction, precludes consideration of such other issues as fear of being on one's own, the giving and taking of parental advice, and anxieties having to do with growth as indicated at the beginning of this chapter. It is not that Pearson may not be correct in some instances in saying that sexual fantasies control the actions of the adolescent, but a theory so narrowly conceived deprives the therapist of an understanding and appreciation of the richness of the multifaceted aspects of growth and development.

An Alternative Approach. To illustrate a method for conceptualization of the problems of the adolescent that does not rely heavily on a restrictive theory, here is a description of therapy with an attractive 14-year-old girl.

Miriam was brought for treatment because she was having considerable difficulty in school: she could not keep up with her work and seemed to have few friends. Because of her physical attractiveness and outgoing nature, I would have expected her to have little difficulty in making friends. Her parents, recently divorced, were both successful professionals. Miriam, an only child, lived with her mother. She was sexually active, although she reported that she had no pleasure in her sexual activities. She smoked both tobacco and marijuana cigarettes and occasionally used hallucinogenic drugs as well as cocaine. Since her accounts of the use of these substances varied considerably in her relating the information to me—at times she seemed to want to impress me with her outlandish behavior and at other times with her compliance and "good girl" qualities— it was difficult to determine the exact degree to which she used them. In general, her behavior had a hysterical quality, and she had frequent panic attacks, as often as two or three times a week. Her relationship with her parents was mercurial, although for the most part she saw them as controlling and oppressive.

As the therapy progressed, the basis of her disorder appeared to be that she had been deprived of a normal childhood. That is, she had been forced to grow up too quickly. A more complete description of how this came about and how it interfered with her development and brought about her neurotic symptoms will illustrate how I conceived of this child's underlying dynamics in the light of her background and developmental pattern.

When they married, Miriam's mother was 29 years old and her father was 32. The father's personality was of a generally obsessional style. While he was not unpleasant in relating to people, he was not cognizant of the emotional aspects of such interactions. His calm demeanor and seemingly knowledgeable approach made him especially attractive to Miriam's mother, who, although fairly organized, was also emotional and intense. In the typical hysteric-obsessional combination they complemented each other, and at the same time, as is also frequent with this combination, the factors that attracted them to each other also caused the most difficulty (Barnett). Miriam's mother was distressed by her husband's apparent inability to "feel," and he was upset by her failure to be always calm and controlled. After twelve years of marriage, when Miriam was 8, her mother decided she could no longer tolerate the relationship with her husband and requested a separation and divorce. Both parties acknowledged their basic differences, and there was little acrimony in the separation. Within a year of the divorce, Miriam's father was living with another woman who had three children by a prior marriage; after living together for about five years, they married. Miriam's mother had a series of relationships with different men. None of the relationships lasted more than a year.

During Miriam's infancy her mother was not unloving but was overwhelmed by her marriage and at the same time was trying to develop a career for herself. Miriam's father remained detached and left the child-rearing to his wife, who, in turn, left the child to grow up herself. Miriam seemed to have caught on to what was required of her through some kind of attunement in infancy and, being quite bright, almost from infancy took on responsibilities more appropriate to an older child. She soon learned to seek little affection or attention and to provide it for herself as best she could. This took its toll: she was left with an intense need for infantile tactile stimulation, which she tried to fulfill with stuffed animals and other "transitional objects." Her mother's preoccupation with her own career and her father's benign neglect left Miriam feeling that no one would notice her no matter what she did. While most of her acting-out behavior was an attempt to connect with friends and to be admired by them for her "grown-up" style, it was also an attempt to be noticed more by her parents.

This bypassing of the freedom and security appropriate to infancy left Miriam with "pockets of childish behavior" (Spiegel). Thus, although in many ways she had been independent from an early age, she frequently had panic attacks when alone, imagining that a thief would enter the apartment, that she would die of a sudden heart attack, just stop breathing, or that other dire, unpredictable things would happen to her.

Miriam suffered most with her interpersonal relationships. She would quickly connect with boys who showed evidence of at least minor psychological disorders and who frequently were quite disturbed. They tended to be somewhat sadistic, but the basis of most of the relationships was Miriam's intense sympathy and empathy and her readiness to take care of their needs. As the sadistic aspects and excessive need demands of the relationships began to become apparent, Miriam would feel some need to end the relationship but be paralyzed by her inability to bring it about. She would feel either terribly sorry for the boy or fearful of sadistic retribution. This left her in a nearly constant state of panic.

When she first started therapy, Miriam was extremely negativistic. In general, interpretation with adolescents is almost never to be recommended, and any interpretations that I offered Miriam were met with loud declarations of how wrong they were and how I did not understand her at all. She treated almost all adults, including teachers and relatives, as parents, and the transference to me was blatantly clear. Many sessions for the first six months were filled with hysterical outbursts and declarations of how miserable and hopeless her life was, punctuated by references to my incompetence. However, each session almost invariably ended with "thank you very much," which seemed to be offered in an authentic manner.

On the average, she missed about one out of five sessions. I explained to her that I did not wish to report her missing sessions to her parents, but that I was concerned about her and asked her to call me if she were unable to attend. She ignored this recommendation at first, but after a while she would call at the time of the session to report that she was sleeping and had just gotten up or that she had missed a bus or that she didn't notice what time it was. I never challenged her explanations, and always thanked her for taking the trouble to report the reason for her absence, which I said would then keep me from worrying. In a way, this had metaphorical significance in that it helped Miriam to understand her mother's concern when she stayed out late and did not telephone to report her whereabouts. Even as the therapy progressed over a period of eighteen months, Miriam continued to miss occasional sessions, but the frequency of attendance increased so that absences were reduced to about one out of six or seven. Her appointments were scheduled on a twice-weekly basis.

At first, the issues discussed in therapy usually had to do with her difficult relationships with boys, her inability to complete school assignments, and her unfeeling and unresponsive parents. Although her descriptions of her parents shifted, she almost invariably objected to her father, while her objections to her mother were minimal. Probably because she was living with her mother, she could not risk being negative about her for very long: it would be as if she had no one. In general, the connection most adult as well as child patients experience between themselves and "the mothering one" (usually the mother) is so filled with an internalized sense of the other that the therapist not allowing for some explanation for the mother's mistreatment or insensitive behavior in terms of external or other mitigating circumstances could result in intolerable guilt and self condemnation by the patient. Therapists are too quick to seize on the "bad mother" as an explanation for pathology. While this must have a certain amount of validity, the parent can also be rescued by noting how, under the circumstances of her own life or history, she probably could not have acted otherwise.

Miriam continued to progress; her relationship with boys became less sadomasochistic. (I use the term here as a description not as an explanation, for I do not feel that as a label it is sufficient to describe or allow for all of the variations of its possible etiology.) Her work in school improved, and her relationship with her parents became less troublesome. She used drugs less frequently, and she became better at separating from difficult relationships with boys and girls. Crises in her life diminished, and she could sustain four or five consecutive therapy sessions without feeling that she was in serious trouble. The content of the therapy still centered on particular difficulties she had in doing school work, getting out of bad relationships, financial arrangements with her parents, her attitude toward her mother and her mother's male friends, and her attitude toward her father and his new wife. However, as therapy progressed she became more able to be critical of her mother probably because she felt she had me as an ally and thus the risk of alienating her mother was not as serious.

Miriam completed high school and faced the difficult decision of choosing a college. Because she was quite bright, the selection was not especially limited. She narrowed the choice to one in the city in which she lived and an out of town college, but she had considerable difficulty in making the final choice. On the one hand, she seemed to feel that it would be better for her to go away to a smaller community where there were fewer urban pressures, but at the same time her problems with separation, particularly from her mother, made it difficult for her to leave. Her parents both felt that it would be better for her to be out of town, but their encouragement in that direction was only interpreted as pressure from them. She finally decided to go to the smaller school, some two-hundred miles away, after making elaborate arrangements to enable her to come home each weekend and to see me at those times. In fact, however, except for the first couple of months, she seldom exercised the option to return on weekends, although she did come to therapy when she was home on vacation. While she was still having considerable difficulty completing her school work, she experienced less difficulty in some of her relationships with boys, and much of her panic in regard to these matters was diminished. She looked forward to a summer job that she had appropriately arranged and during which she would be able to return for twice-weekly therapy.

To what can we attribute Miriam's progress? How did therapy contribute to her change? The literature is filled with explanations for the effectiveness of therapy (Strupp 1973, 1978). It appears to me that the major changes in Miriam can best be conceived of in terms of her self-esteem, which was greatly enhanced through psychotherapy. She had a way of getting a considerable amount of mileage out of failures and little from her successes. When she was enabled to see her accomplishments and failures in terms of their probable and actual causes, she was able to feel at least a little better about herself. I offered few interpretations during the course of the treatment and probably the only two she actually subscribed to were that she had been forced to grow up too quickly and did not have sufficient opportunity to enjoy the carefree aspects that are usual to childhood and that in providing her own self-mothering, she became quite adept at mothering others, which was most often the basis of her relationships with friends, particularly boys. Other concepts such as her competition with her girlfriends and mother, her basic conflict about her own prettiness, and a feeling that she might have been a cause of her parents separation were not directly addressed and would have only been met with denial and a feeling that I did not understand her.

However, we did address those areas tangentially. Often Miriam talked about her friends and what they looked like as well as the basis of her parents' separation. As a result of questions mostly directed toward her friends' attitudes toward such matters it is likely that she modified some of her views. Still, Miriam was so negativistic that she tended to disagree with any direct statement. Over a period of time, as therapeutic progress was made and with some discussion of the probable origin of her negativism, she became less negativistic.

As a therapist, I worked hard at being nonjudgmental, but this did not mean that I always approved of Miriam's behavior; nor did I indicate that I did. No doubt support and encouragment for genuine accomplishments went a long way toward helping Miriam to feel better about herself and provided inspiration for further success.

The ability to regress within therapeutic sessions without being criticized for "being a baby" was probably very significant in enabling her to abandon her more childish behavior. In keeping with the principle that people are not free to change until they are free to be what they are, she chose only infrequently to act childishly when it was clear that she would be allowed to do so. On a transferential and less apparent level, perhaps I provided a corrective emotional experience in as much as I was, unlike her father, quite empathic and unlike her mother, more consistently available.

Conclusion

As noted at the beginning of this chapter, adolescents are difficult to work with. Their frequent changes, their high vulnerability, and their often negativistic attitudes make for an uneven course of treatment. Therapists of all persuasions would agree that adolescents, like all other people, need to be treated with respect and dignity. Nevertheless, it is especially true with adolescents, and the point cannot be overemphasized if one seeks to do good treatment. Respect for the integrity of very vulnerable teenagers must be thoroughly woven into their therapy.

If one assumes that therapy can change a person at teenage or later, then one accepts the premise that the personality formation that took place prior to that time did not result in an immutable character. Further, if the formation of genuine self-esteem is of vital importance to maximum mental health, it must take prominence as a goal of treatment.

The essence of this book until this point has been concerned with issues of principles and their application in establishing treatment with children as well as some of the special problems one encounters in working with adolescents. In the next chapter attention will be paid to some of the issues that need to be attended to as treatment progresses.

8

Ongoing Treatment
and Special Issues

Once established, treatment may go smoothly or be punctuated with difficult moments. In general, it can be assumed that most of the more difficult problems such as the setting of limits, arrangements with parents and schools, problems of fees, transportation, and schedules will be fairly well worked out. It is not that different aspects of the above issues should not and will not appear from time to time but that the relationship between therapist and child and therapist and parents tends to become more comfortable and the work of the therapy tends to become more regular.

Dealing with changes of circumstances that affect the therapy requires the cooperation of the child's parents, and if regular sessions with them have been arranged, the matters can be taken up with them at one of these meetings. If a significant matter occurs when no meeting is scheduled and the parents have access to a "hotline" to the therapist as suggested by Schimel (1979), such concerns can be handled efficiently and effectively. At times there may be concerns of the therapist that require him or her to contact the parents, and of course the therapist should be free to do so.

The course of treatment varies considerably with different children. There is, however, a phenomenon which occurs with sufficient regularity that it needs to be noted: that is, therapeutic improvement usually appears first in school. When school problems seem to be cleared up, problems at home and relationships with family begin to show improvement. This sequence is not unlike a comparable sequence with adults in therapy in which their problems at work are diminished before the problems with significant others are. Being aware of this probable sequence can be comforting to the therapist, and conveying it to the child's parents can reduce some of their anxiety about what they might expect.

Parents, who usually see their children behave remarkably well when visiting relatives or as guests at the house of other children but not when they are at home, find it difficult to understand this apparent contrast. The pattern is frequently similar in therapy in that children are quite cautious with the therapist until the therapy has proceeded for a number of sessions. This behavior can probably be best explained in terms of the child's willingness to take risks with relationships. It becomes clear to children that neither parents nor therapists are likely to desert them because of misbehavior. Particularly with young children, the bind to the parent is of sufficient intensity that the belief in likelihood of their parents deserting them because of their behavior is only present in relatively pathological situations. Unfortunately, therapists as well as parents unwittingly misuse this information and threaten abandonment as a form of punishment. In a department store or park parents often recite the all too familiar phrase: "If you don't come with me now, I'm going to leave you." With therapists it is: "If you don't stop [misbehaving in some way] now, you're going to have to leave the playroom." Only the most uncontrollable behavior should result in this course of action. It is a statement of utter defeat for a parent or therapist to declare that their only recourse is abandonment, and it is quite frightening to children to feel that their behavior is such that even adults feel it is out of their control.

During the process of therapy with children, many varying special problems occur. Not all of them can be discussed here, but several will be considered in detail, along with clinical examples. As I have frequently noted, it is important that the therapist make every effort to be alert to all apparent and all underlying dynamics. Above all, he must be inventive and flexible, able to take therapeutic advantage of all opportunities.

Ethical Problems

There is no formula that can cover all of the special difficulties regarding ethical issues that arise in therapy with children. What does one do with information that a child presents about being molested by a parent or relative? Family dynamics involving child molestation often include an attempt by other family members to deny or cover up the ongoing or previous behavior. Uncovering such information requires a sharp ear and direct questions particularly when obtaining a history. The first thing to be sure of is that the behavior does not continue. But what then? What about issues of drug use? Drug dealing? Alcohol? Shoplifting?

Maintaining the belief that one's first obligation is the health and the welfare of the child is a useful code to follow. There are, however, exceptions to this guiding view. For example, if a child is selling narcotics to other children, he is then endangering their lives, and one's first responsibility is to protect society. The ethical principles in the codes of the varying mental health professions are generally helpful but there can be no blanket application for all occasions. Several situations along with methods of dealing with them will be described in this chapter as evidence of some of the dilemmas resulting from specific issues. Therapist anxiety is a necessary concomitant with most of them.

Sexual Issues. The issue of child sexual molestation or other abuse is not something parents volunteer information about in their interviews with the therapist. However, a careful interview might lead the therapist to suspect and to investigate further. One should inquire about sexual attitudes in the family, about the degree of nudity on the part of all members. Do they close bathroom doors when using the toilet? Where do people get dressed or undressed? What clothing is worn in bed? Do children join parents in bed? When? Who wears what at the time? When is there sexual involvement between the parents? What information is conveyed to the children about sex? By whom? How? Do children sit on parents' laps? When? Who else lives in the house? What relatives visit? What about babysitters? All of this is vital information to be obtained in a complete form, albeit with tact and caution. While the values and standards of the therapist regarding such issues as nudity may be different from the family of the patient, and certainly the therapist needs to be tolerant of attitudes that are different from his own, the point of investigation is to seek out the derivation of the pathology of the patient, and in this regard the therapist must be exceptionally curious and comprehensive in his investigation. If the possibility of child abuse or molestation exists, it must of course be dealt with directly. The family structure may well be one that uses sexual abuse or violence as an attempt at solutions to specific problems, but of course such behavior does not solve the problem and cannot be tolerated. Unfortunately, particularly with teenage girls who may be sexually involved with their fathers, there is often more awareness of the problem in the family than meets the eye, and a kind of mass selective inattention for such behavior may be part of the delicate balance that keeps the family together.

If the therapist suspects that a young child has been molested, an interview can frequently reveal a good deal of information without engendering excessive anxiety in the child. Young children can be asked such questions as "How does your father [uncle, brother, mother, etc.] show you he loves you?" "Does anyone touch you in a place that you don't [or do] like?" Careful use of anatomically correct dolls can be helpful in determining the nature and extent of the involvement. Still, because they might be startling to children or perhaps too suggestive, one must be especially careful in using these.

One instance of child molestation was revealed in a child's reporting a dream to the therapist. A 7-year-old girl spontaneously reported the following dream:

I was sitting on the floor coloring in a coloring book. A friendly dog came along and started to lick my ear. I didn't like it but my parents didn't make the dog stop. They thought it was cute and funny.

The therapist asked how the child felt about the dream. She said it was a cute and friendly dog, but that she didn't like having her ear licked. "How do you know you don't like it?" the therapist asked. "Because sometimes when I sit on my father's lap he licks my ear. He thinks it's cute but I don't like it." "Did you ever tell him you don't like it?" asked the therapist. "No, it might make him mad," the child said. The therapist said simply, "Well, he gets mad at other things and that doesn't bother you too much and he gets over it, so I think you ought to tell him, or I'll tell him next time I see him if you like."

Here is an instance when the child was able to reveal through a dream parental behavior that she did not like. Obviously, it had seductive implications, and perhaps her behavior in not telling her father to stop had implications about her own enjoyment of it, but on some level she also recognized that it was wrong. A simple statement to the child's father that the girl did not like it and he ought to discontinue such "play" behavior stopped it. It is quite probable that the father was aware of its seductive quality, but with no direct reference to that aspect and a simple statement that it was wrong, the therapist conveyed the message. The father may or may not have noted the therapist's concern as an indication of his awareness of the sexual aspect. This approach further conveyed the information that the therapist was in effect "watching him," which apparently caused the father to exercise some restraint. The therapist noted the child's own, perhaps conflicted, behavior, which may have been considered in some later metaphorical play, but in keeping with the principles of this book, the therapist did not inquire directly about her own sexual excitement, if indeed it existed. In many ways much like hysterics, children tend to dream in a relatively straightforward manner—although they are not aware of the significance of the dream—so that, as in this incident, therapists' comments to children about their dreams should be reassuring but minimally interpretative.

The issue of the child's complicity in sexual molestation leads to complicating problems. It is difficult for a young child who does not really have a concept of love to perceive a significant difference in the verbal threat of withdrawal of love by a parent or sibling from the threat of the punishment of being deprived of television viewing. Children who cooperate because of one or the other threat may know the behavior is wrong but don't want to be deprived of television or to hear that Daddy doesn't love them.

If the sexual behavior involves the children in sexual arousal or even just curiosity, the possibility of their feeling that they themselves have brought on the molestation is increased. It is unlikely for them to permit themselves to become involved simply because the message that the behavior is perfectly all right is adequately conveyed by the offending adult. Some seriously psychopathic adults who are exceptionally clever might be able to accomplish this, but it is almost certainly likely that the adult insists that the child keep the matter quite secret, and such secretiveness most likely engenders a feeling of guilt in the child—a feeling that in turn helps to keep the matter a secret. Thus, sexual involvement between daughters and fathers often continues into later teen years (O'Brien 1987). The reasons for this continued liaison are quite variable, and therapy regarding the matter can be exceedingly complex.

There are certain legal aspects to this issue that need to be considered. In some states it is required that the therapist report the matter to appropriate authorities. When state law does not do so, the specific discipline of the therapist may determine whether or not he is legally bound to. There are times when reporting does not seem to be the best way of dealing with the problem, and, if he has the option, the therapist may decide to deal with it in another manner. Of course, how and when the therapist reports the information becomes an individual matter.

Theft. In the issue of theft, formula methods of treatment are ineffective. Stealing from the playroom can usually be handled more easily than other thefts. For example, if the therapist discovers a theft after the child has left the session, he might say to the child in the next session, "Last time when you left you took the red car with you; next time you come bring it back." Therapists should be clear and definite in a statement of the facts, if indeed they are known. To say to children, in the hope of helping them maintain self-esteem, "There was a small red car missing from the playroom; did you by any chance pick it up and put it in your pocket and forget to leave it at the end of the hour?" is inadvisable. While this statement is somewhat exaggerated, the point of the matter is that instead of helping the child to maintain self-esteem, this kind of statement teaches a child to lie, to say that he "accidentally" picked it up or "forgot" to put it back.

If the theft is committed outside of the playroom, other action is called for. The following dialogue between Peter, a 9-year-old who had been in treatment for three months, and his therapist, indicates one way in which the problem might be revealed and dealt with:

PETER (*taking a jacknife from his pocket*): Look at this neat knife I just got, Dr. Y.

THERAPIST: It looks new, and quite sharp. [At this point giving the child an opportunity to pick up on either aspect.]

P: My parents don't know I have it.

[A nine-year-old doesn't often have such items that his parents do not know about. It would appear that Peter has successfully kept the information secret, but wishes to reveal this information to the therapist. What does he have in mind? Is he questioning the therapist's ability to keep a confidence? Is he asking the therapist to reveal it to his parents? Is he simply indicating that there are things he does that he does not want his parents to know? Is it his way of revealing his attachment to the therapist?]

T: How come?

P: I haven't told them.

T: Where did you get it?

P: In school.

[Peter is usually much more talkative than this. Why the simple answers? He hasn't changed the subject, and he brought the matter up, so there is something he wants to convey.]

T: Yeah?

P: Yeah, I got it from Jimmy.

T: I thought you didn't like Jimmy. [The therapist is somewhat slow to catch on.]

P: I don't.

T: [Still a little dense.] So how come he gave you the knife?

P: He didn't.

T: [Finally getting the message.] You took it? Does he know?

P: Of course not.

T: What will you do with it? [Hoping that he will give it back.]

P: Keep it, of course.

T: [This one isn't going to be easy.] What would your parents do if they knew about it? [This isn't a threat, only an attempt to bring the issue into a moral realm.]

P: They'd make me give it back.

T: What do you think Jimmy will do?

[A careful inquiry rather than some kind of moralistic lecture is obviously in order. One can hardly be sure where it will lead.]

P: He's going to be pretty sad, but it will serve him right.

T: How come?

P: He got me in trouble yesterday when he told the teacher I threw the paper airplane, and I didn't.

T: Did you tell the teacher that?

P: No, he never listens to anything I say anyway so what's the sense in telling him?

T: How come he doesn't listen?

P: He always says I think I'm a big shot just because I once told him to shut up.

T: What was that about?

P: Jimmy dared me to do it.

T: Jimmy sounds like quite a troublemaker.

P: Not all the time.

[Why is Peter defending Jimmy? Does Peter envy Jimmy? Perhaps this is a situation where Peter is identifying with the aggressor. Children frequently allow themselves an escape clause by saying "not all the time."] (*At this point Peter stops throwing a Nerf ball at the basketball hoop and begins to play with Play-Doh, shaping it into the form of a person.*)

T: Sometimes you like Jimmy?

P: Only sometimes. (*Peter starts to pound the clay figure down against the table.*)

T: You sure hit that clay hard.

P: Yeah.

T: Sometimes you can pretend it's someone you don't like, and then pound on it.

P: If it were Jimmy, I'd sure hit him.

T: Yeah, how hard?

P: This hard. (*Peter hits very hard at the clay.*)

T: You're that mad at him, huh?

P: Sometimes. [The ambivalence and conflict become more apparent.]

T: Sometimes you like him and sometimes you hate him?

P: Yeah, that's right.

T: You know that's the way people often feel about other people, even good friends.

P: Yeah, maybe we could be friends.

T: Do you suppose you could ask him?

P: Yeah, I think I'll give him back his knife. Maybe we can be friends.

In keeping with the rationale of assisting children to be aware of their feeling and conflicts, the therapist has gotten Peter to accept his conflicting feelings about Jimmy and enabled him to change his mind about his attitude without feeling that he has lost face. Peter may well have applied the implication of this changed view or tolerance for conflicting feelings about other people, particularly his parents, with or without conscious awareness.

Not all questions of theft can be handled so easily or work out so well. For example, if the child is part of a small gang who steal from houses or shoplift from stores, the therapist may have to violate confidence to end the illegal action. The first step in doing so is to take the matter up with the child and attempt to get him to discontinue the theft and to reveal the matter to authorities and make restitution. There may be some instances when it is appropriate for the therapist not to request restitution, but many factors must be considered before such a conclusion can be reached. Basic ethical principals and good judgment on the part of the therapist are of course assumed.

Colleagues and Ethics. Issues regarding such matters as the ethical practice of colleagues are illustrated by the following case:

A woman in treatment with a·psychologist reported to him that her daughter was seeing a therapist once a week and that at this time the child's therapist reported that he felt his patient was seriously suicidal and that he wished for a psychiatric consultation regarding the possible use of medication. The parents gave permission for this examination, and the consulting psychiatrist concurred in the diagnosis and wished to prescribe medication. The child's parents did not believe that their daughter was seriously depressed and questioned the psychologist about the matter. They requested further consultation, and the psychologist who was seeing the child reluctantly gave his permission, although he did not provide any recommendation for whom the child should see.

The mother's therapist asked for permission to speak with the psychologist, and when he did so, the treating psychologist was quite cooperative. When he was asked if it might be useful to see the child more frequently than the once a week she was being seen, the therapist answered that he did not feel that would be of any value. In addition, when the mother's psychologist asked questions about transference that might be taking place, the therapist did not seem to understand the issue. On the basis of this relatively brief contact the mother's therapist speculated that the man was kind and pleasant, but did not appear to be skilled; in general, he appeared to be marginally trained and seemed to have little understanding of the dynamics of the disorder. Against the child's wishes, the parents decided to remove the child from the therapist's care and send her to someone the mother's therapist recommended.

The mother's therapist made the appropriate referral. The child, Ellen, a 14-year-old, reluctantly entered into treatment with the new psychologist. She spent the first two sessions complaining of how unfair it was of her parents to remove her from Howard's care. She referred to the previous therapist by his first name, which she had used with him throughout her prior six months of treatment. The new therapist did not feel that the child was suicidal, although he believed she was depressed, but he did consider her to be essentially hysterical and hypochondriacal. He decided that a medical consultation was not indicated. He was sympathetic to her anger with her parents and her feeling of loss at the separation from the therapist, but explained that the decision was not his and that her parents would not permit her to return to Howard; therefore, it was best if they tried to make the most of it.

At the fourth session, Ellen said she realized that Howard may have erred in his recommendation for medication, but that he was very nice to her and used to take her on his lap and read stories to her. When the therapist inquired further about this behavior, he tactfully inquired if this had any sexual quality. Ellen, who had lost her virginity shortly after she started treatment with Howard some six months earlier and had a fairly continuous sex life, said she saw his behavior as purely affectionate and caring and saw no sexual implications in it. The therapist said that while he could understand that this might be innocent in intent, it might still have sexual overtones and in general it was not considered essentially ethical behavior for a male therapist to have a 14-year-old girl sit on his lap.

Two sessions later Ellen reported that she still missed Howard very much and that while she realized his behavior may have seemed unethical, it was not so intended since "Howard kissed all his patients good-bye" when they left the session. When asked how Ellen knew this, she reported that she had two girlfriends who were also in treatment with Howard.

What was the new therapist supposed to do with such information? The decision was not easy. Was he to tell Ellen's parents? Should he discuss it with the prior therapist? Was it a matter for an ethics committee? Being critical of Ellen's former therapist would not make working with her any easier. At this time she was only seeing the new therapist because her parents insisted, not because she wanted to. It appeared that the most appropriate course for the therapist to pursue would be to discuss the matter with the previous therapist, and then, following this, he would consider reporting the matter to an ethics committee. But what would he do with this accusation? Would he reveal it to Ellen's friends who were still in treatment, and would it then get back to Ellen that her present therapist did not maintain a confidence?

Finally the therapist decided to discuss it with Howard. His questions were received with denial: Howard said he never placed patients on his lap and did not do so with Ellen. The therapist was more inclined to believe Ellen than Howard, but he thought that just raising the issue might be enough to discourage Howard from further behavior of this sort. The fact that he denied it indicated at least that, assuming that such were his practice, he felt it was basically wrong. The new therapist then reported the matter, including the interchange he had with Howard, as accurately as he could to the ethics committee of the national association and sent a copy of his report to Howard. While the committee did not have sufficient evidence to investigate the matter on the basis of this report, any additional reports would certainly have resulted in some action.

Drugs and Alcohol. Many children exaggerate their use of drugs or alcohol for varying reasons having to do with the impression they wish to give the therapist. In some instances they may even wish that the therapist report the matter to parents so that the matter will be ended. The therapist can remind the child that while he feels he can be most helpful by maintaining confidentiality, he is concerned with the child's health and cannot encourage such behavior. Most children are quite aware of the position of the therapist as another adult, and it is not unreasonable for the therapist to declare at some point that he cannot condone "such behavior" and that if it continues, he will have to report it to the parents. The child may simply continue to use drugs and stop reporting it to the therapist or may then declare that if the therapist does report it to his parents, he will discontinue treatment. In some instances the discontinuance of treatment may be preferable to allowing the offending behavior to continue.

If the relationship between the therapist and the child is sufficiently established, the child may be able to hear some of the possible unfortunate consequences of the use of drugs, where such information imparted by parents would only be received with reluctance, if heard at all. The therapist can also engage in a discussion with the child to help the youngster determine the basis for his use of the drugs. It is not always simply a matter of peer pressure, but as with all symptoms—and the principle that common symptomatology does not assume common etiology—children may use drugs to be important or daring with their peers, or they may use them to demonstrate what they feel to be evidence of their ability to be in charge of their own lives. It may be that they use the drugs to crowd out anxiety or to explain their lack of discipline and inability to do their school work. If the initial-history taking with parents and/or the child was complete, it should have included questions about how people handle physical discomfort or pain in the family. Who went to the doctor? When? What use was made of medication? Does the family illustrate an attitude that aspirins, cold medicines, cigarettes, and antacids are quick and ready answers for their ailments? Of course, none of this is sufficient explanation for a child's use of drugs, but an attitude that a pill or

alcohol, for example, is the answer for worries can be readily transmitted in the family.

Certainly parents cannot be completely alert to all the subtle
messages they are giving their children at all times, but a parent
who comes home from a difficult day and says, "I need a martini,"
may be conveying a different message from the one who says, "I'd
like one."

Abortion. When one deals with questions of abortion, the issue of
confidentiality can become quite complicated at times. For example, the following is an incident regarding an abortion that raised
special questions.

Kate, a 16-year-old who had been in treatment for about one
year and who was originally referred because she was doing badly
in school, reported to the therapist that she thought she was pregnant. A pregnancy test confirmed her suspicion, and she informed
the therapist that she did not wish for her parents to know. She
decided she was going to get an abortion. What was the therapist
to do with this information—at least from an ethical and legal point
of view? While a teenager could at that time and in that state seek
an abortion without parental permission, the ethical and possible
legal obligation of the therapist was to take the position of a responsible adult and report to parents behavior that they might consider contrary to the ultimate welfare of the child. The therapist's
responsibility in such a situation is a debatable, but nevertheless
real question, and with the highly litigious orientation toward therapy prevalent at this time, this issue cannot be taken lightly.

The therapist did not immediately report Kate's pregnancy to
her parents. During the week when the matter of what to do, including the possibility of an abortion, was being discussed, Kate went
with a friend to a reputable abortion clinic without telling her therapist. At the clinic she began to cry and had what clinic personnel
labeled a hysterical fit, not unlike much of Kate's behavior when
under stress. The personnel at the clinic refused to proceed further
until they spoke with a responsible adult and obtained permission
from a parent. When Kate informed them that she was in treatment
with a therapist, they telephoned him. He spoke with Kate and
indicated that he was told that she would need the permission of

her mother before the abortion could be performed. Kate did not feel able to call her mother, so the therapist volunteered to do so, and Kate, with relief, gave her permission. Kate's mother was fortunately available by telephone. On the advice of the therapist but not unwillingly, she telephoned Kate at the clinic and spoke with her supportively. She then met Kate at their home and discussed abortion, arranging for her to have the procedure at a later time with her mother present to provide support.

Undecided about the position he ought to take, the therapist had allowed himself to be caught somewhat unwittingly in a kind of conspiracy with Kate, initiated by Kate's taking action herself. This situation was somewhat like those when one parent maintained secrets from the other parent on Kate's behalf. That is, when Kate informed the therapist of her pregnancy and planned abortion and did not inform her parents, he might readily have entered into a conspiracy with her by not telling her parents. In this instance, the therapist effectively worked his way out of the dilemma of responsibility and confidentiality by informing Kate's mother with Kate's permission. The therapist's recognition of how he got "caught" in the dynamics occurred more after the fact than at the time of the event. However, his acting in good faith and from a vantage point of relative objectivity and good will were obviously of major importance to the outcome. It should be noted here I use the term "relative objectivity," for pure objectivity is a myth. (Greenberg 1986a) It is Levenson's (1972) position that it is essential that the therapist get "caught" in the dynamics of the disorder and then work his way out of the situation—which is akin to what happened here.

If one were to follow a classical Freudian view of this work with Kate, the underlying theory would have been quite different. The Freudian might have assumed, for example, that Kate was acting out a fantasied impregnation by the therapist who transferentially represented her father and that informing him in secret would have been necessary to prevent revelation of her sexual involvement with him to her mother. Still, it is conceivable that the therapist might have acted in an identical way as the therapist described in this account. The Freudian might have felt that his informing Kate's mother would be reassuring to the girl because it would arouse less guilt for the fantasied oedipal involvement. Thus the outcome would have been the same, but the explanation might have been quite different.

Contact With Parents and Others

Contact between parents and therapists is not as distressing to children as some therapists imagine and in fact may be quite comforting to them. If the child gets into difficulty during the day, such as being sent out of class or home from school or in an incident with a playmate or in the household, it is essential that the therapist be informed as soon as possible and that he does not have to depend on a report from the child at the child's next session. I make no distinction regarding this kind of information between child and adolescent. If a parent reports such an event, it is best that the therapist start the next session (unless something the child has to say obviously must take precedent) by saying, "Bill, your mother called yesterday and told me you got into trouble in Mr. Allen's class. She said Mr. Allen called, and . . . ," et cetera, telling the child the essence of what was reported to him. The child can then be asked what happened. In spite of continuing transferential problems, children soon learn that the therapist is not just another parent—that the therapist is not there to chastise them for their "bad" behavior and will in fact listen to their side. Sometimes a sympathetic ear can be the most therapeutic aid provided. Some parents might frequently report what they consider to be rule infractions that the therapist ought to know about. When it is clear that the therapist will tell the child of the parent's call, such calls will probably diminish in frequency.

Of course, there might be information that a parent wishes to report that cannot be immediately told to the child but that affects his life, such as illness in the family or a parental problem that might involve separation or divorce. If parents are contemplating separating, it is an unnecessary burden to have a child share their deliberations. If they have decided that in fact they are going to separate, then of course the child should be told, the parents themselves should tell their child and tell the therapist; but it is not the job of the therapist to tell the child. It is unlikely that a brief telephone call to the therapist will be made by one of the parents to impart this information. News of serious illness or death also must come from the parents. It is not that the therapist should not tell the child that he heard the bad news, but it is that the therapist should not be the first to tell the child of such events.

Most parents seek advice during their regular sessions with their child's therapist, when the issues of ways of conveying serious information to the child can be handled in a straightforward manner and advice can be clearly given.

As a child progresses in therapy, new problems seem to arise. It would appear at times that the new problems are themselves a result of the course of the treatment and, in fact, at times this may be true. If, for example, a child has been extremely phobic and unable to stay in his own room at night, attempts at staying alone may arouse new fears. The therapist should always be alert to the practical aspects of such problems and be free to make suggestions. To follow the above example further, if the child is now able to stay alone in his room but requires having a lamp turned on, the next step toward sleeping without a lamp on would be to have the child keep a flashlight next to his bed so that should he become frightened or imagine that there is something menacing in his room, he can readily check on it.

In contrast to therapy with adults, there is a considerable amount of contact between child therapists and significant others. This is a burden and responsibility the child therapist must be prepared to take. It requires continued judgment about the degree of confidentiality involved in terms of the child, the parents, and those others with whom contact is made. For some therapists the solution is easy. They simply avoid all contact with schools and other agencies and keep contact with parents at an absolute minimum. While this attitude may be essentially workable, it is not in the interest of the most effective treatment for the child. A competent therapist can be most helpful in conveying information to schools and others in a manner that lends authority and reason to suggestions for beneficial changes. But in addition to being something of a burden on the therapist in terms of time needed to make appropriate contact, communicating with schools and other agencies is fraught with other risks.

Most elementary and high school systems have their arranged "chain of commands." Bypassing them can result in considerable difficulty and hurt feelings. While the therapist may have need for contact with the teacher of the child with whom he is working, protocol may require that contact be made only with the principal of the school or the superintendent of the system or someone from the guidance department. It is best that the therapist be aware of the arrangements of particular systems before he steps in. Offending people who may directly affect the welfare of the child may readily have deleterious results. Dodds (1985) wisely suggests that if the therapist knows no one in the school, it is best to contact another therapist through his professional association who knows the appropriate procedure for that discipline. In addition, it is likely that this person probably also knows the teachers involved and can make suggestions most congenial to their methods of education. In an incident in which this procedure was not followed, direct contact with the teacher resulted in a complaint from the school superintendent and which then required several meetings to unravel the problems and to smooth ruffled feathers (Spiegel 1959).

The therapist must judge how much information is shared. Confidentiality of school records, like confidentiality in certain work situations and insurance companies, cannot be assured, so, however well-meaning breaches of therapists' confidential revelations may be, therapists should be aware of the possibility for such breaches. Therapists themselves should, of course, have an appropriate signed release of information.

Physicians, particularly pediatricians who are also concerned with the child's welfare can do their jobs more effectively, if they are provided with information that can assist them and they should certainly be provided with appropriate information. Many, however, are not skilled in methods of child psychotherapy and may inappropriately share information with a child in psychotherapy or with his parent. Such information must be conveyed with special caution and competence, or serious damage might be done.

In general, there appears to be a built-in proprietary sense about information relevant to the child, and many therapists are reluctant to share their impressions. Of course some of the above reasons—failures in confidentiality or misuse of the information—make therapists appropriately cautious. However, in this inexact science, with its heavy reliance on "intuition," it is best to maintain an attitude that therapists need all the help they can get, and parents, teachers, and pediatricians can contribute a good deal to therapeutic endeavors, as therapists can contribute to theirs.

Often well-meaning individuals directly or indirectly connected with the child telephone either to ask questions about the child or to contribute information that they feel will be useful in the therapist's work with the youngster. Of course, caution and tact are required of the therapist in receiving and acting on such information, and it is best to remember that in principle the therapist does not wish to get caught in some kind of conspiratorial arrangement where information that might be helpful to parents or child cannot be shared. Unsolicited telephoners who wish to speak about the child should be told that the information they give will probably be shared with parents and child or both, and that they are free to go ahead and provide such information with that understanding.

Occasionally, one parent may wish to share information with the therapist but not with the other parent. If the parents are separated or divorced this does not pose as much difficulty as it does if the family is intact. Such information might include matters relating to divorce or extramarital relationships or different attitudes about punishment and discipline. A parent who fears that the other parent might be too harsh with a youngster if she or he knew of certain misbehavior may wish to share the information with the therapist privately. All of these matters require individual judgment, and one cannot maintain rigid rules about procedure. Orderliness and an inclination toward logical procedural thinking are certainly good traits for an effective therapist to have: obsessionalism that does not allow for some flexibility may be easier for the therapist but is not always the best policy or procedure for effective treatment.

Parental Resistance

Because children tend to be straightforward in their attitudes and revelations—or at least therapists work toward keeping them that way or getting them to be that way if they have already learned too much repression or suppression—their resistance to being in therapy is often expressed directly and can be dealt with in a straightforward manner. Unfortunately, the situation is frequently quite different with parents. They may be either unaware of their resistance to maintaining their child in therapy or for varying dynamic reasons unwilling to express it directly.

There are many reasons for such resistance. A common phenomenon that causes resistance occurs with children whose basic problem was symptomatically revealed by timidity and reticence. While the parents may have brought the child to treatment because of his inability to "stand up for himself," with siblings and peers, they are somewhat surprised that as he recovers from his disorder, he not only stands up for himself with peers and siblings but also with parents—which is something the parents do not always readily tolerate. If the parents are aware of the reason for their concern and can discuss it with the therapist in their regular meeting with him, the matter can usually be handled satisfactorily. However, if for varying personality reasons of their own, they cannot discuss the matter directly or if they are given to passive aggressive behavior as a characterological method of dealing with situations, they may express resistance in other ways.

Another form of resistance may arise if the parents are in disagreement with each other about methods of raising children and the balance is tipped so that the child's behavior is changed to favor the preference of the parent whose view was not the prevalent one in the past. This could readily result in resistance to further therapy on the part of the now unpopular parent. The degree to which such resistance can be expressed or discussed openly depends on the family dynamics, the particular characterological structure of that parent, and the skill of the therapist.

People who have special problems in dealing with financial issues may decide, realistically or unrealistically, that the cost of therapy is more than they can or wish to bear. Of course, if they can discuss the matter openly, the therapist can either make other financial arrangements or refer the child elsewhere. However, the fact that the parents initiated therapy and then decided about financial limitations may lead the therapist to suspect that other factors are operating. It may simply be that the family financial situation has changed, or it may be something more subtle such as the treatment taking more time than the parent(s) had anticipated. With a careful and complete initial evaluation, many of these potential problems can be uncovered before treatment starts and prevented from interfering with the course of the treatment. Nevertheless, given the problems people do have about dealing with money, they may be unwilling, or unaware, or unable to express their concern. Or even the opposite may be true: there may be no financial problem, but the parents may be more comfortable saying that the financial aspect is the problem when in fact it may be, for example, one of the other reasons described above.

Parents may have not anticipated the problems involved in providing transportation for their child or in appearing for their own occasional meetings with the therapist, and they may feel the strain of disrupting their own schedules. They may or may not be willing or able to discuss the matter.

Discovery that the child is in therapy may have resulted in criticism by other family members or by friends, and some parents are unable to deal with such issues directly or might well be influenced to believe that continued therapy only reflects their own inadequacy.

There are many reasons for resistance—the above are just a few. The therapist must be alert to all signs of parental resistance. If they directly express that they do not wish their child to continue treatment, the therapist has a good opportunity to discuss the matter at some length and deal with the real or assumed reasons and issues. It is with parents who do not deal with the matter directly that the therapist must be especially alert and skillful.

Methods of indirectly resisting are limited only by the complex imaginations and personalities of the human species. A few of the more frequent and obvious ones will be discussed here. Confusing schedules is probably the most usual way of showing what is commonly referred to as "passive resistance." Often parents have an order of priorities in their minds and, depending on their attitude toward the therapy at a particular time, the child's appointment time may come somewhere between a haircut and the dressmaker or the post office and a tennis game. If it is more valued it may be below the pediatrician but above the veterinarian. However it is placed, with resistant parents it often takes a relatively low priority. Of course, just forgetting the therapists appointment or believing that "today couldn't possibly be Thursday, it must be Wednesday" is not infrequent and on par with children forgetting to bring their book home from school or leaving their homework on the piano. Other reasons include having the car serviced on that day, although the matter could have been postponed, or getting so involved in the book they were reading that they didn't notice what time it was. That's only slightly better than forgetting to set the alarm to get up in the morning.

Parents who are dissatisfied with the treatment sometimes express their dissatisfaction by failing to pay their therapy bill or delaying it or sending to the wrong address or failing to sign checks or sending the wrong amount. Therapists must always be alert to the unconscious or underlying reasons for such "acting out" so that they can help to alleviate the problem and not merely get caught in it. Therapists who are themselves reluctant to bring up the matter of payment irregularity and discuss it, feeling that it is some kind of oversight or that bringing it up would make them appear too interested in the financial aspect of their occupation, only contribute to the problem and in effect enter into a conspiracy conveying some other message such as the problem doesn't really exist or it is so serious that it would be too embarrasing to talk about.

Depression in Childhood

It is not my intent to enter into a debate or lengthy discussion about the possibility or existence of depression in children. Indeed, children can be depressed, and while young children do have difficulty in sustaining a mood of unhappiness, they are not immune to such aspects of the human condition. For a substantial review of the literature having to do with depression in children and adolescents, see Arieti and Bemporad (1978).

I shall discuss instead, some of the factors that appear to me to predispose children to depression. Given the view that childhood is in itself a plastic developmental process, I recommend that treatment with depressed children be oriented toward assisting them to develop methods of dealing with the viscissitudes of life that are constructive—depression not being one of them.

In homes where the atmosphere is fundamentally depressing,

where there is little joy, children may well feel that they are be-
traying the family if they show moods of elation or enthusiasm. Fortunately, moods do not often prevail for all members of the same
family. Characterologically depressed moods are usually confined to
only one member. Thus, while the family atmosphere is certainly
part of the total influence on the child, only in relatively rare instances does the whole family reflect a single mood.

I am particularly interested in some of the specific factors that
lead to depression. Being able to deal satisfactorily with separations
is probably one of the most significant factors that influence depression. Temporary separations or permanent ones, such as those resulting from death, are usually precipitating factors in adult depression. How the family deals with such matters is vitally important.
The significant event may be overstated or understated. Is every
separation, such as leaving the child with a baby-sitter when parents go out for the evening, considered in the category of an overseas flight? What does the family do when a child's pet dies? Little
respect is conveyed for the meaning of life if dead birds or goldfish
are flushed down the toilet or if the child's parent responds to the
news of a dead kitten by saying, "Tomorrow we'll go out and get
another one." Children subjected to those kinds of experiences have
little preparation for separations in later life. Protecting children
from the disappointments in life by pretending they are of little
significance does not prepare them for an adult life when they must
deal with such matters realistically—as the following case illustrates.

Alice, a woman of 29 who had been in intensive therapy for eleven
months, appeared for a session very tearful and distraught. When
asked to add language to the tears, she explained that Morton went
out with another woman. The therapist expressed surprise at her
extreme reaction and said, "But you haven't seen Morton in over
a year." A little of Alice's history gives us some indication of the
cause of her extreme reaction.

When Alice was 16 years old, her mother was in the hospital
with terminal cancer. Alice knew that her mother was quite ill but
had not been told of the full gravity of the disease. She vaguely
remembers hearing the telephone ring one morning at about 4 A.M.,
that her father answered it, and that she went back to sleep. When
she got up for school and had her breakfast, her father ate with

her as usual and then walked her to the bus stop, which he also did fairly habitually. She had an examination scheduled in school that day, and she remembers her father leaving her as she got on the bus and his having said, "Do well on your exam for your mother." When she came home from school, her father told her that her mother had died during the previous night.

This extreme example of the way in which Alice's father dealt with bad news in the family was representative of the manner in which the whole family treated issues of loss and disappointment. It is any wonder that Alice had difficulty in integrating the loss of Morton? Effectively, he still existed in her head.

Families who protect their children from death and separation as realities of life do them no favor in preparing them for the requirements of maturity and independence, and it is my impression that such protection may well be preliminary to an inclination for depression in later life.

Additionally, if a family engenders guilt and shame for poor grades or other school or achievement failures, children will certainly find it difficult to think well of themselves, and their resulting lack of self-esteem is hardly compatible with feelings of joy and optimism. Lifestyles and reactions can be only understood in terms of the unique history of the development of an individual.

Therefore the methodology of dealing with depression must be unique for every child. For example, Larry, a boy of 7, was brought to therapy because he sometimes threatened to jump out of the window and kill himself, using this threat as a kind of blackmail to obtain toys and privileges he might not otherwise have received. The parents felt themselves to be in a bind. While they did not wish to provide unlimited privileges, they were fearful that he might carry out his threat. Indeed, as all therapists know, all suicidal threats must be taken seriously. Psychological tests were a useful part of the evaluation procedure with this child. When I saw from the testing and play examination that it was highly unlikely that the child would in fact kill himself, I handled the matter in a relatively conservative manner: I told Larry that, while of course we did not want him to, if he intended to kill himself, there really was no way of preventing him if he were left alone in his house. Therefore, to be sure that he would not kill himself he would have to be placed in a hospital where he could be protected twenty-four hours a day. He then said he really did not want to kill himself and later reported to his parents that I had told him that if he continued to say that he was going to kill himself, he would be put in a hospital. He then reassured them that he did not want to be in a hospital and did not want to kill himself. While the same information might have been revealed without the benefit of psychological tests, the tests' providing a relatively clear answer in a short period of time made them a useful procedure. Therapy with the child proceeded in a productive manner, often centering on issues of entitlement and competitiveness.

Ongoing problems and special issues have been considered from the viewpoint of individual, play-oriented child therapy. Other techniques, while not the subject of this book, are nonetheless useful in the hands of skilled practitioners and are not to be understated. Some of these treatment variations are the subject of the next chapter.

9

Treatment Variations

There are a number of variations to psychotherapy with children that must be considered. Alternative forms of treatment include behavior modification, family therapy, group therapy, and medication. Some therapists combine different approaches in their own practices, while others refer children to different experts. Problems of economics and time limitations and special problems that are not generally amenable to individual treatment require alternative considerations. Some of these are discussed in this chapter.

Behavior Modification

Referral to a behavior modification therapist might be made, for example, for a child who has a specific phobia that does not appear to be connected to any apparent complex dynamic other than, say, having had a single traumatic experience related to the phobia and whose parents seek a kind of specific and quick solution and do not wish to become otherwise involved in therapy. Although it is my impression that there are complex dynamics underlying such symptoms as stuttering, bedwetting, addictions, and obesity, patients who display them frequently respond well to behavior modification. It is more than likely that a therapist's decision to make a referral would await a more complete evaluation of the problem, and this usually requires an evaluative session with the parents.

Family Therapy

I do not usually make referrals to family therapists unless the parents specifically request it. A separate and well-documented discipline assumes that emotional difficulties exhibited by a child are a matter of family dynamics, which should be considered as a whole, and that those, rather than individual, dynamics are the source of the pathology (Johnson, Rasbury, and Siegel 1986; Bowen 1976; Guerin and Pendergast 1976; Haley 1979; Minuchin 1974). Some believe that individual pathology can be worked out only within the family unit. While the family does operate as a unit and such concepts as designated roles within the family may be quite valid, I do not believe that dealing with the problem through the family unit is the most appropriate and efficacious method. On occasion I do see a family together for one or two sessions because I find such meetings most revealing of dynamics that I might not otherwise observe, but I do not see this as the arena in which to bring about therapeutic change.

One of the more significant reasons for my position is that exposing family dynamics to children can be quite confusing and much too revealing to them. It is likely that revealing some of the complex conflicts the parents have with each other and varying family members, including grandparents, cousins, uncles, aunts, and pets, might, at the least, force information on children that they are unable to integrate and that would have a deleterious effect on their relationship with family members.

It is also likely in family therapy that parents will reveal information about their relationship with each other, including such matters as their sex life, which would best be kept private. Children have enough fantasies about what goes on in their parents' bedroom; there is no need to elicit additional ones. I am certainly not opposed to appropriate sex information for a child, but, again, the information should not go beyond the level at which the child is capable of understanding and integrating it.

Additionally, if the family therapy is psychodynamically oriented, it is likely to reveal information about the specific life history of the parents, including the relationships they had with their parents and siblings, which they may not wish other members of their family to know. In fact, because of this inherent danger, I prefer not to see parents separately who live together (with the exception of an occasional uncontroversial consultation with an individual parent); a parent might reveal information that he or she does not wish to have known by other family members, and this puts me into a duplicitous position. I believe that people have a right to privacy about their own lives, their sexual affairs, their fantasies, their past experiences and family relationships, and for me to see each of them separately and hold such information as private would make me become part of a conspiracy. In separate sessions, as in family therapy, the rivalries among members are revealed, and I do not wish to be used to widen schisms or reinforce sides, for ultimately, this is not likely to be to the benefit of the child. While perhaps some of my colleagues may indeed maintain neutrality, I find such neutrality more in keeping with the requirements and talents of a legendary wise man or guru and not in keeping with my own qualities and skills.

Finally, I have enough difficulty understanding what goes on between me and another person, and to sort out the complex dynamics of several people in the room at the same time is more than I can deal with. Those of my colleagues who are experts in family therapy tell me that such specific understanding is unnecessary, but perhaps for reasons having to do with my own personality structure, I find attempting to do therapy without such understanding to be entirely unsatisfactory.

Parent Guidance Groups

A frequently satisfactory way of working with parents in addition to or instead of individual sessions is to arrange for parent guidance groups (Slavson 1958). These can meet on a regular basis and include all parents of children in treatment. Parents find it helpful to talk about some of the problems they probably would not have been able to reveal to friends or neighbors on a casual or individual basis, to discover that they share difficult, although common, problems; and they often help each other work out solutions. A guidance group is more educative than therapeutic, since group member interaction is not the focus, and private lives are revealed to only a very limited extent. In addition, if one or more members must miss a session, it is not as significant as it would be in a therapy group and in the way the group experiences such an absence.

The Home Visit

Most therapists do not make home visits except for emergency situations when the child may be unable to come to the therapist's office for treatment. In other instances, the home visit is an unconventional approach that is worthy of consideration, especially when the therapist feels that the parents and/or the child in treatment are not sufficiently revealing or present a puzzling picture about the specifics of the family situation. I have on occasion made home visits. It is an unusual practice that requires considerable forethought, but I have found such meetings to be immensely helpful. If the parents and the child accept the idea, sharing dinner with the family provides an optimal opportunity to observe the family in their own comfortable setting.

Children frequently welcome an opportunity to show the therapist their room, pets, and playthings. It is an ideal opportunity for an observant therapist to see the children and their family on their own territory. How do family members treat each other in their own home, even in the presence of a nonfamily guest? One can observe the placement of furniture and objects, the presence or absence of photographs and art, issues of neatness, table manners, and the like. Repeated visits are not recommended because they would complicate and further change the relationship in a way that might compromise the therapist's role, but for a single and singular experience I find a home visit remarkably useful.

Group Therapy

While this book is essentially about individual treatment of children, it is not my intention to overlook the valuable therapeutic gains that can be accomplished in group therapy. For a lengthy discussion of group work with children, see the works of Ginott (1961b) and Slavson and Schiffer (1975).

Adolescent group therapy is frequently quite useful and, because space requirements are not as extensive as required for young children, can often be readily arranged. On the other hand, except in clinics, where space may be available, group therapy for young children who require activity space is hard to come by. Children younger than 5 or 6 generally do not play too well together, and the possibility of therapeutic gains from each other is limited. Very young children tend to engage in parallel play. Groups seem most appropriate for children after the age of 7. If there are enough children to form several groups, then the age range can be fairly narrow. Because emotional and physical growth is inversely proportional to the number of years the child has lived—that is, one year is a quarter of the life of a 4-year-old but only a tenth of the life of a 10-year-old—the significance of age differences among children diminishes as the individual gets older. Therefore, for children to have similar interests and developmental problems, they should be close in age to each other.

A good arrangement for a child play group is a room equipped with a fairly large assortment of play materials, particularly those items which lend themselves well to cooperative play. Such materials might include clay, construction materials, and some selected games. Additional items not generally found in the playroom but useful with groups are hand tools, wood, and other items used for construction. A more detailed description of the function and use of various play materials was given in chapter 4.

The major function of the therapist in a group is to be a facilitator, available for specific difficult tasks and trained to take advantage of therapeutic opportunities indicated by the play and conversations of the children.

The Use of Puppets With a Large Group

The writings of Woltmann (1964) and my own (1959b) indicate the ways in which puppetry can be used with larger groups of children where the age range can be as much as 4 or 5 years.

In a community mental health clinic I had the good fortune of being able to enlist the volunteer aid of an actress. In this setting I utilized puppets for a kind of group therapy. My general method for conducting these sessions was to present a puppet show for the children using hand puppets and a simple platform stage. My assistant and I provided the puppet voices and manipulations, and the children were invited to engage in dialogue with the puppets during the play. It is particularly helpful to have scripts written with an orientation toward the specific problems the children of the group have, such as problems related to school, siblings, parents, and so on. The technique might be especially useful for groups of children in distinctive situations, such as handicapped children or children in a general hospital ward. The following script illustrates the general method of conducting these sessions. This is a clinical account and includes remarks of the children.

Act I

CASPER: Hello, boys and girls, good morning, good afternoon, good evening, good day. Today I'm going into the woods near my house. I like to go there sometimes by myself and sometimes with my friends. I like to make believe the woods are Africa and then I'm in the jungle. I'm going to call my mother and ask her if I can go. Mother . . . Mother.

(*Mother comes on stage*)

MOTHER: Hello Casper, I'm glad you're home from school. I'd like you to go to the store for me.

[Note that Casper addresses the audience as well as his mother while his mother does not, so that it is as if he is in private communication with the children.]

CASPER: I want to go down the street to my jungle. I don't want to go to the store.

MOTHER: Yes, Casper, you don't want to go but you have to. I'm all out of sugar, and you'll have to go down and pick some up.

CASPER: Do I have to go to the store, boys and girls?

AUDIENCE (*variously*): Tell her you don't want to go.

Run out of the house.

Go and get it over with.

You've got to obey your mother.

CASPER: I guess you're right. Sometimes you have to do things you don't want to do.

MOTHER: I'll check and see what else I need and get the money for you. Here, Casper, here's three dollars. Get a dozen eggs and two pounds of sugar, and when you come home, you can go down to your jungle.

(*Mother exits. Casper leaves on the opposite side of the stage and reappears this time with the storekeeper.*)

STOREKEEPER: What can I do for you Casper?

CASPER: I want a dozen eggs and two pounds of sugar.

STOREKEEPER: O.K. I'll get them for you.

(*leaves stage*)

STOREKEEPER: (*calls out, but not visible to the audience*): That will be two dollars and forty-five cents, Casper. I'll have to go to the back to get them.

CASPER: Two dollars and forty-five cents, and I've got three dollars. That leaves me fifty-five cents change. If I bought a candy bar for forty cents, I'd still have fifteen cents left over. But I'm supposed to bring back all of the change. But my mother didn't say that. I'd sure like a candy bar. Should I buy it, boys and girls? What would my mother say if I didn't bring her all of the change? What should I do?

AUDIENCE (*variously*): Buy it.

Don't do it, you'll get in trouble.

Tell her you lost the change.

Tell her it cost more.

STOREKEEPER (*returning*): Casper, while I was back getting the eggs, your mother called to tell me it would be all right for you to buy a candy bar and take it home with you to eat after supper.

CASPER: Mothers and daddies always seem to know what we want and when we want it even when we don't tell them. They must be mind readers.

AUDIENCE: It's magic.

CASPER: I'm sure glad she called and sure glad I didn't buy it without telling her. (*To storekeeper*): Thank you, Mr. Storekeeper. (*Takes bag and leaves.*)

STOREKEEPER: Good-bye, Casper.
(*Casper leaves. Storekeeper leaves. Mother and Casper reappear.*)

MOTHER: Thank you for going to the store for me. Now you can go out and play.

CASPER: Good-bye, I'm going to the jungle. (*Both go, and Casper returns with a stick.*)

CASPER: Here I am in the jungle. It's sure spooky in here. I wonder if there are any wild animals or mean natives in this jungle. I'm sure glad I got this stick to protect myself.
(*Cat appears behind Casper. Casper turns around, but the cat disappears.*)

CASPER (*to audience*): Did you here a noise? Where? (*Casper and the cat keep missing each other, with children telling Casper where to look.*)
(*Cat spits and hisses.*)

CASPER: A tiger. What did you say?
(*Cat hisses and spits more.*)

CASPER: Go away. You scare me.

AUDIENCE (*variously*): He'll bite you, Casper.

Don't trust him.

Watch out.

It's just a cat.

CASPER (*raises stick*): I can see you're a mean tiger. I'll hit you if you come near me.
(*Cat backs off and raises paws defensively.*)

CASPER: I guess he doesn't want to bite me after all. Let's be friends. (*He pets the animal, and the cat rubs up against him. A female puppet appears.*)

JANE: Hello, Casper. Whose pussycat is that?

CASPER: Hello, Jane. It's not a pussycat. It's a tiger. But he's my friend. (*Animal pulls at Jane's hair.*)

CASPER: Don't do that. (*Animal stops.*) Sometimes it looks like fun to pull a girl's hair but you're not supposed to do that because it hurts. That's the rule.

JANE: It's all right Casper, he didn't know.

CASPER: He's strong. He can do lots of things we can't do. I'll bet he'll help us if we want him to.

JANE: Maybe he can knock down the school house. Then we wouldn't have to go to school.

CASPER: That would be good. But if my daddy found out it wouldn't be so good.

JANE: Yes, anyway, sometimes school's fun, but sometimes it's not.

CASPER: If we get him to help us, we can run away, and then we wouldn't have to go to school at all.

JANE: Yes, Casper, let's run away from home. Let's start this way.

Act II

(Casper, Jane, and the cat are on the stage.)

JANE: Gee, it's getting dark, and I don't even know where we are.

CASPER: Don't be afraid. We'll find a nice place in the woods to stay tonight.

JANE: Yes, then tomorrow we'll go far away. Gee, I'm hungry.

CASPER: I've got an orange we can share *(gives each a piece)*.

JANE: Thank you.

CAT: Meaaow.

CASPER: You're welcome.

JANE: I'm still hungry and I'm scared.

MOTHER *(voice in the distance)*: Casper, Casper.

AUDIENCE *(variously)*: Your mother's calling you.

You have to go home, Casper.

Don't run away.

Be quiet, and she won't hear you.

CASPER: Shooosh. Don't say anything. Maybe she'll go away.

JANE: Casper, your mother doesn't want us to run away.

CASPER: Yeah, but I don't want to go to school.

JANE: But your mommy and daddy will miss you.

CASPER: Oh, they can get along without me, and they have my baby sister. She'll keep them company.

JANE: Are you still mad at your baby sister? You know she's little and she needs to have big people take care of her. Anyway, I'm still scared.

CASPER: Girls are always scared.

JANE: Not always, and sometimes boys are scared too, so that's not true.

CASPER: Well, I'm not scared now, but I am hungry.

MOTHER: Caaasper. Jaaaane.

CASPER: I guess if you're scared, maybe we better go home. Tiger, you better go.

(*all three wave good-bye, the cat leaves the stage, mother appears.*)

MOTHER: Your father and I were worried about you. I'm sure glad I found you. What are you doing here?

CASPER: We were running away, and we had a tiger to help us.

MOTHER: Oh Casper, you know there are no tigers here.

AUDIENCE (*variously*): There was a tiger.

I saw him.

(*As usual, the mother ignores the audience.*)

MOTHER: Anyway Casper, we don't want you to run away. We love you. Come on home, and I'll call Jane's mother, and she can have dinner with us . . . and ice cream too.

JANE: Goody. Good-bye, boys and girls.

CASPER: Good-bye.

MOTHER: Good-bye.

(*All leave stage*)

Dynamically oriented psychotherapy has been considered from a number of approaches. The ending of treatment with children also poses its own special problems. Of course, there is much variation in the way in which treatment ends, and the next chapter describes some of these and points to guiding principles for therapy having to do with termination of treatment.

10

Termination of Treatment

The end of treatment, it is hoped, results in a satisfactory achievement of a goal. Important issues to be considered in making the decision to terminate child and adolescent therapy include the basis for the decision, the method of terminating, and the aftermath of the completion of treatment. There is considerable variation in the content and in the manner of dealing with these issues, depending on whether or not the child's termination is planned or unplanned and the special considerations necessary in dealing with an adolescent. Each of these circumstances will be described and explored.

Planned Termination With Children

The Decision to Terminate. The presence or absence of the problem that brought the child to therapy initially is foremost in making the decision for termination. Therapists should not look for children to show uniformity of behavior with no qualities of distinctiveness as criteria for deciding on termination. In fact, such uniformity is almost impossible, and, at best, it certainly is less than desirable. People are entitled to their own dynamics and individuality, and uniqueness may well be a desirable quality and not pathology. If the child has reached the point where he may have his own style but is essentially free of the pathology that brought him into treatment, it is time to end therapy. The problem, presumably, was the existence of behavior or ideation inappropriate not only to a child of that chronological age but perhaps to all children. If the problem no longer exists—if, for example, the child is no longer enuretic or does not sleepwalk or have nightmares or is not phobic or does not exhibit tics or does his school work—then the job can be considered finished. Good therapy should be like good surgery. One should enter the problem area, do the job as efficiently and effectively as one can, and then leave. The task, at least with children, is to repair, not to remake.

The questions of whether or not to terminate and when to terminate require a good deal of careful consideration. Characterological style is not the same as pathology. There is a point where the therapist is able to say this is a quiet child or a shy child and differentiate this from a child who is withdrawn or schizoid in a continuum of pathology from mild degrees of problems of living to severe pathology (Spiegel 1987; Sullivan 1953b). In the same way, children who tend to be more active than others may not merit the label "manic" or even "hyperactive," and their higher level of activity may not call for psychotherapeutic intervention. As I noted at the beginning of this book, there is a difference between a child who occasionally wets the bed and one who is decidedly enuretic; the symptom itself must be placed on a continuum. An occasional nightmare is not the equivalent of regular, nightly bad dreams or sleepwalking. Chastising the family dog for soiling the rug is not the same as spanking a younger sister; certainly, it is not in the same category as throwing darts at the family cat. A child who tends to be talkative is not the same as a compulsive talker.

The symptoms that brought the child to treatment must always be kept in mind, and regular meetings with parents should always include direct inquiry about those symptoms. Although a brief return of the initial symptoms is possible after the announcement of termination (a matter which will be discussed later in this chapter), in general, the major indicator of the appropriateness of termination of treatment is the cessation of such symptoms.

A second major criterion for termination is that the child should have reached an emotional level that is essentially appropriate for his age. In this regard I wish to emphasize that children should be neither ahead nor behind most children of their own age. As I noted throughout this book and especially in discussions on metaphor, limit setting, and principles, it is fundamental that children do not have the insight and knowledge of their dynamic processes that one might expect of adults. More insight than is appropriate for the child's age gives rise to cynicism, depression, and an inability to enjoy the freedom of expression of feelings one should expect of children.

Ideally, the decision to complete therapy is made by the therapist. Help from and cooperation of the parents is important, but the therapist is the expert and best equipped to make such decisions. I do not agree with some therapists such as Dodds (1985) who believe that the cues of the patient as to when he thinks he is through are the ones to be most attended to in terminating treatment with children. Ending treatment is much too important a decision for it to be made by a child. Just as children should not decide if they should be in treatment (chapter 3), they should not decide when treatment is to end.

Given the option, children may decide to end treatment for any number of reasons. Because most children have little concept of the basis or need for therapy, their having the idea that the work of therapy is "complete" strikes me as the least likely reason for a child to wish to terminate. This is especially true if the treatment has followed the kind of pattern suggested in this book, in which the orientation is not to focus on symptoms and "cure" in any direct fashion. Effectively, except on some deep, unconscious level, the child does not know why he has been in treatment; he knows only in some vague way that his life isn't as it should be. Therefore, if the child does not fully understand why he is there and such conscious understanding is not considered germane, how can he decide that the job has been completed?

Informing the Child. Once the therapist has made the decision to terminate treatment and has conferred with the child's parents, the therapist, not the parents, must convey the information to the child. The parents should be informed first, as they might present information that would lead the therapist to alter his decision.

The method of giving such information to the child is likely to show considerable variation, depending as it does on the child and the circumstances. Whether one subscribes to an attachment theory that defines a sequence of separation and individuation or some other developmental sequence, separations are the most difficult events in life. Death, the ultimate separation, is usually *the* most difficult. But the ending of psychotherapy—as of any relationship that has little prospect of continuation, even though the individual will continue to be alive—requires considerable thought and preparation and is likely to result in feelings of loss and abandonment as well as possible guilt, anger, and remorse. Children, unlike adults, usually have had little experience in separations. They are bound to meet such events with these complex feelings, even more so than adults.

In the discussion of depression in chapter 8, there is some exploration of the history of separations that might contribute to the pathology of depression. Youngsters may react similarly to termination in psychotherapy. Moreover, because children are usually psychologically as well as chronologically closer to the state of infancy than are adults, there is often a feeling that if someone cannot be seen or otherwise contacted, she or he does not exist. Children, then, need a transition from treatment that is gentle and helps them to realize that even when people are not present, they still exist. They need to understand that there are varying degrees of relatedness, and while there may be some grief as a result of physical and or geographic separations, such separations can be accepted as a part of life.

Timing Termination. The timing of the actual termination should ideally be arranged to coincide with a natural break in the treatment. Probably the most appropriate time is the end of the school year. Some children go off to camp or have other summer vacation plans at this time or just go into "summer mode," and usually treatment is at least temporarily discontinued. Many children, particularly younger ones (probably because of the likelihood of identifying therapists with teachers), tend to place therapy in a class with school and expect that if school is not in session, neither is therapy. If a natural break does not coincide appropriately with termination of treatment, then, of course, the therapist has to follow the dictates of practicality and necessity.

The most frequent procedure in terminating therapy with adults is to set a tentative date from one to three months in advance and orient the therapy with that date in mind. Issues that are relevant to the impending separation are usually considered during this final period of the treatment. While the termination date can be postponed or advanced, the selected date usually works out about right. There are certainly times when new issues arise or some error was made in the course of the treatment that is uncovered, which may require postponement of the termination date; or the work may be completed sooner, and the date advanced. But, in any case, adjustments with adults are relatively easy to arrange.

The termination procedure and its ramifications are quite different with children. To begin with, the termination date is usually not a mutual decision. Young children are frequently reluctant to discontinue treatment because they have enjoyed it, having experienced therapy as an opportunity to play with an understanding and accepting adult. Thus, the setting of a termination date may be quite a disappointment for them. In addition, although they may well have known when the treatment began that it would end, children have trouble with time concepts, so that the aspect of termination often gets lost as the treatment progresses. As a result, the announcement of the possibility of terminating may come as a surprise to the child. As noted before, as in the process of terminating treatment with an adult, there may be a return of symptoms either as an unconscious way of staying in treatment or, more likely, simply as a regression resulting from the stress of discontinuing therapy. If parents are properly informed about this possibility, the appearance of such symptoms need cause no alarm and, because they are not likely to last long, can be readily tolerated.

Further Issues of Separation. Soon after the decision for termination is made, it should be shared with the child. The therapist should make a clear, simple statement about the pending end of therapy and give the child a complete opportunity to express his feelings about the separation. For children who have special difficulty expressing their feelings, this is an excellent opportunity to utilize play with puppets in which different separation scenarios can be enacted. Dollhouse activity is additionally useful in this context. Also, children can be encouraged to call the therapist if they wish to talk with him in the future. While in fact few children do so, it is quite reassuring for them to know that they can. In one of the final sessions, toy telephones can be well utilized for the rehearsal of such calls. Assuming the therapist is flexible, whatever material seems appropriate to this situation is suitable.

While in general I do not believe in gift-giving as a regular part of therapy, in terminating treatment I often give the child a gift at his last session. An appropriate gift might be an item such as a favorite puppet or a car or truck that the child frequently used. In this manner I hope to provide a transitional object so that the child can feel he still has a part of me with him.

In view of the child's inability to deal with abrupt change, I am more inclined, if given the opportunity, to taper off the treatment rather than to set a fixed number of consecutive sessions and then end therapy suddenly. This seems to work best if the termination takes about three to four months to complete. An appropriate sequence for a child seen once a week might be arranging for the next two sessions to be on consecutive weeks, then three or four sessions at two-week intervals, then one session three weeks later, and a final one six seeks later. This sequence is an arbitrary one, but the progression gives the child the opportunity to get used to being without regular sessions. For therapeutic reasons it is sometimes useful to set a kind of check-up date about six months later. Even if the child is not seen at that time, the parents can be encouraged to telephone so that the therapist has an opportunity to learn how the child has progressed.

Return to Therapy

As a result of varying developmental problems, children, more frequently than adults, may come back for a "refueling" of some eight or ten sessions six months to a year later. Children may return several times throughout the adolescent years. Return to treatment need not be seen as a failure of the therapy; since one is dealing with a developing personality, the possibility of future problems is far less predictable with youngsters than with adults—although it is also occasionally true that future problems may be predicted with some children.

To illustrate, a child of 8 may show evidence that enables the therapist to predict that when the child reaches puberty he or she will probably have additional difficulties. A child who tends to be overweight, say, or is somehow considered physically unattractive is likely to have difficulties when those characteristics become especially significant to his contemporaries, and this is likely to affect relationships with friends. Or, likewise, a child who is timid or physically poorly coordinated is likely to have difficulty when peer relationships become more competitive and based on daring.

The problems that brought the child to treatment at age 8 might be readily cleared up in ten or eleven months, but to continue treatment in anticipation of the problems likely to arise when the same child reaches 14 would not be prudent. Therapy as a regular way of life is inadvisable.

Just as children are not generally consciously aware of the effect of treatment, they do not always consciously feel a need to return. However, there is an almost unconscious connection between their feeling good about themselves and being in therapy, so that if they start to feel badly about themselves, it is likely that they will also feel a vague need for treatment. What they probably perceive is a recollection of the feeling of warmth and comfort they had in treatment and therefore a need to return to it. I suspect this feeling could not be articulated by most children even as I have described it here. A child might be able to announce that he would like to see Doctor X, but when asked why, he might invent some reason, such as a project they worked on together that he would like to finish or that he may be able to help him with some particular game or toy or even a school problem. Parents would be well advised not to interrogate the child, who would be unable to supply an accurate answer and may become confused or simply embarrassed, but rather to act on it and arrange an appointment.

Clinical Illustration. An example of a child's terminating therapy and of some of the resulting problems just noted is as follows:

Michael, an 8-year-old who had been in therapy for a little over a year, had made substantial strides and was ready for termination. He originally entered treatment approximately five months after his mother gave birth to another boy. Michael already had a sister two years younger than he; and, with a mother who was hypochondriacal and not sufficiently nurturing, the additional sibling was almost more than his mother could handle and more than Michael could endure. He started bedwetting six weeks after his brother was born, and this continued for several months, to the point where the parents brought him for consultation, and he was entered into play therapy.

While the bedwetting as a major symptom became less frequent about four months after he started treatment (and effectively stopped after about eight months), other symptoms, including aggressiveness toward his infant brother and increased disobedience, persisted until Michael had been in treatment a little over eleven months. At this time reports from school as well as from the parents indicated that, while in some ways Michael was more aggressive than most children, his behavior could hardly be considered pathological. Termination of treatment was clearly in order.

The treatment process had originated with much emphasis on water play, including the "drowning" of a small, infantlike, plastic doll. Michael was imaginative and frequently used puppets, making up stories to represent plays he said he would like to present at school. In fact, with some puppets he had at home he presented short plays to his parents and younger sister. His parents, who were psychologically sophisticated, were cautioned against interpreting his plays, which were filled with messages of feelings of deprivation and anger, and to confine themselves to enjoying the plays. His favorite puppet was a dog he at first called "Louis" (the reason for the choice of that name never became apparent to me). He later changed the name to "Tuffy," which in Michael's mind probably should have been spelled "Toughy." The dog obviously represented Michael; many of his feelings were expressed through the words that emanated from the mouth of this "animal."

As the therapy progressed, his play indicated considerably less anxiety and more freedom to enjoy life at home, at school, and with friends.

The following is an account of the session when Michael was told of the intent to terminate treatment:

> Michael entered the playroom and went directly to a project he had been engaged in on and off throughout the last two months and during the previous session. The project was folding paper to make paper airplanes. He proceeded with deftness to construct an airplane, which he announced would be powerful enough to fly to Switzerland, where it would then load up with Swiss cheese and return to this country.

MICHAEL: Help me find a red crayon. I'm going to color this real bright so everyone will see it.
THERAPIST: Here's one, Mike, at the bottom of the box.
M: It will have to have big wings to fly that far.
T: Do you think it can make the trip by itself?
M: Well, it has a powerful motor.
T: What if it runs out of fuel?
M: It's got a big gas tank.
T: Maybe if it needs fuel, a "tanker plane" can provide a mid-air refueling.
M: Yeah, if there's one around.
T: I suppose if there isn't any, the pilot could radio for one.

Michael continued to color the airplane for a while and then announced that he was going to knock over some bowling pins (a plastic set of playroom size). While he was setting up the pins and getting ready to bowl, the therapist said, "Michael, we're going to be stopping your regular visits here soon."

M: Why?
T: Well, you've been coming for about a year and children don't usually come here longer than that.
M: But I like to come here on Thursdays.
T: Yeah, and I like to see you here.

M: But that's the way it is?

T: Yes, that's the way it is. I'll miss you.

(*Michael threw a bowling ball exceptionally hard but only knocked down three pins.*)

M: Shit! Those pins just skipped out of the way.

T: Yeah, I guess they can take care of themselves pretty well.

M: Can I come next week?

T: Oh, sure, you can come for the next three weeks, and then I'll see you two weeks after that, and later on a couple of more times.

M: And that's all?

T: No, you can come back another time a few months from now, and you can call me if you want to talk to me sometimes.

The therapy tapered off as planned, and at the last session, the therapist gave Tuffy (the dog puppet) to Michael as a gift.

A detailed examination of this session reveals an interesting dynamic progression. Of course, I do not clearly know the meaning of Michael's play with an airplane; the material has many possibilities, and the underlying dynamic meaning may have been any one or more of a number of alternatives. The airplane play may well have represented freedom and escape from the regular requirements of life, much as flying dreams frequently do. Along with the concept of freedom, the activity carried with it possibilities of independence and all the fears it may entail. It was this possibility that the therapist considered in his metaphorical use of the material. Why Switzerland and Swiss cheese? Perhaps this was related to some recent experience having to do with lunch, or a geography lesson, or a casual conversation, much as the manifest content of a dream relates to daily experiences.

Michael's first communication, asking for assistance in finding a red crayon, was a request for aid. His remark was given in neither a dictatorial nor a helpless manner; it was merely a reasonable request, as one might make of a friend who could be helpful. Ever aware of the possibility of injury to self-esteem, after finding the crayon, the therapist pointed out that the crayon had been at the bottom of the box, implying that it would not have been particularly easy to find. Thus, there was no implication that Michael should have found it himself. The therapist's reply was unlike that of a disparaging person who says, for example, "If it were a snake, it would have bitten you," or "If you just looked a little harder, you would have found it." Such derogatory statements are often made by well-meaning teachers and parents who fail to consider that the child has a tender sense of self; they can be disparaging almost without thinking about it.

Noting Michael's emphasis on the distance of the trip, the therapist decided to use the material metaphorically and reasonably assumed that the airplane represented Michael. Being a little unsure of the child's ability to "fly on his own wings," he tested out Michael's concept of himself by asking if Michael believed the plane could make the trip. Seeing an opportunity to represent his own supportive presence, the therapist checked a little further and then offered the possibility of being available for "refueling." His additional suggestion that the pilot could radio for help was intended to represent the possibility that Michael could telephone the therapist if the need arose.

None of this was ever interpreted to the child, although the therapist did tell Michael that he could call if he ever felt that he wanted to. The metaphorical message in the airplane play was in a sense intended for the unconscious, just in case Michael ever did telephone—although it was unlikely that he would (in fact he did not). Had he telephoned, it probably would have been in response to some kind of almost unconscious prompting, and it is very unlikely that he would have made a direct request for help with an emotional issue that bothered him. Most likely, he would have experienced a kind of vague uneasiness and a desire for some kind of comfort and a recognition that such comfort could be provided by the therapist. Perhaps Michael would have had a recollection of the good feeling he had had when he was in therapy. As adults, we recall experiences of doing or sharing something with a loved one that was "fun," like visiting a zoo or building a wagon or learning to identify stars. Most of the time it is the quality of the experience that we recall; its details, which may, in fact, be inaccurate, are only a way of representing the relationship quality. A memory of such an experience is much like a screen memory in that it is used as a good example for illustrating and recalling a particular relationship, even though the experience itself may not have been of any major significance or in fact may be apocryphal.

What is the propitious moment for the announcement of termination? The time chosen for Michael was deemed appropriate because he seemed happy and relaxed. Michael asked the crucial question "Why?" How can this question be answered? Some therapists might say, "Because you no longer need help, or treatment." But this answer would probably only confuse the child, who does not conceive of being in play therapy as help for his emotional problems. Some therapists might have simply explained to the child his reason for being there—that is, that his parents and therapist had felt he had not been having enough fun and now believed that he was. This explanation would likewise not make too much sense to the child and would probably result in a response such as "I have fun here, so why can't I come?"

In the example, the therapist's reply that children do not usually come any longer than a year was both a way of stating reality and a reminder that life is a process of change. Michael's response, that he liked coming on Thursdays, was a weak bid to continue and a response appropriate to an 8-year-old: if one likes something one should be able to do it. At this point, the therapist added support by saying "and I like to see you here" and that he would miss Michael. Such sharing of genuine feeling, while it did not result in a literal "I'll miss you too," was an example, a form of modeling for Michael, to show him that such feelings were acceptable and could be openly and easily stated. Michael had not yet acquired the sense of social conformity and politeness that might have prompted him to say that he would miss the therapist too, even if he had genuinely felt it.

Why did Michael shift from his airplane construction to bowling at the time he did? Perhaps it was a response to his general restlessness. It was certainly in keeping with his regular pattern of shifting to two or three different activities during each play-therapy session. Michael made the shift before being told that therapy would be ending, so his knowing that therapy was to end soon, unless he already understood at some unconscious level, could not account for it. It is possible that the feeling of strength and independence he experienced in talking about the coming airplane flight prompted him to more aggressive activity as a way of showing his strength.

The shift to bowling fortuitously gave him the opportunity to put some of his resentment or anger into forcefully rolling the bowling ball. The therapist used the opportunity to provide further metaphorical support by saying that the bowling pins could take care of themselves. Michael inquired further about the termination, and the therapist provided reassurance in showing how therapy would be tapered off.

Premature Termination

Treatment with children, as with adults, does not always stop in a manner that therapists feel is most effective. It is often discontinued for any one of a number of reasons, many unavoidable, such as a patient's moving out of town. While it is conceivable that some adults might even postpone changing their residence to continue in therapy, it is unlikely that a family will postpone moving or nct move in order to keep a child in treatment with the same therapist. It is also rare for a therapist to recommend that a family do so.

Other reasons for discontinuing that have little do with the course of the treatment include serious economic changes, severe illness, or the therapist's moving or retiring. Whatever the reason for premature termination, there are usually a few sessions in which to conclude treatment, and the reason may become the central issue to be dealt with in the closing sessions.

When termination is not in the best interest of the child and when treatment must be concluded without being completed, the emphasis in the treatment for the concluding sessions is likely to be on the inevitability of certain situations and changes in life over which one has little control. The feelings engendered by such experiences are likely to include anger, disappointment, sadness, hurt, and helplessness. The last is a feeling that does not get sufficient attention in dynamic formulations, which tend to emphasize the hurt and anger. Hurt and anger are, of course, significant, but it is the sense of helplessness that often leads to the inability to make significant moves in later life because of the individual's foregone conclusion that whatever has happened to him, "nothing can be done about it." In effect, inability to exercise control over one's life is almost tantamount to denying the validity of one's existence and frequently is accompanied by pervasive depression. Unfortunately, the realities of life do not make it appropriate for children to make decisions about some consequential issues such as in what house or what city the family lives, and so it is especially important that significant adults show special care in presenting such matters to children. For this reason alone, parents should be encouraged to permit children to make decisions about matters that affect them if it is at all practical to do so and the issues are within the scope and level appropriate to children. Making even such apparently inconsequential decisions as choosing the flavors of ice cream not only gives children the feeling that they are responsible for their own fates but also gives them practice in the process of making decisions.

Case Illustration. Danny, a slight, timid, only child of seven, was brought into treatment because he was generally frightened, particularly in the presence of other children. If they fought with each other, he would readily start to cry. He was fearful of injury and became quite apprehensive when he heard emergency sirens. He tended to cling to his mother and avoid his father, whose idea of encouragement was to call Danny a "sissy" or a "momma's boy." Danny's father was an engineer with a large chemical company where he had been employed for the two years since they had moved to their present location. His style was highly obsessional, and he attempted to solve most problems at home with paper and pencil lists.

After Danny had been in treatment for seven months, his father's corporation moved its headquarters to another city several hundred miles away. Danny's father was transferred with only one month's advance notice. He was enthusiastic about the move and announced it to his wife and son with eagerness. Although Danny's mother was quite frightened about moving—she had just begun to establish friendships—her attitude was not to complain but to accept the move as one of the many disappointments she had to sustain in life. Danny was obviously unhappy about it but said little. Danny's father could not understand their restrained, unenthusiastic reaction.

The therapist was informed of the move the following day, and two days later Danny appeared for his regular weekly session.

For the past five weeks Danny had played with cars and trucks, setting up scenarios involving accidents, ambulances, and wild automobile rides to the hospital. Accidents were frequently caused by aggressive drivers whom Danny referred to as "crazies."

The following is an account of this session:

Danny entered the playroom and went directly to the cars and trucks and began to set them around on the floor.

THERAPIST: I understand your family is going to move to J———.

D: Yeah, we're going next month.

T: What do you feel about that?

D: My mother says it's a nice city and it's warm there.

T: What do you think?

D: She says that's the way it is and there's nothing we can do about it.

T: It sounds like you don't like the idea.

D: It doesn't matter.

Danny proceeded to set the cars on the "street" in front of the dollhouse. When in his typical manner Danny had two cars crash in front of the house, the therapist intervened by saying, "What happened?"

D: They crashed, it was another "crazy."

T: Anybody hurt?

D: Yeah, the woman driving in the blue car. We'll have to get her to a hospital.

T: Who's going to call an ambulance?

D: Maybe a friend will pass by in another car. The car that hit her just drove off.

T: How about someone in the house who heard the crash?

D: They're strangers. This isn't her neighborhood.

T: When people are hurt, lots of strangers will help. I think I see a man looking out of the window. Look, I think he's opening the door.

(*The therapist takes a male figure from the house and moves him out through the door to the accident scene. Then he has him run back into the house.*)

T: I'll pretend I'm the man. (*The therapist then goes to the toy telephone.*) Hello, operator, there's been a terrible accident here and there is a lady that looks like she's hurt bad. Send an ambulance quick.

D: Yeah, that's you. But nobody else is going to do that.

T: Sometimes it's hard to know what strangers in a strange neighborhood will do. But you know, there really are a lot of nice people and we just don't know everybody.

(*With the arrival of the ambulance, the therapist helps to put the lady into the ambulance and mimics the sound of an ambulance in a somewhat muted tone.*)

Danny had only three more sessions, and the therapist, having located a colleague in J———, did his best to arrange for extended help with Danny. He told Danny something about his friend who would be continuing to work with him, attempting to make the transition as smooth as possible and to indicate that sometimes nice things happen in new or strange situations. Obviously Danny would need continued therapy for some time, which, it was hoped, would be provided in J———.

Several observations can be made about the therapeutic session just described. The therapist initiated the conversation at the very beginning of the session by announcing his awareness of the pending move. The information about the transfer was too important for the therapist to wait until Danny brought up the subject and told him he was moving, which indeed he might have done. Not talking about it might imply that the therapist also thought it was an awful thing and might indicate that perhaps he was willing to enter into a conspiracy not to discuss it as a way of denying its reality.

By acknowledging the move, Danny made it easy for the therapist to ask a direct question about feelings. Danny's response was simply to repeat his mother's words. The identification with her was obviously quite strong. When asked again about his reaction, Danny once more resorted to his mother's statement about the matter. The therapist made one more attempt to get Danny's reaction, and the child's response was one of resignation and hopelessness, hardly in keeping with the reaction one would hope for from a 7-year-old. The therapist believed that further verbalization about the matter would probably only have resulted in reflections of the child's feeling of resignation and that more could be accomplished through the metaphor of play.

Knowing that he needed to make full use of the analogous possibilities, the therapist entered into the play by asking what happened. Cognizant of the general scenario that Danny usually acted out, the therapist asked if anyone was hurt. Danny immediately made it apparent that he expected little from strangers. His dialogue indicated his feeling that one could not expect any help from a passing stranger or even from someone who knew the injured woman; the person must more than know her, he or she must be a friend.

Thinking in terms of the impending move, the therapist suggested the possibility that strangers (new neighbors) might be helpful. Obviously, Danny was very skeptical, but the therapist almost intrusively played through the idea that strangers could be nice people in the hope that the message would be conveyed on a level that might assuage Danny's suspicious attitude. Because the therapist was aware of Danny's fear of his father, he made the helpful neighbor a male, hoping to influence the image Danny may have had of men, at least to the extent that his father served as a model. It is interesting that in Danny's conviction that strangers were not friendly or helpful and perhaps even people to fear, he made an exception of the therapist, as indicated by his response to the therapist's comment that when people are hurt, lots of strangers will help. Danny said, "Yeah, that's you. But nobody else is going to do that." It is as if this belief system the 7-year-old child had already established had sufficient strength to require him to deny an alternative point of view.

This illustration dramatizes one scenario for dealing with unplanned termination. By virtue of the termination's being unplanned, the result can never be entirely satisfactory. Unplanned termination usually does not give therapists enough time to ease the separation. While the transferential aspects of therapy with adults can make therapists parental symbols, with children therapists take on positions of greater importance than they do in their relationship with adult patients. Therefore, children are likely to show considerable distress as a result of a precipitous ending to the therapeutic relationship. However, because of their tendency to see issues as black or white—that is, to show evidence of splitting to a far greater degree than do most adults—their severe reaction is likely to be shortlived, and they soon deal with termination as if the therapist no longer existed.

Termination With Adolescents

Termination with adolescents is somewhat different from termination with children. Their treatment is usually short term, and allowing teenagers to plan the termination date of treatment on their own volition, so long as it is not impulsive, often contributes to the usefulness of the therapy. Encouraging teenagers to play an active part in the decision can have the benefit of indicating the therapist's faith in the young patient's judgment and respect for his or her maturity. Constantly questioning the judgment of adolescents makes them uncertain of their own decisions, about which they are only beginning to have a sense of security. Such inquisitions may result in their having greater doubts about their competence, and they may thus become more dependent. Or, excessive questioning of their judgment may make them become more rebellious and negativistic. Unfortunately, because of their rebelliousness, there are times when therapy with adolescents can hardly get started.

A particularly rebellious 15-year-old announced after a single session that he liked the therapist well enough—although he had only gone because his parents insisted—but that if they did not buy him a motorcycle, he would not return to treatment. The fact that he was not legally able to operate one was of no significance to him; he announced that he would only use it on private property to which he had access. The parents were advised to insist that he return for treatment and that they were not about to bribe him for what they considered essential visits to a therapist. Unfortunately, they were neither forceful nor consistent with their children and could not stand behind their decision, being readily intimidated by such threats as running away or refusing to go to school. Therefore, the parents were seen for regular counselling about ways of dealing with the child and independently for treatment for themselves.

Pine (1988) compares termination of treatment with children to leaving home for an adolescent. He notes that it is important for the youngster to know that the home is still there and that he can go back to it. Analogous to the dynamics of separation from therapy is the situation of children who go off to college and during their senior year in high school or their freshman year in college become especially concerned with the state of their room at home. While for years they may have apparently enjoyed living in a state of disarray, they suddenly attend to their room and fix it up as if it is going to be their home for life. Similarly, the treatment that was a part of life and apparently taken for granted becomes much more important when adolescents become aware that they must separate from it.

During their first year in college, when they visit home on vacations, adolescents attend to their rooms with almost loving care. It is only by the second or third year of college that most will not protest vehemently if their parents use the room as a guest room or react almost violently if it takes on another function such as a den, sewing room, or library. The explanation for this is that with some teenagers, particularly those who have been overprotected at home, their rebellion prior to leaving home must be rather extreme. That is, it is necessary for them to establish that their parents are bad parents, never did them any good, and "who needs them anyway?" Such complete denouncement enables them to leave without having to acknowledge their fears of being on their own, which they would see as demeaning and injurious to their self-esteem. Likewise depending on the basis and extent of attachment they have to the therapist, they frequently play out the same behavior in treatment.

For the teenager, the separation from therapy has some of the same quality of conflicting feelings as leaving home: in both cases they give apparently contradictory messages about wanting to be off on their own and at the same time having no intention of leaving home. As with parents, to the therapist they convey mixed messages in an almost unconscious attempt to assert that they no longer have a need for therapy while protesting that therapy was never of any benefit to them anyway. The core of the message is that they can rebel and do what they wish (by showing the therapist how outrageous they are) and at the same time indicate that there has been a significant change in their adjustment.

Clinical Example. An interesting configuration having to do with termination is indicated by the experience with Tracy, a 16-year-old girl who had been in treatment on a once-a-week basis for about fourteen months. She came to treatment somewhat reluctantly after making a quasisuicidal attempt by taking a moderate overdose of her mother's tranquilizer. Her behavior was always characterized by rebelliousness, cutting classes at school, failing to do her homework, occasionally being suspended, coming home at late hours, and smoking marijuana. She frequently practiced brinksmanship: while she came close, she was never picked up by the police nor was she dismissed from school. Tracy was always argumentative about her conduct and always rationalized her behavior as some kind of accident: she missed the last bus, or forgot to bring a needed book home, or misunderstood a regulation. She could always devise an excuse that almost made sense.

In therapy Tracy was always polite, seldom missed a session, and was almost never late. She used the time to brag about her dangerous exploits and seemed delighted if the therapist showed any concern for her health or safety. The validity of her reported exploits was never clear, although the impression was that for the most part they were true, but slightly exaggerated. Tracy kept many secrets from her mother that she shared with the therapist, knowing that the information would be kept confidential.

While Tracy's recitations of her behavior continued in pretty much the same manner, she reported almost sheepishly that her grades had improved. She never explained this improvement except to say that an examination was easy or that it was some kind of a fluke. One day, when it was apparent that treatment was nearing completion, she reported that she had done well on a biology exam. When I asked how that happened, she said that she had had coffee and NoDoz the night before and then she was unable to sleep. Being unable to sleep, she had nothing to do, so in an effort to keep from being bored she studied for the examination. She presented this preposterous story as if it had validity and as if she expected the therapist to believe it. The therapist did not say he believed it, but neither did he question it. For Tracy to have admitted that she was actually concerned with grades or an achievement of that kind would have been an admission of some kind of conformity and a loss of her independence and individuality.

It is evident that Tracy improved in her adjustment and that therapy had something to do with the improvement. How did this come about? It is here that our theories suffer most: they are essentially theories of development and dynamic personality structure, but they fail to provide a basis for explaining therapeutic change (Witenberg 1987; Chrzanowski 1986a). One can, however, speculate that a major factor in the process was that the therapist was able to tolerate her sometimes outrageous behavior; he was appropriately appalled, but unlike her mother, he did not prohibit it. Because he gave her no flack that she had to oppose, Tracy was enabled to be open enough to see that she did truly have impact on a significant adult, which added to her self-esteem. Tracy also really wished for adult approval, and once she could establish that she was indeed an independent individual, she could set about realistically preparing for her future. She believed that her ultimate goal would require completing college and that successful high school work would be necessary to enter an appropriate college. Having established her "rights" and the validity of her existence, she was free to pursue socially acceptable goals.

As with all aspects of child therapy, the problems of termination show considerable variation. Unlike that of adults, the attitudes of children in making the decision to terminate are not of major significance. Emphasis must be placed on the importance of bringing the child to a level commensurate with his chronological age, not to exceed that level or to discontinue treatment before it is reached.

Epilogue

In this book I have presented a view of the treatment of children from an interpersonal orientation. Because of the emphasis on the requirement for a complete understanding of psychodynamic history unique to each individual, there is a considerable amount of overlap in the subject matter of the individual chapters. Had the book been organized in a manner oriented toward diagnostic categories or developmental issues, it would have appeared more orderly, but would not have done justice to an approach that must truly consider the whole individual in seeking the source of maladjustment or problems of living.

Refining techniques is an admirable goal, and in the hard sciences the resulting precision leads to better understanding and greater possibilities for the utilization of information in the furtherance of knowledge. Within the field of behavioral sciences such refinement is also admirable but carries with it the increased danger of oversimplification and an illusion that we know far more than we do. As our theories and methods of treatment advance, we must always be vigilant, ready to examine what we ordinarily view as the exception in behavior not as an exception but rather as an illustration of the complexity of the human condition. As a final statement, I wish to emphasize that therapy with children should be oriented toward correction of warps in growth processes, not toward remanufacture of the individual. For example, in a maze study with rats, the animal who finds a shortcut to the goal by jumping over the fence may be treated as an anomalous nuisance and his particular solution discounted in collecting the data. With a person who arrives at a unique solution, it is the very uniqueness of the individual that must be understood. It is this that will add to our comprehension of human behavior.

References

Alexander, F. and T. French. 1946. *Psychoanalytic Therapy*. New York: Ronald Press.

Allen, F. H. 1942. *Psychotherapy with Children*. New York: Norton.

Anchin, J. C. and D. J. Kiesler. 1982. *Handbook of Interpersonal Psychotherapy*. New York: Pergamon Press.

Arieti, S. 1974. *Interpretation of Schizophrenia*. New York: Basic Books.

Arieti, S. and J. Bemporad. 1978. *Severe and Mild Depression*. New York: Basic Books.

Axline, V. 1947. *Play Therapy*. Boston: Houghton Mifflin.

Axline, V. 1964. "Recognition and Reflection of Feelings." In M. R. Hayworth, ed., *Child Psychotherapy*, pp. 262–264. New York: Basic Books.

Barnett, J. 1971. "Narcissism and Dependency in the Obsessional-Hysteric Marriage." *Family Process*. 10:75–83.

Bellak, Leopold and Sonya Bellak. 1949, 1974. Children's Apperception Test (C.A.T.). New York: The Psychological Corporation.

Bergin, A. E. and H. H. Strupp. 1972. *Changing Frontiers in the Science of Psychotherapy*. Chicago: Aldine-Atherton.

Bixler, R. H. 1964. "Limits Are Therapy." In M. R. Hayworth, ed., *Child Psychotherapy*, pp. 134–147. New York: Basic Books.

Bowen, M. 1976. "Theory in the Practice of Psychotherapy." In P. J. Guerin, ed., *Family Therapy: Theory and Practice*. New York: Gardner Press.

Chrzanowski, G. 1986a. "Changing Modes of Neurosis and Changing Therapeutic Approaches." *Contemporary Psychoanalysis* (April) 22(2):241–251.

Chrzanowski, G. 1986b. "Interpersonal Psychoanalysis." *Contemporary Psychoanalysis* (July) 22(3):445–451.

Cohen, N. 1980. "Integrating Pharmocotherapy with Psychotherapy." *Bulletin of the Meninger Clinic* 44:296–300.

Dodds, J. B. 1985. *A Child Psychotherapy Primer*. New York: Human Sciences Press.

Ekstein, R. 1983. *Children of Time and Space of Action and Impulse*. New York: Jason Aronson.

Elkin, I., M. B. Parloff, S. W. Hadley, and J. H. Autry. 1985. "NIMH Treatment of Depression Collaborative Research Program." *Archives of General Psychiatry* March 6 42:305–316.

Epstein, L. and A. Feiner. 1979. *Countertransference*. New York: Jason Aronson.

Freud, A. 1946. *The Psychoanalytic Treatment of Children*. London: Imago.

Freud, S. 1900. *The Interpretation of Dreams*. In *The Collected Psychological Works of Sigmund Freud*, J. Strachey, ed. and trans., vols. 4, 5.

Freud, S. 1909. *Analysis of a Phobia in a Five-Year-Old Boy*. C.P.3, 149; In *The Collected Psychological Works of Sigmund Freud*, J. Strachey, ed. and trans., vol. 10.

Freud, S. 1949. *An Outline of Psychoanalysis*. J. Strachey trans. New York: Norton.

Fromm, E. 1941. *Escape From Freedom*. New York: Avon.

Fromm-Reichman, F. 1950. *Principles of Intensive Psychotherapy*. Chicago: University of Chicago Press.

Gardner, R. A. 1969. "Mutual Storytelling as a Technique in Child Psychotherapy and Psychoanalysis." In J. Masserman, ed., *Science and Psychoanalysis*, 14:123–135. New York: Grune and Stratton.

Gardner, R. A. 1973. *The Talking, Feeling, Doing Game*. Cresskill, N.J.: Creative Therapeutics.

Gardner, R. A. 1973b. *Understanding Children*. New York: Jason Aronson.

Gardner, R. A. 1975. *Psychotherapeutic Approaches to the Resistant Child*. New York: Jason Aronson.

Gardner, R. A. 1986. "The Game of Checkers in Child Therapy." In C. E. Schaeffer, and S. E. Reid, eds. *Game Play*, pp. 215–232. New York: Wiley.

Gilbert, L. J. 1964. Personal communication.

Gill, M. M. 1982. *Analysis of Transference*, vol. 2. New York: International Universities Press.

Ginott, H. G. 1960. "A Rationale for Selecting Toys in Play Therapy." *Journal of Consulting Psychology*, 24(3):243–246.

Ginott, H. G. 1961a. "Play Therapy, The Initial Session." *American Journal of Psychotherapy* (January), 15(1):73–88.

Ginott, H. G. 1961b. *Group Psychotherapy with Children*. New York: McGraw Hill.

Ginott, H. G. 1963. Personal communication.

Ginott, H. G. 1964. "Problems in the Playroom. In M. R. Hayworth, ed., *Child Psychotherapy*, pp. 125–130. New York: Basic Books.

Ginott, H. G. 1966. Personal communication.

Greenberg, J. R. 1986a. "On The Analyst's Neutrality." *Contemporary Psychoanalysis* (January) 2(1):87–105.

Greenberg, J. R. 1986b. "The Problem of Analytic Neutrality." *Contemporary Psychoanalysis* (January) 2(1):76–86.

Groddeck, Georg. 1929. *The Unknown Self*. London: C. W. Daniel.

Groddeck, Georg. 1976. *The Book of the It*. New York: International Universities Press.

Guerin, P. J. and E. G. Pendergast. 1976. *Evaluation of Family System and Genogram*. In P. J. Guerin, ed., *Family Therapy: Theory and Practice*. New York: Gardner Press.

Guntrip, H. 1969. *Schizoid Phenomena: Object Relations and the Self*. New York: International Universities Press.

Haley, J. 1979. "Family Therapy." *International Journal of Psychiatry* 9:233–242.

Jernberg, A. 1979. *Theraplay*. San Francisco: Jossey-Bass.

Johnson, J. H., W. C. Rasbury, and L. J. Siegel. 1986. *Approaches to Child Treatment*, pp. 271–305. New York: Pergamon Press.

Kaplan, L. J. 1987. "Discussion [of] The Interpersonal World of the Infant (A Symposium)." *Contemporary Psychoanalysis* (January), 23(1):27–44.

Katz, C. 1987. "Discussion [of] The Interpersonal World of the Infant, (A Symposium)." *Contemporary Psychoanalysis* (January), 23(1):17–26.

Klein, M. 1932. *The Psychoanalysis of Children*. London: Hogarth Press.

Kohut, H. 1977. *The Restoration of the Self*. New York: International Universities Press.

Kritzberg, N. 1975. *The Structured Therapeutic Game Method of Child Analytic Psychotherapy*. Hicksville, N.Y.: Exposition.

Levenson, E. 1972. *The Fallacy of Understanding*. New York: Basic Books.

Levenson, E. 1983. *The Ambiguity of Change*. New York: Basic Books.

Loomis, E. A., Jr. 1964. "The Use of Checkers in Handling Certain Resistances in Child Therapy and Child Analysis." In M. R. Hayworth, ed., *Child Psychotherapy*, pp. 407–411. New York: Basic Books.

Mahler, M. S., M. Furer, and C. F. Settladge. 1959. In S. Arieti, ed., *American Handbook of Psychiatry*, 1:816–839. New York: Basic Books.

Marshall, R. J. 1979. "Antisocial Youth." In S. I. Harrison, ed., *Basic Handbook of Child Psychiatry*, pp. 536–554, New York: Basic Books.

Marshall, R. J. 1982. *Resistant Interactions*. New York: Human Sciences Press.

Minuchin, S. 1974. *Families and Family Therapy*. Cambridge: Harvard University Press.

Moustakas, C. E. 1953. *Children in Play Therapy*. New York: McGraw Hill.

Murray, H. A. 1943. *The Thematic Apperception Test*. Cambridge: Harvard University Press.

Munroe, R. L. 1955. *Schools of Psychoanalytic Thought*. New York: Dryden Press.

Normand, W. C. and H. Bluestone. 1986. "The Use of Pharmocotherapy in Psychoanalytic Treatment." *Contemporary Psychoanalysis* (April) 22(2):218–233.

O'Brien, J. D. 1987. "The Effects of Incest on Female Adolescent Development." *Journal of the American Academy of Psychoanalysis* 15(1):83–92.

Paves, M. 1986. "The Children of the Dream Revisited: The Object Relations Perspective." Paper presented at the Ninety-Fourth Annual Convention of the American Psychological Association. Washington, D.C. (August).

Pearson, G. H. J., ed. 1968. *A Handbook of Child Psychoanalysis*. New York: Basic Books.

Pine, F. 1988. Personal communication.

Rabin, A. I. and B. Beit-Hallahmi. 1982. *Twenty Years Later, Kibbutz Children Grown Up*. New York: Springer.

Rogers, C. R. 1942. *Counseling and Psychotherapy*. Boston: Houghton Mifflin.

Rogers, C. R. 1951. *Client-Centered Therapy*. Boston: Houghton Mifflin.

Schachtel, E. G. 1959. *Metamorphosis*. New York: Basic Books.

Schaefer, C. E. and S. E. Reid. 1986. "Therapeutic Use of Childhood Games." In C. E. Schaefer and S. E. Reid, eds., *Game Play*. New York: Wiley.

Schimel, J. L. 1979. Annals of Adolescent Psychiatry, vol 7: *Developmental and Clinical Studies*, S. Feinstein and P. Giovacchini, eds. Chicago: University of Chicago Press.

Schneidman, E. S. 1949. *The Make a Picture Story Test*. New York: The Psychological Corporation.

Searles, H. F., ed. 1965a. "Dependency Processes in the Psychotherapy of Schizophrenia." In H. F. Searles, *Collected Papers on Schizophrenia and Related Subjects*, pp. 114–156. London: Hogarth Press.

Searles, H. F. 1965b. "Positive Feelings in the Relationship Between the Schizophrenic and His Mother." In H. F. Searles, ed., *Collected Pa-*

pers on Schizophrenia and Related Subjects, pp. 216–253. London: Hogarth Press.

Singer, E. 1970. *Key Concepts in Psychotherapy.* New York: Basic Books.

Slavson, S. R. 1952. *Child Psychotherapy.* New York: Columbia University Press.

Slavson, S. R. 1958. *Child-Centered Group Guidance of Parents.* New York: International Universities Press.

Slavson, S. R. and M. Schiffer. 1975. *Group Psychotherapies for Children.* New York: International Universities Press.

Spiegel, R. 1980. "Manic-Depressive Syndromes in Light of Sullivanian Theory." *Contemporary Psychoanalysis* (July), 16(3):320–334.

Spiegel, S. 1959a. "Obstacles to Non-Clinical Roles of Mental Health Clinics." *Mental Health in Virginia* (Winter), 10(2):24–26.

Spiegel, S. 1959b. "The Use of Puppets as a Therapeutic Tool with Children." *Virginia Medical Monthly* 88:272–275.

Spiegel, S. 1973. "Psychoanalytic Intervention with Children." *Contemporary Psychoanalysis* (February), 9(2):166–170.

Spiegel, S. 1987. "Discussion [of] The Interpersonal World of the Infant (A Symposium)." *Contemporary Psychoanalysis* (January), 23(1):6–17.

Stern, D. N. 1985. *The Interpersonal World of the Infant.* New York: Basic Books.

Strupp, H. H. 1973. "On the Basic Ingredients of Psychotherapy." *Journal of Consulting and Clinical Psychology* 41:1–8.

Strupp, H. H. 1978. "Psychotherapy Research and Practice: An Overview." In S. L. Garfield and A. E. Bergin, eds., *Handbook of Psychotherapy and Behavior Change: An Empirical Analysis.* New York: Wiley.

Stumphauser, J. 1973. *Behavior Therapy with Adolescents.* Springfield: Charles Thomas.

Sullivan, H. S. 1953a. *Conceptions of Modern Psychiatry.* New York: Norton.

Sullivan, H. S. 1953b. *The Interpersonal Theory of Psychiatry.* New York: Norton.

Sullivan, H. S. 1956. *Clinical Studies in Psychiatry.* New York: Norton.

Sullivan, H. S. 1962. *Schizophrenia as a Human Process.* New York: Norton.

Sullivan, H. S. 1970. *The Psychiatric Interview.* New York: Norton.

Szalita, A. 1968. "Reanalysis." *Contemporary Psychoanalysis* (Spring), 4(2):83–102.

Weil-Malherbe, H. and S. I. Szara. 1971. *The Biochemistry of Functional and Experimental Psychosis.* Springfield, Ill.: Thomas.

Will, O. A. 1967. "Schizophrenia: Psychological Treatment." In A. M. Freedman and H. I. Kaplan, eds., *Comprehensive Textbook of Psychiatry*, pp. 649–661. Baltimore: Williams and Wilkins.

Will, O. A. 1983. "The Relationship of Psychopharmacology and Schizophrenia." In M. Greenhill and A. Gralnick, eds., *Psychopharamacology and Psychotherapy*, pp. 97–112. New York: Free Press.

Winnicott, D. W. 1971a. *Playing and Reality*. New York: Basic Books.

Winnicott, D. W. 1971b. *Therapeutic Consultations in Child Psychiatry*. New York: Basic Books.

Winnicott, D. W. 1977. *The Piggle*. New York: International Universities Press.

Witenberg, E. G. 1987. "Clinical Innovations and Theoretical Controversy." *Contemporary Psychoanalysis* (April), 23(2):183–198.

Wolf, S. 1969. *Children Under Stress*. London: Penguin Books.

Wolstein, B. 1988. Personal communication.

Woltmann, A. G. 1963. Personal communication.

Woltmann, A. G. 1964. "Psychological Rationale of Puppetry." In M. R. Hayworth, ed., *Child Psychotherapy*, pp. 395–399. New York: Basic Books.

Zaphiropoulos, M. L. 1985. "Harry Stack Sullivan." In H. I. Kaplan and B. J. Sadock, eds., *Comprehensive Textbook of Psychiatry*, 4th ed., 1:426–432. Baltimore: Williams and Wilkins.

Zaslow, S. 1985. "Countertransference Issues in Psychotherapy with Adolescents." In S. Feinstein, ed., *Adolescent Psychiatry, Developmental and Clinical Studies*. Annals of the American Society for Adolescent Psychiatry. Chicago: University of Chicago Press.

Index